Protest, Politics and Work in Rural Engl

Rural workers in eighteenth- and early
passive victims in the face of rapid socia
that they deployed an extensive range of resistances — from ~~~~ ~~~~
poaching to the Swing riots and Chartism – to defend their livelihoods and
communities.

Thematically organised, *Protest, Politics and Work in Rural England, 1700–1850*
analyses:

• cultures of work, worklessness, the poor laws and poverty
• relations between law, the evolving state and rural labourers
• enclosure, land use and changes in the environment
• religion, custom and the politics of everyday life and resistance
• rural protest movements, trade unionism, and popular radical politics.

Locating protest in the wider contexts of work, poverty and landscape change,
this lively and approachable volume offers the first critical overview of a growing
area of study.

Carl J. Griffin is Senior Lecturer in Historical Geography at the University of
Sussex, UK. His previous publications include *The Rural War: Captain Swing and
the Politics of Protest* (2012).

Social History in Perspective Series
General Editor: Jeremy Black

Social History in Perspective is a series of in-depth studies of the many topics in social, cultural and religious history.

PUBLISHED

John Belchem Popular Radicalism in Nineteenth-Century Britain
Andrew Brown Church and Society in England, 1000–1500
Sue Bruley Women in Britain Since 1900
Anthony Brundage The English Poor Laws, 1700–1930
Simon Dentith Society and Cultural Forms in Nineteenth-Century England
Joyce M. Ellis The Georgian Town, 1680–1840
Paul A. Fideler Social Welfare in Pre-Industrial England
Peter Fleming Family and Household in Medieval England
Ian Gazeley Poverty in Britain, 1900–1965
Kathryn Gleadle British Women in the Nineteenth Century
Harry Goulbourne Race Relations in Britain since 1945
Carl J. Griffin Protest, Politics and Work in Rural England, 1700–1850
Anne Hardy Health and Medicine in Britain since 1860
Tim Hitchcock English Sexualities, 1700–1800
Sybil M. Jack Towns in Tudor and Stuart Britain
Helen M. Jewell Education in Early Modern England
Alan Kidd State, Society and the Poor in Nineteenth-Century England
Peter Kirby Child Labour in Britain, 1750–1870
Arthur J. McIvor A History of Work in Britain, 1880–1950
Hugh McLeod Religion and Society in England, 1850–1914
Donald M. MacRaild The Irish Diaspora in Britain, 1750–1939, 2nd Edition
Donald M. MacRaild and David E. Martin Labour in Britain, 1830–1914
Christopher Marsh Popular Religion in the Sixteenth Century
Michael A. Mullett Catholics in Britain and Ireland, 1558–1829
Christine Peters Women in Early Modern Britain, 1450–1640
Richard Rex The Lollards
George Robb British Culture and the First World War
R. Malcolm Smuts Culture and Power in England, 1585–1685
John Spurr English Puritanism, 1603–1689
W. B. Stephens Education in Britain, 1750–1914
Heather Swanson Medieval British Towns
David Taylor Crime, Policing and Punishment in England, 1750–1914
N. L. Tranter British Population in the Twentieth Century
Ian D. Whyte Migration and Society in Britain, 1550–1830
Ian D. Whyte Scotland's Society and Economy in Transition, c.1500–c.1760
Andy Wood Riot, Rebellion and Popular Politics in Early Modern England

Please note that a sister series, *British History in Perspective*, is available, covering key topics in British political history.

Social History in Perspective
Series Standing Order ISBN 978–0–333–71694–6 hardcover
Series Standing Order ISBN 978–0–333–69336–0 paperback
(outside North America only)

You can receive future titles in this series as they are published by placing a standing order. Please contact your bookseller or, in the case of difficulty, write to us at the address below with your name and address, the title of the series and the ISBN quoted above.

Customer Services Department, Macmillan Distribution Ltd,
Houndmills, Basingstoke, Hampshire, RG21 6XS, UK

Protest, Politics and Work in Rural England, 1700–1850

CARL J. GRIFFIN

palgrave
macmillan

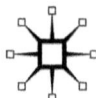

First published 2014 by
PALGRAVE MACMILLAN

Palgrave Macmillan in the UK is an imprint of Macmillan Publishers Limited,
registered in England, company number 785998, of Houndmills, Basingstoke,
Hampshire RG21 6XS.

Palgrave Macmillan in the US is a division of St Martin's Press LLC,
175 Fifth Avenue, New York, NY 10010.

Palgrave Macmillan is the global academic imprint of the above companies
and has companies and representatives throughout the world.

Palgrave® and Macmillan® are registered trademarks in the United States,
the United Kingdom, Europe and other countries.

ISBN 978-0-230-29968-9   ISBN 978-1-137-37301-4 (eBook)
DOI 10.1007/978-1-137-37301-4

A catalogue record for this book is available from the British Library.

A catalog record for this book is available from the Library of Congress.

For Andrew Charlesworth

Contents

List of Abbreviations

AgHR	*Agricultural History Review*
BPP	*British Parliamentary Papers*
EcHR	*Economic History Review*
IRSH	*International Review of Social History*
JPS	*Journal of Peasant Studies*
P&P	*Past & Present*
RH	*Rural History*
SH	*Social History*
TNA	The National Archives

Acknowledgements

Book writing is supposedly a lonely business. My experience was rather different. For if the words have flowed from my pen – or rather the somehow still functioning keys on my laptop – the intellectual work was always shared. The debts, then, are many. First, my students, most recently at Queen's University Belfast, have continued to force me to think more critically about the nature of social conflict. They have listened to my thoughts, engaged me in debate, and challenged many of my preconceptions about the nature of popular protest. Truly, they have been an inspiration. More materially, this book would not be without the support and time offered by staff in the School of Geography, Archaeology and Palaeoecology at Queen's. It is hugely appreciated. I would also like to recognise the staff at the British Library at St Pancras and the British Library Newspaper Library at Collindale, the National Archives at Kew, the Kent History and Library Centre, the Hampshire County Record Office at Winchester, the Dorset History Centre in Dorchester, the East Sussex and West Sussex County Record Offices in Lewes and Chichester respectively, the Somerset Record Office, and the Wiltshire and Swindon History Centre for the help and patience extended to me.

Many colleagues – or rather friends and co-workers – have borne my arguments and frustrations with remarkable grace. Your company, critical commentary and feedback have shaped this book in ways I can barely begin to comprehend. I would especially like to thank Peter Jones, Briony McDonagh, Katrina Navickas, Steve Poole, Adrian Randall, Iain Robertson, Samantha Shave and Rose Wallis. My colleagues at Bristol, Southampton, Oxford and Queen's all deserve thanks, especially Edwin Aiken, Bruce Campbell, Paul Glennie, Nuala Johnson, Keith Lilley, Steve Royle, Ian Shuttleworth, and Sarah Whatmore. I am fortunate in that I can call all my colleagues and collaborators friends. But without the support of my family and their allowing me to give so much of my life over to people they (and I) will never truly know, I am most grateful. My sister Katie and her family, my aunt Ann Francesconi, and Martin Blandy and Libby Beech have all gone out of their way to support me, for which I am humbled. My parents, Mary and Roy Griffin, have lived with the ideas central to this book for as long as I have – and have somehow put up with the all too infrequent visits and calls from its author. Suzanne: thank you for your support and encouragement – and for being so understanding when I had to spend more time with my laptop than with you. Soon it will be your book. My final thanks, and my eternal gratitude, go to Andrew Charlesworth. Not only have you shown me great kindness and support, but you have blazed a trail for historical geographers. You have shown me what can be done. Truly, you are an inspiration. This book is dedicated to you.

CARL J. GRIFFIN
Belfast

Preface

We hear a great deal now and then of the wickedness that abounds in manufacturing localities; but it may be pretty safely affirmed that those demoralizing practices for which our land is unhappily notorious, abound to a greater extent in country places than in crowded towns ... the lot of the village labourer is very different. His work is in the fields or farm yard all day long: it is laborious, and performed often in solitude and silence. He is not educated: he cannot enjoy the most interesting book, or even the newspaper: village politics are the only politics he cares to discuss: of the great questions which agitate the nation, he knows literally nothing.[1]

So wrote the Reverend John Eddowes, vicar of Garton-upon-the-Wolds in the East Riding of Yorkshire, in 1854. His *The Agricultural Labourer as He Really Is; Or Village Morals in 1854* was one of many mid-Victorian tracts concerned with 'improving' the morals of agricultural workers.[2] Locating the 'problem' with cheap and readily available beer, cramped and poor quality housing, inadequate educational provision, and the annual hiring fairs that persisted in the East Riding but had largely died out elsewhere, Eddowes suggested that, reduced to a brute state, agricultural workers duly became animalistic.[3] If they were 'capable' of thought, it was a lumpen, reflexive response rather than independent, something rooted in the fields and farmyards as opposed to the nation and the world.

Such was the received perception of rural workers in Victorian England. By the 1850s, and arguably as early as the 1820s, they had long since ceased to be viewed as a subject of national pride, the sturdy, independent backbone of the nation, but instead being subject to both derision and moralising pity. The fieldworker had become 'Hodge', 'a cross between hedge (where he spent much of his time ...) and clod (the substance on his boots and in his brain)' as Jan Marsh put it.[4] As Mark Freeman has suggested, the 'Hodge' stereotype might never have been universal but it was the dominant representation of the labourer in the mid-nineteenth century, a conception shared not just by urban dwellers but also by the rulers of rural England and even some farmers too.[5] Central to this discourse was the idea that 'know[ing] literally nothing', the 'clodhopper' might feel injustice but was unable to theorise it or do anything to alleviate it. As John Dent, Liberal MP and agriculturalist, put it: the labourer was not only 'unimaginative, ill-clothed, ill-educated, ill-paid, [and] ignorant of all that is taking place beyond his own village' but also 'dissatisfied with his position and yet without energy or effort to improve it'.[6]

Yet, the English rural worker throughout the eighteenth and early nineteenth centuries *was* often to be found protesting his (or her) lot. Few are the studies of the making of modern England without some reference to the totemic moments of rural protest that both shook and shaped the social and political nation: opposition to the enclosure of commonable land; the largest ever rising of rural workers in the so-called Swing riots of 1830; and the case of the Tolpuddle Martyrs in 1834. These moments, as an ever-increasing volume of historical scholarship attests, were but the tip of the protest iceberg. For rather than being passive and rapt by lassitude, workers in the English countryside frequently resorted to a plethora of practices, from the seemingly petty acts of psychological release such as back chatting and foot-dragging, to such 'dramatic' practices as riot, machine-breaking and incendiarism. Moreover, these acts of resistance, from the 'everyday' to the exceptional, framed rural social relations and the experience of work (and hence also the form of agrarian capitalism), as well as the making and remaking of public policy. This book seeks to make sense of these diverse protests and practices, to help better understand the roles and function of resistance in eighteenth- and early-nineteenth-century rural England, and to examine their effects (and affects). Ultimately, then, it attempts to show that English rural workers were not forelock-tugging victims of capitalist change, but instead were active agents in the making of the modern world.

This book represents the first attempt to survey our understanding of the resort to protest in rural England in the eighteenth and early nineteenth centuries. Earlier surveys by John Stevenson – in 1979, usefully revised in 1992 – and by Archer in 2000 have in many ways stood the test of time, but both are more general accounts concerned as much with the protests of the London artisan or the Leeds factory worker as they are of the Cornish miner and the Norfolk labourer. Both are also more concerned with dramatic protest episodes – and in the case of Stevenson's book, the emergence of 'industrial' forms of protest – at the expense of the local and the quotidian. Nor do they necessarily cover the recent upturn in interest in protest studies. Charlesworth's innovative *Atlas of Rural Protest* (1983) in many ways provides a closer intellectual cousin to this book, but adopts a wider spatial and temporal frame while only providing short contextual essays to support the maps.[7]

The time period covered means that the study is neither exclusively focused on the early modern or modern periods. Nor is it a study of the becoming modern; besides, as Bruno Latour has argued, the term is conceptually and politically problematic.[8] As with many long(er) duration studies, the timeframe is in some senses arbitrary: the world did not shift on its axis on 1 January 1700 or 31 December 1850. Indeed, the start date of 1700 means that the protests in the post-'Glorious Revolution' ferment of the 1690s are not analysed directly. Nor is the book a *complete* account of protest in the period. It does not, for instance, offer a *systematic* analysis of the 1715 and 1745 Jacobite Rebellions, or of the attempts at rural campaigning by the Anti-Corn Law League.[9] Rather, the seven chapters are driven by, and structured around, themes in the study of protest as well as protest practices and protest events. By contextualising the resort to protest in the realms of work, worklessness and poverty as well as custom and beliefs, the analysis is also a study of politics. This politics is both that of everyday life and, to use Keith Wrightson's phrase, of the parish, as well as, in the later chapters, of participation, the many attempts to extend the electoral franchise beyond the rich and landed. The argument is not arranged chronologically – though several of the chapters and chapter sections are – instead it is arranged around critical themes in the study of past protest. Necessarily, this means that some major episodes of rural protest are noted in passing before being fully analysed later in the book. In such instances, the reader will need to follow the cross-reference.

The analysis starts with an overview of the emergence and current state of understanding of protest, politics and resistance in eighteenth- and early nineteenth-century rural England, starting with Victorian conceptions of the ability of rural workers to resist their lot and ending with an attempt to 'unpack' conceptually what we mean by 'rural'. In so doing, this introductory chapter explores the relative importance of 'riot' and 'overt' forms of protest compared to more 'covert' and everyday forms of resistance, as well as the importance of microhistories in better understanding the local contexts and complexities that underpin all acts of protest.

Chapter 1 continues this theme with an examination of the centrality of the experience of labour to the lives of English rural workers. It
starts with a consideration of the idea that by 1700 the rural worker was
already a landless pauper. While agricultural labourers were numerically
the dominant constituent of the rural workforce, especially in the highly
capitalised south and eastern cornlands, it is shown that by 1800 many
individuals and families still lived off the land, often combining smallholdings with other occupations and occasional labouring. Such petty
producers were not the only individuals who did not get their primary
subsistence from agricultural labour; rather, a host of artisans, beer-
shop keepers, builders, higlers, industrial workers, miners, specialist
wood-based trades, among many others, were all important members of
rural working communities. If all rural workers, including those remnant peasants, were all subject to the vagaries of the market their experiences of being at – and without – labour were necessarily quite different.
As such, the chapter goes on to consider the regionality of work and,
especially post-1750, worklessness. In particular, it analyses the impact
of the many parish and poor law union-based attempts to 'deal with'
un- and under-employment as generators of protest. Moving from the
effects of the old poor laws, the chapter ends with an analysis of rural
protests against the imposition and operation of the post-1834 Poor Law
Amendment Act, the so-called New Poor Law that shifted the working
of the poor law from the parish to 'unions' of parishes providing relief
institutionally in workhouses.

Chapter 2 shifts from the parish state to examine how policies devised
and managed by the central state provoked unrest. It takes four different
but interrelated foci of protest: extensions of the criminal code to protect
political interest (and capital); extensions of the criminal code to outlaw
customary practice and define private property; to gather revenues; and
finally, compulsory militia enlistment acts. The first section analyses the
context of the passing of the notorious Black Act of 1723, an attempt to
clamp down on the politically informed protests of the forest-dwelling
gangs of Berkshire, Hampshire and Surrey against the exploitation of
forest management by Whig office holders and sinecurists. The second
section develops the theme in examining Hobsbawm's concept of social
criminality, with a particular emphasis on poaching and wood-taking. It
is argued that the persistent breaking of such property laws represented a
key way in which authority and the concept of ownership was challenged
in the countryside. The third section analyses the importance of smuggling as a critique of excise law, and thus state policy, and as an assertion
of plebeian strength against the combined force of the state, itself also
often underwritten by a libertarian ideology. The chapter ends by briefly

considering other forms of protest that offered a more direct challenge to the authority of the state, specifically opposition to the Militia Acts first enacted in response to the internal 'threat' of Jacobitism.

The third chapter returns to that most enduring field of rural historical enquiry, enclosure. As noted above, much of the foregoing debate has hinged on the economic and labour impacts of enclosure. The chapter deviates from this argument by arguing that the enclosure of commons and wastes always represented a profound dislocation in the *way of life* of rural workers, and as such on whatever scale it was enacted received some degree of opposition. It also contends that the huge emphasis placed on enclosure in rural history tends to shadow the important effects other major land use and environmental changes had on rural society. Chapter 3 therefore, after beginning with an analysis of opposition to enclosure, goes on to examine resistances to other land use changes. It ends with a shorter consideration of the importance of technological projects and technologies of change as generators of conflict.

Chapters 4 and 5 examine the cultures that underpinned protest as well as offering a detailed examination of several important protest practices. Chapter 4 begins with a consideration of what it meant to protest, paying particular attention to more subtle forms of everyday social 'dissent'. It then moves on to examine the ways in which religion both underpinned popular protest – for instance, the Bible was often invoked by food rioters – and through the adoption of 'dissenting', non-conformist religious practice. Religion also underwrote the customary calendar of rural communities, the many saints and feast days offering an opportunity to engage in various customary rituals that 'legitimately' turned the normal social order topsy-turvy. Such physically assertive, rumbustitious acts were central to a plebeian culture that, as E.P. Thompson argued, remained an important wellspring of popular opposition to those who transgressed accepted community codes of behaviour. Chapter 5 offers a more detailed analysis of specific protest forms. The first section examines that most iconic form of eighteenth-century protest, the food riot, and the second section analyses incendiarism, arguably the archetypal rural protest in the early nineteenth century. Both practices, so it is shown, could be used interchangeably in subsistence crises but whereas food rioting, while always socially catastrophic, represented an attempt to redress imbalances, incendiarism was a tool of terror.

The penultimate chapter moves beyond consideration of protest practices to examine the form and importance of those landmark 'protest movements' in the English countryside: the 1816 Bread or Blood riots in East Anglia, the 1822 East Anglian rising, and the Swing riots of 1830.

Before this, it offers a critical reading of the meanings of social movements and protest movements, loaded terms that have tended to be
used rather uncritically. It also considers the rural manifestations of the
Luddite disturbances of 1811–13, a series of protests associated with the
urban but often occurring in the countryside. What united the Luddite
attacks with the protest movements of 1816, 1822 and 1830 was a plebeian
suspicion of labour-sapping machinery, the Bread or Blood riots representing the first sustained assault on agricultural machinery in England,
and Swing the most significant and widespread rural rising since the
Peasants' Revolt. In comparison to 1816 and 1822, Swing was also a more
broadly based and widespread movement. Swing, it is shown, was many
different things: an outpouring of feeling; a joyous moment when rural
workers could reassert their self-belief and confidence; a proto-insurrec-
tionary movement; and the final nail in the coffin of the old paternalist
rural system. The chapter ends with an assessment of Swing's achieve-
ments, both in relation to the immediate and longer-term gains – higher
wages and the delay of agricultural mechanisation, respectively – and
the unforeseen consequences – a massive upturn in rural terror; the
imposition of the New Poor Law and rural police constabularies; and the
further politicisation of rural workers.

Chapter 7 begins where Chapter 6 ended, with an analysis of the ways
in which radical participatory politics, first, gave form to rural protests
and, second, and examined in more detail, was in itself an important
form of rural conflict. It contends that while the key national political
movements that swept through the countryside occurred in the aftermath of Swing – specifically Chartism – rural workers had long engaged
in popular politicking in support of parliamentary reform. Evidence for
the involvement of rural workers, it is shown, was marked during the
1790s reform crisis and then, after several decades of relative abeyance,
again gained vitality in the 1820s, finding voice and vigour during Swing
and its aftermath. Disenchantment with the fact that the reformed parliament of 1832 betrayed the reform movement by passing the New Poor
Law in turn acted to further politicise rural workers and led to the adoption of new organisational forms, creating fertile recruiting grounds
for the General National Consolidated Trade Union – most famously
at Tolpuddle in rural Dorset – and Chartist missions. Trades unionism
had a long history among farmworkers but flourished post-Swing, a factor of changing social relations in the countryside and encouragement
from urban unions. Similarly, while Chartism was ostensibly an urban-
based mass membership organisation, it *was* active in the countryside
and attracted significant numbers of rural workers through its powerful
critiques of agrarian capitalism.

It is also important to note that the chapters are not grounded in a traditional 'ploughs and cows' approach to rural history, but instead are concerned with all those who worked in the fields, yards, workshops and factories, whether far from the cities or on the urbanising fringe. The distinction between the rural and the urban worker, then, is a hard one to draw. Indeed, in some senses it is a false distinction, for the experiences of work existed on a spectrum of occupation – from farmhand to merchant banker – rather than a spectrum of location. However, it is arguable that there was something culturally distinctive that forged a divide between rural workers and those of the town. For not only were those who lived and worked in rural communities subject to rule and control by those who made their living in the working of the land, but their shared customs and traditions were defined by this same bond with the soil. Besides, equating the countryside with the agrarian is truly an anachronism, for between 1700 and 1850 the rural was as much equated with the industrial as it was with the agricultural. This simplification was a development outside the temporal frame of this study and therefore it plays no part in the ensuing analysis.

Introduction: Understanding Rural Protest

Against repeated evidence that rural workers not only *could* conceive of alternative social worlds and did protest their lot, social commentators in eighteenth- and early-nineteenth-century England often asserted that such protests were either mere rebellions of the belly – the reflexive reactions of the animal – or the acts of the instigated. As Hannah More, in her patronising *Village Politics* (1793), attempted to 'prove', the seduction of the seditious words of Tom Paine was incomplete, for Tom Hod the village mason could not understand the complexities of politics let alone decode the *Rights of Man*.[1] 'Instant' histories of the so-called 'Swing riots' of 1830 – against the mechanisation of agricultural practices and the immiseration of rural workers at the hands of penny-pinching farmers and poor law officials (see Chapter 6) – were also quick to assert that this most intensive and widespread of all rural rebellions could not have been the work of agricultural workers and artisans alone. The mythical leader of the Swing rioters, 'Captain Swing', was variably reported to be a decayed small farmer, the son of a tenant farmer, and a former farmer with Irish connections, his followers either smugglers, 'the most lawless men in the village', or simply those mindlessly swept along.[2] Even against attempts by Victorian antiquaries to better understand the major revolts and rebellions of medieval and early modern England,[3] the protests of Georgian England obdurately remained in the scholarly mind the work of foreigners, Jacobites attempting to restore the House of Stuart to the monarchy, revolutionary Jacobins attempting to mimic the 1789 French Revolution, and the asinine. As Hobsbawm and Rudé noted, mid-nineteenth-century parsons were more at home deciphering medieval manuscripts than attempting to understand their plebeian flocks.[4]

1

This is necessarily to paint with a broad brush, for one *can* find evidence of more critical and nuanced early histories of protest. The *Westminster Review* of 1836, for instance, called Reverend Gleig to account for his representation of Captain Swing as 'a well-dressed person, with black whiskers and insinuating manners ... with the secret purpose of smuggling, and instigating fires and riots' when 'the causes were unfortunately too obvious in the condition of the people'.[5] Moreover, as the ensuing chapters show, foreigners, Jacobins, Jacobites and the easily led all assumed an important part in protests in Hanoverian England. But the exceptions serve to prove the rule.

Arguably it was not until the publication of John and Barbara Hammonds' *The Village Labourer* in 1911 that the cosmos of the rural worker was subjected to analysis, the causes of their poverty and discontent, their worldviews and protests all deemed worthy subjects of critical study. The Hammonds' book has often been read as the first proper study of Swing, the several chapters on the 'village' before, during and after enclosure, food riots, poor law reform are all a teleological prelude to the several chapters on the 'Last Labourers' Revolt', aka Swing. But to claim that this was just the first systematic account of Swing is to do this pioneering book a profound disservice. If the model adopted served their own Fabian political ends well (the decline of the sturdy labourer as affected by capitalist imperatives and given voice in social decay), it also opened up several other fields to critical enquiry. Enclosure, for instance, had hitherto been the subject only of quantifying and Whiggish impulses, the huge areas of 'champion' England enclosed in the late eighteenth and early nineteenth centuries a matter of great national pride rather than something worthy of critical social analysis.[6] If this was not a truly national study of either Swing or the resort to protest in general, what mattered was the fact the Hammonds located protest in the wider social (and political) context, enclosure and pauperisation located at the root of both the food riots of the 1790s and Swing.[7] Read in tandem with the similarly pioneering work of Sidney and Beatrice Webb on the English poor laws and trades unionism (also a central theme in the Hammonds' *The Skilled Labourer*), here was a seemingly emergent historical canon, a critical social history focused on the 'people' rather than the nobility.[8]

In some senses, the prolific output of the Hammonds and the Webbs can be read as a dead end in the study of English history. Indeed, few were the studies in the ensuing decades that took direct inspiration from their work in furthering understandings of rural social change in Hanoverian England, let alone the resort of rural workers to protest. Beyond a small number of inspiring but initial and localised studies,[9] the new rural social history appeared to be stillborn, partly a function of two world wars and partly a function of the stranglehold of (elite) political history in British academe. It was not until the early 1950s, and emphatically so from the 1960s, that the baton was well and truly taken up by a new generation of scholars who took inspiration not from radical liberalism but instead from Marxism. And betraying both this ideological baggage and a devotion to no-holds-barred critique, the Hammonds' foundational text was not above criticism. Their chief critic was Eric Hobsbawm. As he put it, while *The Village Labourer* was both groundbreaking in its emphasis on social change and protest and a pioneering work of history 'from below', it suffered from innumerable flaws. Their account, he claimed, underestimated the extent and intensity of the landmark events of rural protest, lacked detail, was driven by emotion, and lacked objectivity. The Hammonds' most heinous crime was – and there is a degree of irony in this statement coming from Marxist scholars – being ideologically predisposed to blindly support the protestors' cause against the interests of the propertied, yet, conversely, taking the Fabian line 'that strong-arm methods in labour action are less effective than peaceful negotiation'. All that happened in the eighteenth and early nineteenth centuries was, in short, a prelude to the labour movement, a crude and violent precursor to the ultimate enlightened state of 'peaceful negotiation'. In such views, Hobsbawm continued, 'there is obviously a good deal of truth', but he essayed they tend to 'obscure a good deal of history ... they make impossible any real study of the methods of working-class struggle in the pre-industrial period'.[10]

The point is necessarily over made. Indeed, some 17 years after the publication of Hobsbawm's 1952 essay 'The machine-breakers', he returned to the theme with crowd historian George Rudé in their landmark study of the events of 1830, *Captain Swing*. The Hammonds' book, he now asserted, suffered from 'avoidable weaknesses'. Besides, 60 years of subsequent scholarship – this being partly a self-referential point – had made their study 'inevitabl[y] obsolescen[t]'.[11] Yet, without *The Village Labourer* there could be no *Captain Swing*, for the analytical and methodological debt owed is obvious, the 'history from below' perspective a striking continuum. More directly, *Captain Swing* betrayed an immediate debt to the earlier works of the two authors, specifically Hobsbawm's aforementioned study of machine-breakers, his treatment of 'bandits', *Primitive Rebels* (1959), and his *Labouring Men* (1964);[12] and Rudé's innovative studies of 'faces in the crowd', *The Crowd in the French Revolution* (1959) and *The Crowd in History* (1964).[13] Another influence was Edward Palmer ('E.P.') Thompson's strikingly original and extraordinarily wide-ranging survey of the emergence of class consciousness in late eighteenth- and early nineteenth-century England, *The Making of the English Working Class*.

This seminal book, published in 1963, was quickly recognised as a land-mark study in social history and 'history from below'. Thompson's claim that his book was an attempt to 'rescue the poor stockinger, the Luddite cropper, the "obsolete" handloom weaver, the "utopian" artisan, and even the deluded follower of Joanna Southcott, from the enormous condescen-sion of posterity', quickly becoming a rallying cry for social historians and fellow cultural Marxists alike.[14]

Beyond the opening chapters that – in obvious debt to the Hammonds – analysed changing agricultural and social systems in the four decades before Swing, the key sections of *Captain Swing* first systematically explored the unfurling of the protests in four regional studies, before in the final section analysing who the 'faces in the crowd' were, how the protest movement was repressed, and its aftermath. In addition, Rudé, by then working in Australia, also reconstructed the new lives of the many Swing protestors transported to New South Wales and Van Diemen's Land (Tasmania) for their involvement in the movement. This was not just seemingly comprehensive in its coverage but also novel in asking new questions of protest, especially the interaction between protestors and the authorities, and the aftermath of the movement.

The thesis posited was deceptively straightforward. The protests of poor farmworkers often supported by artisans and small farmers revealed the fissuring of English rural society into three distinct classes: the landed classes and clergy; tenant farmers; and the landless labourers, artisans and residual peasantry. This fracturing was further rendered by, so they claimed, the collapse of old patriarchal systems, though the labourers still clung on 'to the ancient symbols of ancient ideals of stable hierar-chy'. Unaware that they were present at the making of the working class, farmworkers had little in the way of political self-consciousness and could not yet call upon the 'modern' practices of the urban worker, such as trades unionism. Instead, their protest tools were 'archaic', their move-ment 'improvised, archaic, spontaneous movement' and easily crushed by the might of the British state.[15] Hobsbawm and Rudé's book has stood the test of time; only very recently has their account of the events of 1830 come under sustained systematic scrutiny.[16] While on its publica-tion in 1969 it was not without criticism – E.P. Thompson questioning the absence of radical politicking and women from their account, others arguing it lacked detail to substantiate their broader points[17] – it is hard to over-emphasise the transformative impact the book has made on the study of rural and protest history. Published in the wake of the 1968 stu-dent riots, anti-war protests and civil rights movements, as well as a grow-ing concern with the impacts of industrial capitalism on the environment and countryside, their book was welcomed by a ready audience. Indeed,

INTRODUCTION 5

it remains one of very few works of academic history to enter the bestsellers charts, a popular 'Reader's Union' edition being rapidly produced. And yet, beyond the popular audience, the influence of Hobsbawm and Rudé's work was neither *immediately* obvious in the study of protest past and remains, as Iain Robertson has recently asserted, diffuse.[18] In part, this is due to the singular focus on Swing. Another factor was the apparent comprehensiveness of their study militating against early revisionist studies, the first serious revision coming with Andrew Charlesworth's 1979 mapping of their tabulation of protest incidents, and Eric Richards' 1974 study of Swing in the West Midlands offering neither critique nor a substantial reassessment.[19]

And yet in a flurry of studies published in the mid-1970s, it was possible to read the emergence of a rural protest studies paradigm, the ideas of Hobsbawm and Rudé being most *directly* manifest in David Jones' 1975 study of incendiarism in 1840s East Anglia.[20] Arguably in this wave of new studies it was a subsequent article by Hobsbawm on 'social crime' and a landmark paper by E.P. Thompson – published in 1972 and 1971, respectively – on the 'moral economy' of 'the English crowd' in eighteenth-century food riots that proved most immediately influential.[21] Hobsbawm's short essay posited that certain acts, while forbidden by law, were deemed permissible by plebeian communities. Typically these were acts that were once customary (poaching and wood-taking, for instance) but had been redefined as criminal as part of wider attempts to solidify the rights of private property. By contrast, Thompson's was a more complex thesis, albeit one based on a distinctly urban reading of protest, the dynamics of the marketplace and urban consumers taking centre stage. Essentially, it rested on the idea that in eighteenth-century England the poor and the authorities shared similar beliefs, as vested in Tudor Books of Orders as to how food markets should operate. Bakers, dealers, farmers, and millers were thus charged with a moral duty to the community to charge a 'fair' price for a quality product. Undermining the old shibboleth that crime was necessarily a practice of the social deviant and that food riots were mere rebellions of the belly, both interventions, while very different, were important for very similar reasons. Both suggested that custom was the wellspring of popular beliefs and values. As such, custom was a – and perhaps *the* – key driver of protest.

This conclusion has proved central to the study of rural protest ever since. But to ascribe all the 'credit' to the two aforementioned studies would be a gross simplification, for Thompson's paper was conceived of at the same time as a far broader project was being hatched among several scholars centred on the University of Warwick. Together, Thompson and Douglas Hay, Peter Linebaugh, John Rule and Cal Winslow sought to better understand both the mentalities of the poor – a clear nod to Hobsbawm and Rudé – as expressed through their 'crimes' and protests, and the interplay between the poor and the emergent eighteenth-century British state. While the fruits of their collective and individual labours are too many to list here, it is important to note that two studies in particular have proved hugely influential. *Albion's Fatal Tree*, a collection of extended essays analysing, among other things, poaching, smuggling, wrecking and coastal plunder, and the sending of threatening letters, is widely acknowledged as the landmark study in the emergence of the social history of crime. A 2011 edition powerfully attests the continued potency of both the overall book and the essays therein.[22] Together, the several essays can be read not only as an attempt to think through the importance of plebeian mentalities but also the central place taken by the operation of the rule of law in shaping social relations. As Hay notes in the introductory essay, the eighteenth century represented a defining moment in the reworking of social relations, the law being redefined as an ideological system which, through 'imagery and force, ideal and practice', attempted to 'enforce the division of property by terror'. Or to put it another way, the ruling classes co-opted the law to both buttress their power and to help annex and define all property as private, and by definition, theirs. The tenor of a slew of statutes against property 'crimes' that made even such petty acts as – brilliantly satirised by Henry Fielding in *Tom Jones* – the taking of a twig punishable by death, together with the Janus-faced combination of occasionally making examples and extending the hand of mercy acted to both internalise terror among the non-propertied and gave the sheen of legitimacy to the self-interest of the ruling classes.[23]

The most brilliant expression of this dynamic was Thompson's *Whigs and Hunters*, his study of the socio-political contexts and effects of the passing of the so-called Black Act of 1723.[24] The British state, as noted, was extraordinarily prolific in legislating against property offences, the sheer number of offences punishable by death leading to the tag of the 'bloody code' being applied to the English and Welsh statute. By the late 1760s, legal chronicler William Blackstone could detail 160 capital crimes, a figure that rose to some 223 crimes leading to the scaffold by the end of the 1810s.[25] If magistrates had considerable discretion in deciding by what statute offenders would be indicted, if they were to be prosecuted at all, it was the very fact that such statutes existed and could be invoked that was material to Thompson.[26] In the context of Jacobite challenges to the nascent early eighteenth-century Hanoverian state and the allied Whig 'ascendancy', and in the fragile politico-economic aftermath of the bursting of the South Sea Bubble, law was used to secure the ascendancy and to protect the interests of those granted potentially lucrative forest offices. The latter point is particularly germane to Thompson's thesis. Against attempts to reinvigorate forest law and to clamp down on the exercise of common rights and customary practices, those who lived in and around the forest and relied on the forest resources of southern England resisted. Their resistances were both organised – the several gangs being known as 'the Blacks', a reference to their going about incognito with blackened faces – and varied, deploying such practices as deer-stealing, the maiming of trees and animals, incendiarism, and the sending of threatening letters. The response of the state, so related Thompson, was the passing in 1723 of the Black Act, a piece of legislation that detailed more capital offences than any other European country had in its entire criminal code.

The argument that changing functions in the state and, more generally, the withdrawing of the landowning classes from direct social interaction with rural workers, was also at the heart of two further hugely influential interventions by Thompson in the mid- to late 1970s.[27] The eighteenth century, argued Thompson, was the period that witnessed 'the erosion of half-free forms of labor, the decline of living-in, the final extinction of labor services and the advance of free, mobile wage labor'. The combined imperatives of the commercialisation of agriculture, rising industrial production, and a huge building programme all necessitated the ready availability of a pool of casual(ised) labour. The rise of such occupational groups as 'the clothing workers, urban artisans, colliers, bargees and porters, laborers and petty dealers in the food trades', not to mention the mechanics and operatives and the many increasingly specialised farm trades, wanted not the close ties of paternalism but freedom. If the nobility and gentry were happy to abdicate responsibility and to withdraw to their grand houses and rely on land agents and bailiffs to extract rent and run their estates, they did not cede power.[28] Rather, the emergence and articulation of a distinctive plebeian popular culture in the eighteenth century was still framed within a deeper cultural hegemony – and here Thompson is in debt to the Italian political theorist Antonio Gramsci – set by the ruling classes. In short, power was exerted not in everyday social relations and interactions but instead through setting the limits to popular action, by setting 'authority and even modes of exploitation' so that they 'appear to be in the very course of nature'. And having withdrawn from everyday social interaction, when resentments and antagonisms surfaced popular opprobrium was targeted not at the ruling classes but instead at the marketmen, farmers, poor law officials and so on. As Thompson put it, 'the gentry might profit from the sale of wool, but they were not seen to be in a direct exploitive relation to the clothing workers.'[29] Or at least until the 1790s, when open rebellion and popular politicking questioned the very basis of the state and the status of the nobility, with the influence of events in revolutionary France to the fore. This cultural hegemony, so Thompson suggested, had absolute limits. It required the constant 'exercise of skill, of theatre and of concession'. Besides, 'even when imposed successfully' it could not:

> impose an all-embracing view of life; rather, it imposes blinkers, which inhibit vision in certain directions while leaving it clear in others. It can co-exist ... with a very vigorous self-activating culture of the people, derived from their own experience and resources. This culture, which may be resistant at many points to any form of exterior domination, constitutes an ever-present threat to official descriptions of reality; given the sharp jostle of experience, the intrusion of 'seditious' propagandists, the Church-and-King crowd can become Jacobin or Luddite.

The rural English worker was not born into subordination without the possibility that they could throw it off. Indeed, for much of the eighteenth century the plebs:

> Maintained their traditional culture; they secured a partial arrest of the work-discipline of early industrialism; they perhaps enlarged the scope of the Poor Laws; they enforced charities which may have prevented years of dearth from escalating into crises of subsistence; and they enjoyed liberties of pushing about the streets and jostling, gaping and huzzaing, pulling down the houses of obnoxious bakers or Dissenters, and a generally riotous and unpoliced disposition which astonished foreign visitors.[30]

What happened in the 1790s snapped the illusion, breaking the power of the cultural hegemony of the landed. It was at this point, Thompson reckoned, that it was possible to view the making of an English working class, the self-identification by workers that their individual and collective interests were not best-served by their social betters but by themselves.

The Legacy of E.P. Thompson, and Hobsbawm and Rudé

The mantle of the great innovators in the study of rural protest was taken up most emphatically by Roger Wells in article published in the *Journal of Peasant Studies* in 1979. Building upon his recent doctoral work supervised by the great scholar of the independent urban artisan, Gwyn Williams, Wells' paper argued that the 1790s were indeed a pivotal decade in the emergence of a 'new' protest culture. The brutal military and judicial repression of the 1795 wave of food rioting meant that the popular response to the chronic dearth of 1800 was not a resort to older moral economic forms of redress but instead to the tools of rural terror. The coincident extension of the systems of social monitoring, control and regulation through the pauperisation of agricultural working families effected by the provision of Speenhamland-style child allowances – in essence being *de facto* wage subsidies – also meant that being seen to openly protest was to risk the loss of parish support and the possibility of being thrown out of work. Moreover, having been robbed of the means of production through the loss of the commons, and having customary rights curtailed by new definitions of property, rural workers became just that, non-property-owning workers, a rural proletariat with no avenues of seeking redress beyond crime and affecting terror. And so the trend was set until the widespread uptake of agrarian trades unionism in the 1870s, the protest landscape now dominated by the destruction of property and the means of production, and attempts to inculcate fear rather than appealing for concessions from the ruling elites.[31]

This striking thesis sparked off a debate in the pages of the *Journal of Peasant Studies*, the series of replies and responses eventually being reproduced with two further influential essays in a landmark book. Much of the 'debate' focused on the somewhat circuitous question as to whether those who lived in 'open' villages – without resident squires and high levels of social control – were more likely to turn to protest and crime compared to those who lived in 'closed' villages – tightly regulated settlements where landownership was in a small number of hands. However, a response by Charlesworth, questioning Wells' identification of the 1790s as the decade in which rural workers effectively abandoned 'overt' protest and took up 'covert' protest, most directly advanced our understandings of the complexity of rural protest. Overt protests, Charlesworth asserted, remained central to the protest landscape in the early nineteenth century. The Swing risings of 1830 were, he noted, the largest single episode of machine-breaking in British history, while the 1816 Bread or Blood riots and 1822 labourers' protests in East Anglia proved the persistence of 'riot' in the English countryside in the years after 1795.[32] Wells promptly countered that the events of 1816, 1822, and especially 1830, were exceptional episodes that proved his overall argument. Accusing Charlesworth of a 'myopic attachment' to these exceptional landmarks, Wells argued that what was needed were detailed studies of the everyday lives of rural workers, analyses of the quotidian resistances rather than the exceptional that hitherto dominated studies of protest. Having established this need, Wells offered an initial 'micro' study of the 'open' Sussex Wealden parish of Burwash.[33] While later contributors argued Burwash was in itself exceptional, Wells' micro-study, together with responses by John Archer on incendiarism in East Anglia and the essays by editors Wells and Mick Reed, served to highlight the wide array of rural protest forms, the centrality of the poor law as a locus of conflict post-1795, as well as the depth of protest, especially arson, in the corn-land counties of the south and east both before and after Swing.[34]

If the question concerning the relative importance of overt and covert protest forms soon reached something of an intellectual impasse, the outcomes of the so-called 'Wells–Charlesworth' debate set the agenda for rural protest studies until very recently. Indeed, this, with the continued influence of Thompson's moral economy and class formation theses, were the key drivers of studies through the 1980s and 1990s. Before considering these trends in relation to studies that focused explicitly on the countryside, it is important to consider briefly several other trends that while not being studies of rural protest per se were pivotal in extending our knowledge of the protest landscape in late eighteenth- and early nineteenth-century England. Analyses of food rioting have remained central to protest studies, Wells' brilliant survey of the food crises of the 1790s and early 1800s, *Wretched Faces*, and the joint work of Adrian Randall and Charlesworth on the culture of food rioting doing much to extend our knowledge of the role of rural workers in food disputes.[35] Elsewhere, again the influence of Thompson was clear in what in the 1980s became a recognisable sub-genre in social history, the study of political radicalism. While almost invariably focused on the urban experience, studies by Malcolm Chase on radical agrarianism, Ian Dyck on William Cobbett's rural constituency, Wells on rural radicalism and Chartism in southern England, as well as myriad local and regional studies, have transformed and begun to challenge the received notion that rural workers were apolitical.[36] Similarly, work on industrial Luddism, most notably by Randall, has usefully reminded us that before the 1830s much in the way of industrial production was located in the countryside, either in the scale of the cottage workshop or in mills and factories located in villages and on the urban fringe.[37]

The period between the late 1980s and the mid-1990s witnessed a flourishing in rural protest studies. But while the work of, among others, Archer, Barry Reay, Charlesworth, Dyck, Jeanette Neeson, Randall and Wells represented a fracturing of intellectual concerns,[38] what united such works was a shift away from nationally focused analyses to detailed regional and, increasingly, 'micro' studies. The influence here has partly been calls to dig deeply in the archive to better contextualise moments of protest – Richard Cobbs' review of *Captain Swing* is often repeated[39] – and partly archival – expedience. In Reay's studies of the wood-bound Kentish communities in which the so-called Battle of Bossenden Wood of 1838 unfurled, a further influence was also at play: the Italian concept of 'microhistory'. This approach focuses on a particular locale – a parish, set of parishes, or a forest, for example – not to write local history per se but instead to test broader theories. Or as Edward Muir puts it, '[to] isolate and test the many abstractions of social thought'.[40] The turn to detailed, contextualised local studies also allowed for a reconsideration of opposition to enclosure, the pioneering work of Neeson on Northamptonshire and of David Eastwood on Otmoor, Oxfordshire, being the most notable examples.[41] This, moreover, was not confined to studies of the eighteenth and early nineteenth centuries, rather, what Alun Howkins has called the 'locality' approach, arguably has deeper roots in broader social histories of early modern England through the work of David Underdown, David Levine and Keith Wrightson, and has similarly emerged as an important trend in studies of post-1850 protest.[42]

As I have argued elsewhere, such microhistories and studies of everyday forms of resistance, while adding hugely to our understanding of the complexity of past rural protests, tends to replace one form of exceptionalism with another.[43] Indeed, the everyday acts that are detailed in the archive are there because either the apparatus of the state or letter writers and newspapers – arguably the most important source for the study of rural protest – deemed them worthy of record: the poacher prosecuted at a summary court, the incendiary fire noted in the county press. Such acts must necessarily be the tip of an iceberg of unknowable size, the vast majority of acts of everyday resistance – the taking of wood or a few apples, let alone back-talking, gossiping or foot-dragging – infrequently if ever recorded. Thus while the history of everyday life *seeks* to uncover the agency of people as opposed to the structures of power, the danger in writing protest is that it acts to replicate structures of power rather than quotidian social lives.[44] Focusing on the local, whatever the implications for the regional, national and even the international, also runs the risk without parallel studies pitched at a wider spatial scale of failing to appreciate and apprehend difference between locales and regions.

After the extraordinary burst of creativity – and productivity – in the 1980s and early 1990s, the field of rural protest studies lost much of its vitality, with what few publications that came out in the mid- to late 1990s tending to either be compendiums of previous writings or reflecting established shibboleths.[45] This sense of frustration was most clearly manifest in an a call to arms issued by Charlesworth in his part review, part polemical piece, 'An agenda for historical studies of rural protest'. Surveying the state of the field, Charlesworth suggested that while much had recently been achieved, there remained several blindspots in previous approaches. There was a need, as Charlesworth saw it, to better understand how power was exerted, by governments, by the rich and landed – as well as by rural workers themselves. Here Charlesworth suggested the adoption of the approach of anthropologist James Scott, and his study of the 'weapons of the weak' might reap dividends, particularly by paying close attention to the protest practices of rural workers. In addition, Charlesworth suggested that future studies of rural protest should be alert to matters of gender, of disguise, and of costume.[46] The first publication to take up this challenge was a book, edited by Randall and Charlesworth, that emerged out of a major Economic and Social Research Council-funded project on market cultures in the south-west of England.[47] If the essays in *Markets, Market Culture and Popular Protest* were rooted in the now dominant localities/microhistory approach, the emphases on the importance of folk and customary cultures – notably drawing on the pioneering work of Bob Bushaway[48] and on Scott's readings of the 'hidden transcripts' of peasant resistance – offered something strikingly different.[49] Thus while the hand of E.P. Thompson's moral economy thesis and his recently published work on custom were clearly evident,[50] these different conceptual stimuli allowed for studies that were both sensitive to local values and more-than-local dynamics of cultural systems. A subsequent book by Randall – *Riotous Assemblies* – returned to these themes in offering a systematic survey of the resort to riot in eighteenth-century England. But Randall's fine book represents not a new agenda but instead the pinnacle of work in the Thompsonian tradition – and one just like Thompson's *The Making of the English Working Class* essentially focused on the town rather than the country.[51]

Towards a 'New' Protest History?

The mantle of the innovative approach adopted in *Markets, Market Culture and Popular Protest* has only relatively recently been taken up in what Katrina Navickas has described as the 'new protest history'.[52] Also inspired by the vibrant field of the study of the politics of social conflict in sixteenth- and seventeenth-century England, not least the work of Steve Hindle and Andy Wood, and literary scholar Kevin Binfield's analysis of the 'writings of the Luddites',[53] a new generation of scholars has firmly taken up Charlesworth's challenge. The relevance of old shibboleths like class and the distinction between 'overt' and 'covert' protest have been called into question, new archives (and technologies) tapped, while new questions have been asked of previously utilised archives. In many ways, it may be premature to herald a 'new' direction given the relative infancy of the recent increase of interest in protest studies. Similarly, it is possible that the 'newness' claimed for this wave of studies – and I would include myself as someone who would make such a claim – is over-played, being if not a case of 'new wine in old bottles', then as much a re-emergence rather than a total rebirth. Either way – and this list is by no means exhaustive – through the work of Peter Jones, Briony McDonagh, Katrina Navickas, Iain Robertson, and the continued work of Robert Poole and Steve Poole, it is evident that the field has undergone an energetic and creative remaking.[54]

In addition to the continued, if problematised, resort to the localities approach, several new trends are also apparent. First, and in no particular order, through the influence of cultural geography, art history and the aforementioned work of Binfield, is an attention to the meanings of signs and symbols. While this has perhaps been evident most explicitly in recent research on urban radicalism,[55] Frank O'Gorman's work on the effigy burnings of radical Tom Paine in the early 1790s, Jones' work on the meanings of Swing, and my own work on the symbolism of violence all attest to the centrality of semiotics in recent protest studies.[56] Second, as Charlesworth implored, considerations of gender have assumed a much greater importance in this 'new' wave. This has not been, thankfully, a case of the feminist-derided 'add women and stir' approach, though several important studies have highlighted the central role of women in protests hitherto thought to have been the exclusive domain of men.[57] The approach is arguably most notable for the more critical unpacking of gender roles, and even sexuality, in protest; recent studies exploring the gendered nature of machines, homosociality among machine-breakers, the use of sexual violence as a form of inter-class protest, and complex sexual statements made in the maiming of animals' genitals.[58] Third, and again following Charlesworth's lead, recent studies have been particularly alert to the ways in which protest was shaped both by other protests, events and agendas outside the immediate locality, and by the interplay between the local and central states. While arguably the most direct application of this approach comes in the several studies by Dave Featherstone on 'militant particularisms' – the phrase is originally Raymond Williams' – in the transatlantic world, Navickas' work is also of importance in demonstrating the ways in which the more-than-local helped to frame protests in industrialising Lancashire and Cumbria.[59] Fourth, and perhaps most radically, though the influence of Thompson's *Whigs and Hunters* and Neeson's work on the cosmos of the commoner have been critical, there has been a shift to consider the material and affective dimensions of rural protest. Such studies have been many and varied: the work of McDonagh on anti-enclosure protests in both the early modern and modern periods; Navickas' aforementioned work on political clothing; Robertson's invocation of the work of Karl Jacoby's concept of 'moral ecology': and my own work on 'plant-maiming' and resistance to land-use changes.[60]

What ties much of this recent work together is an understanding that protest was never just about actions. Rather, as the so-called linguistic turn suggested, the power of the written, spoken and sung word was of considerable importance in motivating, diffusing and mobilising protest. Also, in the sending of threatening letters, the use of graffiti, in the making of speeches – something brilliantly delineated by Janette Martin – in the uttering of seditious and inflammatory words, in the singing of songs and the printing of popular ballads, and the cursing of employers behind their backs, language was a powerful weapon of resistance.[61] Beyond language, other systems of codes – for that is ultimately what language is – have also been to shown to express (and embody) resistance. The carrying of flags and banners, the aforementioned wearing of political clothing, even the making of certain gestures, have been shown to be important, expressive forms of resistance.[62] Another welcome shift comes in the geography of the locales studied. As Charlesworth noted in his now over 20-year-old agenda (1991), the '[rural and] agricultural historiography in Britain has always been shot through with southern English insularity'. The papers of the Wells–Charlesworth debate containing 'hardly a reference … to any event north of Birmingham or west of Gloucester'. This is, as Charlesworth suggests, a function 'of the shadow cast by the Hammonds' *The Village Labourer,* a book he believed should have been titled "The Southern English Village Labourer"'.[63] If this has started to change – the work of the late Timothy Shakesheff on Herefordshire, of Robertson on Gloucestershire, of Soderlund on Yorkshire, and of Navickas on Cumbria and Lancashire offering vital corrections to this historiographical imbalance[64] – then it is important to note that these are exceptions that prove that the rule still broadly holds. What follows, reflecting the field as it does, is skewed towards the communities of the south and the east, the cornland communities where agrarian capitalism was at its most voracious and where the major rebellions started and were most intense. The need for further studies of the counties of the East and West Midlands and the North-East is especially great, but it is important not to forget that the so-called Home Counties of Bedfordshire, Buckinghamshire and Hertfordshire also remain little studied in terms of pre-Swing protest histories. In making such a plea there is an inherent danger, though.

Just because the southern and eastern counties have hitherto dominated studies of rural protest does not mean that we know everything there is to know, as the several recent revisionist studies of Swing attests.[65] And there remain significant gaps in our knowledge of large parts of Cornwall, Devon, Somerset and Gloucestershire, though the ongoing work of Rose Wallis and Robertson for the latter two counties, respectively, will significantly redress this issue. Moreover, we – and again Charlesworth alongside John Bohstedt provides the inspiration[66] – need more than ever to undertake comparative studies, whether between regions, counties, or between communities.

Scholars of protest need to be especially alert to definitions of the rural. Indeed, this is a particularly pertinent issue for a book that purports to offer an analysis of 'rural England' that ends at the mid-point of the nineteenth century. In 1851, the census authorities declared that for the first time over half of England and Wales lived in towns, some 50.1 per cent to be precise. Thus, while the population had risen to 16,738,495 souls by the time of the 1851 census compared to an estimated 5.2 million in 1700, the period covered by this book saw not only rapid urbanisation but also a huge increase in the rural population. Indeed, by 1851 agricultural workers were still by far the dominant occupational group. And yet such figures are problematic because the distinction between the rural and the urban necessarily rests upon definitions. For the 1851 census, a 'town' was considered to be a settlement of 2,000 individuals or more but as enumeration occurred on the level of the parish this meant that the distinction was hard to delineate meaningfully. For example, in 1851 the Sussex parish of Mayfield had a population of 3,055 individuals, making it, according to the census definition, a town. Yet at 13,604 acres this was a huge parish with very low population densities. Its social structure was dominated by agricultural workers and those who worked in rural trades. It was, in short, an agrarian parish, an archetypal rural settlement.[67] Other parishes might have pockets of high population density, for example around a mine or a mill, but were essentially rural, lacking any facilities of a town. Similarly, some extensive town parishes also contained not only large numbers of agricultural workers and those engaged in agricultural support trades but also a majority of the acreage in farmland. Conversely, some parishes contained settlements that assumed all the functions of towns, and even had borough status, but whose overall population was below 2,000. Steyning in the Adur Valley of Sussex had a population of 1,464 in 1851 yet was a fully functioning borough town with a bank, grammar school and had, until the 1832 Reform Act, returned an MP to the House of Commons. Yet, of the 3,100 acres in the parish, the borough made only a slight imprint.[68]

Another definitional problem relates to the fact that many suburbs spilled over from 'town' parishes into neighbouring 'rural' parishes, some of whose parishioners were therefore truly urban yet still classified as rural. Drawing the line between rural and urban is therefore not only difficult but also poses many definitional questions as to what makes a town and what makes the countryside. Moreover, some rural workers might have had stronger ties with those working in the market towns, and some in the towns a more intimate connection with the workings of surrounding villages and hamlets than their immediate urban environs. For example, during the summer many industrial and urban workers would assist with the harvest, and the practice of Londoners coming down to Kent and the Weald to pick hops continued into the 1950s.[69] As the next chapter explores, many industrial workers lived and worked in the countryside. Most mineworkers before the 1820s lived in small, quasi-industrial settlements near their mines in the countryside, with many miners often combining such work with agricultural work. The same was true for many manufacturing processes, the cottage and small workshop being a more typical site of production than the emergent large manufactory until at least the late 1820s. Even some of the new factories were located among fields in the heart of the countryside or on the urban fringe rather than being surrounded by other factories and high-density housing.[70]

What follows, taking Barry Reay's lead, acknowledges that there were many rural Englands.[71] The 'rural' did not stop at the field and forest edge and the farm gate, but rather could encompass the industrial and enfold provincial market towns and even the semi-agricultural suburbs of such metropolitan places as Birmingham, Manchester and London. As such, when rural workers' protests took them into the towns, as often occurred during subsistence crises, the analysis that follows does not stop at the city gates. Nor does it ignore, where the archive allows us to make the distinction, the protests of urban residents in the countryside. After all, many urban workers, through work and kinship networks, were still financially and culturally tied to the countryside.

Chapter 1: Work, Worklessness and the Poor Law

Until recently our received historical understanding was that, by the start of the eighteenth century, the English rural worker was already landless, reliant on his/her own labour and the poor laws. Those who toiled in the fields and farmyards, woods and workshops were wage labourers whose fortunes were dependent upon the mercies of a powerful landed elite, parish officers and the market. Rural society was thus clearly divided into three groups: the landed nobility, the farmers, and the poor.[1] In contrast to continental Europe, England was famously a country of capitalist farms, much of the country already being enclosed. Kent was by then all but bereft of open fields, while, according to J.R. Wordie, by 1600 Cheshire, Cornwall, Devon, Essex and Lancashire were also 'enclosed counties'.[2]

Before parliamentary enclosures, that is to say enclosures supported either by a dedicated act of parliament or from 1801 the General Enclosure Act, large parts of agrarian England were still farmed in common. By the mid-eighteenth century some three-quarters of cultivatable land in Northamptonshire and Oxfordshire remained under the open system. Indeed, it has been calculated that between 1760 and 1820, 30 per cent of agricultural land in England was enclosed under Enclosure Acts, transforming not only the Midland counties but also large parts of East Anglia, East and West Yorkshire, Derbyshire and Gloucestershire.[3] While it is important to note that huge areas of commonable open moorland and fells remained unenclosed in the North-East, North-West, Welsh borders and South-West, by 1850 the remaining half of the open-field systems that had persisted to 1750 had been extinguished by enclosure.[4] This chronology of enclosure is now long-established – and more-or-less accepted. Indeed, Leigh Shaw-Taylor has recent reasserted that '[p]arliamentary enclosure did not represent the last decisive stage in the development of agrarian capitalism. Capitalist farmers *and* proletarian labourers dominated English agriculture before parliamentary enclosure'.[5] But this is to mask a complex regional picture. In some places enclosure transformed local societies, while in others it had occurred long before. Moreover, as Henry French's study of the 'town moors' of Clitheroe in north Lancashire has revealed, after enclosure the already market-driven agricultural system operated in a more-or-less unchanged way notwithstanding that an important 'second income stream' for labourers had been lost.[6]

This matters because throughout England a variety of pre-enclosure landscapes, albeit in varying levels of concentration, remained. With the provisos in mind that enclosure did not necessarily lead to new social alignments, while even pre-enclosure there was a tendency towards larger farms,[7] small-scale family farming persisted. Indeed, Shaw-Taylor's claim that by 1850 in the South-East the family farm had disappeared, while being fundamentally true, masks an uneven picture. Using census records, Reay has shown that by 1871 family labour still accounted for over 40 per cent of the agricultural workforce in the counties of Cornwall, Cumberland, Derbyshire, Lancashire, Westmoreland and West Yorkshire. Only in the area south of a line from the Wash to the Bristol Channel was the figure under 20 per cent, but in no county were there *no* farms where most of the labour demands were met by the family.[8]

The huge wave of parliamentary enclosure and enclosure by agreement – the process whereby enclosure was effected without recourse to parliament by virtue of the agreement of those who had a claim to the land – physically and socially transformed vast swaths of the English countryside in the eighteenth century. In so doing, it acted to all but eliminate the old semi-cooperative agrarian system, and all but eradicated those agriculturalists who were as reliant on the exercise of common rights as they were of market exchange. But where old systems persisted, often on the marginal lands and on the, as broadly defined, geographical margin, so did a more complex array of agricultural and work forms. In short, even by 1850, the English countryside was not just tended by landless wage labourers but also by petty agriculturalists. As Jeanette Neeson and Brian Short have so powerfully shown for Northamptonshire and Ashdown Forest (Sussex), respectively, before enclosure, the exercise of common rights to both pasture, stock and the collection of food and fuel from commons and wastes supported economically independent and culturally distinctive communities.[9]

Many such individuals, though, were not classic subsistence 'peasants' solely reliant on their common rights and their small plots of land. As the work of Mick Reed and Michael Winstanley, among others, has demonstrated, by the early nineteenth century many were dual occupationalists, often also assuming roles as publicans and shopkeepers. Many others also had to turn to labouring to supplement their living from their smallholdings. What is particularly striking is that it was not only areas with remnant commons that supported this heterogeneous social mix. In some areas long-term copyhold tenancies maintained the presence of smallholdings, while in others landlords continued to let small farms.[10] It is important also to remember that a 'small farm' might have many different connotations: an advert for a lease placed in the *Taunton Courier* in 1816 suggested the 217-acre farm was 'truly eligible for a capitalist, who wishes to farm on a small scale'.[11] Charles Searle's work on Cumberland and Westmoreland also sheds light on a system that by the late eighteenth century was part capitalist and part feudal, a system that still made feudal demands on customary tenants yet enabled peasants to build up significant capital in their holdings.[12] The persistence of small farms might also simply be a reflection of landlords meeting particular local demands. For example, John Rule has noted that in the more remote parts of Cornwall, miners often also kept smallholdings. Similarly in rural Lancashire by the mid-eighteenth century, full-time weavers complained that competition from 'farmer-weavers' was deflating piece rates.[13]

These examples serve as a useful illustration of the fact that whatever the often highly localised complexities of systems of landholding, rural England was not just a place where tillage and pasture was tended by hired hands. There were many other forms of work. Large parts of the country were covered in woods that supported a series of quasi-agricultural systems. In Dunkirk, Kent, four out of every five acres of the parish was wooded, supporting a variety of trades from bavin and faggot cutting; timber milling; hop pole, fence and hurdle making; charcoal production; and bark stripping for the tanning industry.[14] Wooded areas were, as will be shown in the following chapter, also particularly active in their defence of custom and customary practice, developing distinctive cultural forms compared to classically agrarian communities.

Nationally, such wood-bound trades were *relatively* unimportant in terms of labour demands compared to that of rurally-based industries. While truly accurate population statistics before the first census are impossible to ascertain, of a population of 5,826,000 in 1701 it has been estimated that between one-quarter and one-third of adults were engaged in mining and manufacturing. Clearly not all these individuals were resident in the countryside, or even employed in what might meaningfully be described as occupations of the countryside. However, when one considers that by the time the first census was taken a hundred years later, only 35.9 per cent of the 8.7 million population were employed in agriculture, forestry and fishing, yet 66 per cent of the population were classified as *rural* residents, that it is to say, that they lived in settlements of fewer than 2,500 inhabitants. This suggests a complex balance between agriculture, 'trades', manufacturing and wood trades.[15] Another complication was the fact that many individuals were dual occupationists, often combining mining and manufacturing with agricultural work, but in official records tended to be recorded as miner or weaver rather than small farmer or labourer. Either way, manufacturing was clearly important in the countryside.

This was already the case by 1700. Indeed, by the start of the eighteenth century the once prosperous cloth trade of the Weald centred on the small town of Cranbrook had already disappeared, production having shifted to the area around Norwich, while the industry in Essex was already in terminal decline and that in Suffolk close to extinction. The weaving trade had a deep history in the countryside, leading many commentators to suggest that rural industry and the weaving trade were synonymous. Daniel Defoe's 1728 *Plan of English Commerce* is particularly telling. In the 'manufacturing counties' – then Devon, Gloucestershire, Norfolk, Somerset and Yorkshire – Defoe reported that 'you see the wheel going almost at every door, the wool and yarn hanging up at every window'.[16] There was something in this claim. By that time, in areas outside of the established zones of rural manufacturing, there were growing numbers being employed in emergent trades; for example, 5,500 cottage-based stocking-knitting frames were reportedly already in use in Leicestershire, Nottinghamshire and Derbyshire. By the 1720s, between one-half and two-thirds of male occupations as detailed in the parish registers of the areas in and around Rochdale, Bury and Colne in Lancashire were those of textile workers. Cotton weaving was also well-established by the middle of the eighteenth century, with 4,674 looms being operated in the area around Manchester.[17]

By 1850 these shifts in the geographies of the cloth trade had hardened: Lancashire and Yorkshire assuming a position of relative strength; the East Midlands remaining important in the stocking trade; but the once dominant West Country cloth trade in a state of long-term decline. This picture, though, obscures the emergence, and subsequent decline, of other important forms of industrial processing and rural manufacturing in other parts of the country. Central to this was 'putting-out', that system that linked a central contractor – and sometimes finishing factory – with usually rural-based domestic 'workshops', the system on which the revolution in industrial output was based.[18] While it is well-established that the early nineteenth century witnessed a shift to the towns from hand-weaving in the countryside, Timmins' study of the Lancashire handloom weavers shows that it was not until the 1860s that putting-out was finally snuffed out by urban power looms.[19] Mechanisation was beginning, though, to put paid to other rural trades. For example, the wire-button industry that in the 1790s had employed 4,000 workers in and around the north Dorset town of Shaftesbury had disappeared completely by the 1830s, supplanted by factory-based production in Birmingham.[20]

The period post-1830 was undoubtedly one of decline for rural industries, but as Reay has shown, a vibrant mixed rural economy persisted in many places into the early 1850s. In addition to agricultural workers, the reports detailed that at Keswick (Cumberland) there were woollen workers, pencil manufacturers and tool-makers; at Tamworth (Staffordshire) there were tape- and paper-mill workers; at Halstead and Grinstead Green (Essex) silk-factory workers, velvet and satin out-workers, straw plaiters and paper-mill workers.[21] 'Cottage'-based industries were rarely ever exclusively the domain of male workers. In many households contracted by agents in the putting-out system the whole family was so engaged, the labour of children being called upon when demand was strong and laid off when trade was slack. As Jane Humphries has recently put it, industrial development in all its forms was powered by child labour.[22] To Daniel Defoe the very merit of manufacturing was that it had the potential to employ the whole family. In eastern and central Norfolk, still an important centre for the cloth trade by the time of his famous *Tour Through ... Great Britain*, he noted that 'there was not ... any hand unemployed, if they would work'. From the age of four or five, so reckoned, a child's labour was enough to 'earn their own bread'.[23] Some cottage industries, though, were entirely dominated by female and child labour, the aforementioned button-making industry in Dorset and the straw-hat trade – which itself had supplanted the lace-making trade – in the Home Counties being important examples. It is particularly telling that in areas where there was not sufficient demand from farmers to employ enough women and children, handicrafts were often encouraged to reduce the poor rates.[24]

One important rural industry that was reliant more exclusively on male labour was mining. The tin and copper mines that developed in Cornwall and Devon in the final decades of the seventeenth century and the well-established lead mines of Derbyshire increased in importance in the early eighteenth century. More dramatically, the amount of coal mined in the North-East coalfield doubled between 1700 and 1750 from one million tons to two million, with significant increases, too, in the West Midlands, Yorkshire, Lancashire and Cumberland. As with Rule's Cornish miners, it was typical in many other mining areas to combine mine work with agriculture, something that persisted well into the nineteenth century.[25]

Such a survey necessarily fails to demonstrate, though, that in almost every rural parish farm work existed side-by-side with trades, whether allied to a particular contractor or simply meeting local demand. As Tony Wrigley has shown, the population boom in the 1810s and 1820s not only led to a massive out-migration from the countryside to the towns, but also to a boom in the number of small-scale rural artisanal producers. Furniture makers, blacksmiths and tool-makers, carpenters and builders, shoemakers, among other trades, all assumed a greater importance in providing rural employment and supporting the rural economy. Many of these tradesmen occasionally also had to turn to agricultural work to supplement their incomes, not only during the harvest when many of those engaged in rural industry worked in the fields, but also when trade was slack. Thus, whatever the changing function and fortunes of rural industry, in the countryside the livelihoods of all were inescapably bound to the soil.[26]

Even by 1851, when only 25 per cent of the workforce were (primarily) engaged in agriculture, many more were reliant in some form upon agriculture. Indeed, if this appears to be the story of the dramatic relative decline of the agricultural *sector* – collapsing to 30 per cent of the workforce from approximately 55 per cent in 1700 – it is worth noting that the actual numbers employed in agriculture actually rose from 900,000 in 1700 to 1.1 million in 1851.[27] Even these figures represent an undercount, ignoring the increasing number of individuals, those reliant on income from multiple forms of work. It also ignores the large number of women and children that Nicola Verdon, Pamela Sharpe and Jane Humphries have shown continued to be employed in agriculture, as well as those domestic servants that Caroline Steedman has shown often spent as much time doing farm work as they did housework.[28] Either way, agricultural workers were engaged in a system that had been through something that was every bit as revolutionary as the industrial sector. According to Gregory Clark, in 1850 the output per acre in Great Britain was greater than anywhere else in Europe, Belgium excepted, while on average the British farm worker produced almost twice as much as a worker in the Netherlands, the next highest country for efficiency in Europe.[29] In short, rural workers in England had truly undergone an industrious revolution.

The Condition of Work

Any reader of the above section would be forgiven for arriving at the conclusion that while the eighteenth and early nineteenth centuries witnessed dramatic changes in the ways in which the land was owned and used, this was a golden age for rural workers. It was not. It has been suggested that until about 1750 labourers were in a good position because of the growth of agricultural production, low and stable food prices, low population growth, and competition for labour from the expanding rural industries. Indeed, to the rural radical William Cobbett, the period before the mid-eighteenth century, while not a golden age, did represent a time when labourers were treated equitably and with respect. Thereafter, their condition spiralled relentlessly downwards, even in the tightening labour markets of the Napoleonic era marked by declining real wages as food prices soared. This supposed shift was a function of population growth, rising food prices and repeated harvest failures.

In some senses, this received understanding holds true. Undoubtedly, after c.1750 things did get worse for those primarily engaged in agriculture, and markedly so after 1780. While the debate regarding the impact of enclosure on the poorest members of rural society continues, it is apparent that the huge wave of enclosures from the mid-eighteenth century increased dependency on waged labour and thus the vagaries of the market. Moreover, it undoubtedly denied rural families other (legal) potential 'sources of subsistence other than wages'.[30] Recently enclosed communities were thereby particularly vulnerable to price fluctuations during periods of dearth. At the same time it is apparent that poor relief became less generous, and parish vestries applied greater stringency in determining relief policy. As Hindle has noted for the parish of Frampton in the Holland Fen of Lincolnshire, enclosure led to the tripling of the poor rate. This was no matter of coincidence: the highest level was in 1769, the year the fen was enclosed.[31] Repeated poor harvests in the 1750s and 1760s were also catastrophic for rural workers, the reduced demand for well-remunerated harvest employment and higher – and wildly fluctuating – prices hitting families hard. Population growth, though regionally uneven, necessarily increased the labour supply and thus tended to force agricultural wages down and increase the chances of un- and under-employment. This, combined with variable harvest lengths, led to, as David Stead has shown, an ever-increasing casualisation of agricultural labour, something supported by Snell's calculation that employment became more seasonal and that living-in service declined nationally by the mid-eighteenth century.[32] But this account denies problems that existed before 1750 – and the improving state of employment opportunities in the second half of the eighteenth century in rural industries.

Our received understanding is that before 1750 male and female wages were increasing while the cost of goods was declining. This hides important variations, though. By the 1720s the golden age for the serge weavers and combers of Devon was already over.[33] Constancy of employment was also not a given, as Peter Bowden has suggested. For the early decades of the eighteenth century 'there must have been considerable underemployment and irregularity of employment during the winter months in seasonal activities such as agriculture'.[34] By and large, though, from the close of the seventeenth century labourers saw their position improve for the first time in 100 years. Labour being in a position of relative power over capital, workers were better able to dictate terms, and even to take more leisure time. This was perhaps best evidenced in the establishment of early proto-trades unions among established trades. At Tiverton in rural Devon, for example, the Society of Woolcombers formed a 'benefit society' in 1700.[35] But there were many employers and commentators who, as Hatcher puts it, believed that it had 'once again became a priority to find means of blocking and reversing harmful tendencies in the labour market'.[36] Cutting wages or paying in truck to maintain – or perhaps improve – employers' margins was one way of testing workers' resolve. During the food crisis of 1740, against a backdrop of hugely inflated corn prices, the master weavers of Norwich reduced their journeymen's wages. This led to an invasion of the town by 'many thousands of the mob', the weavers taking the lead in the ensuing riot.[37] An attempt in November 1738 by the chief clothier at Melksham, Henry Coulthurst, to cut his piece rates led to one of the most sustained and bitter series of riots that Wiltshire had ever witnessed. Over three days of rioting, Coulthurst's house and mills were sacked, with the military having to be called from Bristol and Salisbury to restore the peace. The Melksham example is of particular importance, for, as Julia de Lacy Mann and, more recently, Randall have asserted, the government reaction to the riots marked a shift in government attitudes to the demands of workers. Having shown themselves to be, in the words of Randall, 'surprisingly sympathetic towards disgruntled weavers in the first two decades of Hanoverian rule', they now showed no mercy or compassion.[38]

As noted above, standard-of-living historians point to the middle of the eighteenth century as a watershed in the fortunes of rural workers.[39] This is not to suggest, though, that come the start of the 1750s, the world changed for rural workers. It did not. There was no sudden end to agricultural service, no sudden rise in unemployment. Besides, as we have noted, localised unemployment was a problem in the first half of the eighteenth century. Indeed, Alan Armstrong's analysis of the final decades of the century serves to remind us that the situation was not only regionally variable but might vary locally too, especially in relation to differences between the terms of employment of the minority employed on estates compared to those more precariously employed on tenanted farms.[40]

Notwithstanding that the fortunes of rural industrial workers were subjected to trade cycles, their position was relatively secure. Farmworkers, though, were now locked into terminal structural decline. Where opportunities for industrial and mining work were strongest – nominally the northern counties, parts of the East and West Midlands and parts of the west – agricultural wages remained strongest. Elsewhere – the south, east and Herefordshire – wages were lower, and alternative employment opportunities fewer. Of course, this is necessarily a crude picture, because in southern areas where commonable land persisted, alternative strategies of making ends meet allowed many families to survive on the fringes of agrarian capitalism, while booming leisure resorts like Bath, Brighton and Weymouth offered significant employment opportunities in construction and service to rural workers prepared to migrate. Conversely, those parts of the north that did not have many alternative employment opportunities were, more like the arable south, riven by structural decline and rural population growth. In Cumberland, for instance, Frederick Eden in his survey of the state of the poor in the early 1790s found that wages were 'very inconsiderable'.[41] This regional difference was in part mitigated by a poor law that was relatively more generously interpreted in the south and east than the north and west, though, as noted, from the 1780s even southern vestries were becoming more stringent in their giving of relief.[42]

All rural workers, regardless of employment and location, were also highly susceptible to acute dearth and bad winters. While, as Prasannan Parthasarathi notes, 'the magnitude of seasonal unemployment is one of the great unknowns in eighteenth-century British agrarian history', the evidence overwhelmingly suggests that wintertime unemployment was a recurrent problem. In particularly harsh winters this problem was chronic, while prolonged severe rain led to flooding of both arable and pasture.[43] In relation to dearth, the problem was not only a short-term one. Peter Linebaugh has suggested that the recurrent crises of the 1760s led to a structural shift from 'underemployment to outright unemployment'.[44] While it is impossible to absolutely verify this thesis, Snell's quantification of settlement records appears to offer empirical support. In the south and east, so Snell asserts, from 1760 the real wages of female agricultural workers declined – as did opportunities for such work – while the real wages of male agricultural workers declined from

1780. This was, with the exceptions of false dawns in the early 1790s and late 1830s and some highly localised revivals during the Napoleonic Wars, a long-term trend.[45] If the patterns of decline were uneven, the structural processes were universal. By the turn of the nineteenth century, according to Barbara Kerr, every parish in Dorset was 'pulling along landless labourers who could not find, or keep, regular employment', a situation that applied almost universally in the south.[46]

Protesting the Poor Law: The Condition of Worklessness

Attempts to put the unemployed to work were relatively few until the 1790s. Where evidence permits, it would appear that agricultural parishes attempting to reduce the cost of supporting unemployed men turned to the workhouse. At Shinfield, Berkshire, the vestry met in December 1768 to consider how to alleviate the cost of supporting the poor that had 'of late years greatly increased to such a Degree as at this Time to become an enormous and insupportable Burthern to the Inhabitants'. The problem, they asserted, was the lack of available work, 'one great Cause of the present great expence'. Their solution? To build a workhouse.[47] Using workhouses to employ those out of work had significant limitations in relation to capacity and the cost of providing materials and supervision necessary for meaningful work. This might be possible for combined parishes, but under the terms of Gilbert's Act of 1782 – something Samantha Shave has shown was adopted far more widely than we have hitherto thought – such unionised parishes were not allowed to incarcerate the so-called 'able-bodied' poor.[48]

Institutionalising the poor was not only an expensive option but also liable to generate protest. Many parishes (and unions of parishes) adopting work- and poor-houses did so with humane intentions and many such institutions were, at least initially, run in a dignified and comfortable way,[49] but they were not always well-received by the poor or the wider rate-paying community. Notwithstanding that studies of opposition to the creation of workhouses are few, Anne Digby and Paul Muskett's studies of the pioneering East Anglian poor law unions are important exceptions. The first such union, or rather rural incorporation, was founded by a dedicated act of parliament at Nacton, Suffolk, in 1756. Being projected by the 'more substantial landholders and local clergy' under the leadership of Admiral Vernon, this first rural poor law 'union' appears not to have initially generated (recorded) resistance and, having produced significant savings, encouraged other Suffolk Hundreds to apply for local acts. By 1765 seven incorporations were in operation and opposition *was* stirring. The construction of the Tattingstone workhouse led to a letter being directed to the 'Gentleman' sponsors, accusing them of attempting to starve the poor, and if the poor were not allowed to 'tak Care of thin Selves' their 'Brains be Blown out ... and the hous shall not be bilt a toyle'. A meeting of the 'directors' for Lees and Wilford led to the assemblage of a crowd estimated to contain some 500 men and a small number of women and children who disrupted the meeting, destroyed the parish poor records, and insisted that the poor be maintained as before. This was, they threatened, only the beginning of their work, for they intended that 'Nacton House and all other buildings of this sort should be levelled with the ground'. Before departing, the ringleaders forced the Directors to sign an agreement to drop their plan to build a workhouse at Melton. Further riots followed at Nacton and at Bulcamp; at the latter place, a 200-strong group demolished the works for the Blything Hundred workhouse, causing some £2,000 of damage. Of the 38 men and women committed to gaol for taking part in the three protests the occupations of 20 are known. Twelve were labourers, three yeomen, one a breeches-maker, another a carter, one a chimney-sweep, one a wheelwright, and a solitary shoemaker who had travelled 30 miles to take part in the protest at Bulcamp. These were not, Muskett notes, individuals who stood to gain directly from the protection of outdoor relief, but instead were doing 'good work' for the community in the defence of what was perceived as a right to outdoor relief. Government intervention in funding the prosecutions also shows a degree of paranoia about the power of rural workers to combine in collective action.[50]

It is also telling that while these protests did not halt the workhouse schemes already in progress in Suffolk and east Norfolk, plans in south and west Norfolk to adopt new systems for relieving the poor were abandoned after the Suffolk disturbances, not to be revived until the mid-1770s. These new plans also faced staunch opposition. A projected parliamentary bill to create an incorporation of the parishes of the Mitford and Launditch Hundred in mid-Norfolk prompted a petition from the 'labouring poor and small occupiers' to stop:

[T]he imprisonment of our persons, that separation from our children, that destruction of our race, that loss to the kingdom, and that curse from the Almighty which must attend establishing a poor house upon the specious fallacy of providing for our comfort, by the breaking of our hearts.[51]

As unemployment increasingly became structural rather than just seasonal, more adaptable and less expensive approaches were necessary to put the workless to labour. One important option was the roundsman scheme whereby those out of employ were sent 'round' to the farmers, or modifications thereon, having their wages paid in full or part from the rates. Whilst urban variations on the scheme date back to the late seventeenth century, their principal application to rural parishes appears to date from the 1770s and 1780s. At North Aston, Oxfordshire, the roundsman scheme was first adopted in 1775 to employ two or three labourers. Nearby Cropredy followed their example in 1785.[52] In neighbouring Berkshire, 1780 appears to have marked the decisive date. The Shinfield workhouse being found not to have answered its initial purpose, the vestry resolved that it would no longer relieve able-bodied men unless they laboured for each ratepayer in turn 'for as many days as shall be in proportion to the rates every man is charged to the poor'.[53] In the ensuing 11 years, the parishes of Drayton (1784), East Hendred (1786), Kingston Lisle (1791) and Tilehurst (1795) all made similar pronouncements.[54] By 1794 it was even said that in Buckinghamshire and Oxfordshire as soon as the harvest was finished the 'abominable practice' was enforced on *all* the labourers.[55]

As the Tilehurst scheme attests, the outbreak of war with revolutionary France in 1792 did not lead universally to a better situation for rural workers. Indeed, the notion that the Napoleonic Wars represented a golden age for rural labourers has been dismissed. Rent and provision inflation more than eroded the temporary, and spatially uneven, increases in labouring wages.[56] The huge transfer of rural workers from the fields of England to the battlefields of continental Europe undoubtedly acted to tighten labour markets and increase wages. In some areas, the unprecedented war effort – the size and effects of mobilisation having a far more profound effect than either the Seven Years War or the American Revolutionary Wars – also led to new employment opportunities. The wartime labour demands of naval dockyards and of other non-agrarian projects, notably canal and turnpike construction, had a profound, if localised, impact upon labour markets. The trade embargo also created opportunities in import substitution, the straw plait and hat-making trades in Hertfordshire 'thrived' to such an extent that farmers complained that it was now difficult to procure servants.[57] Demand for labour remained, however, seasonal and insecure, with unemployment and under-employment being, as Samantha Williams has suggested, 'pervasive for the many men and boys employed in agriculture.'[58] Indeed, the example of Tilehurst was far from unique in the south. Roundsman type systems were also deployed in Dorset and Hampshire, while many parishes found employ on an ad hoc basis for those out of work.[59]

While historians are unanimous in agreeing that tensions over food were the foremost generator of popular protest in eighteenth-century England, in an early response to Thompson's 'Moral economy' paper, Elizabeth Fox Genovese suggested that from the late eighteenth century wage levels replaced the price of basic foodstuffs as the fundamental component in plebeian living standards.[60] Hence, if the economic and cultural importance of the wheaten loaf was on the wane among wage-earners, then, *ceteris paribus*, we would expect that protests were increasingly concerned with wages and, where appropriate, poor relief entitlements. This shifting emphasis is evident in the changing discourses and demands made during eighteenth-century food crises. During the national crises of 1740, 1756–7 and 1766 protestors focused their attentions almost exclusively upon manipulations in the marketing of food. From the 1790s, though, the demands of protestors made during subsistence crises started to focus less on food – though this remained the primary focus – and more on wages. Perhaps the best example of the juxtaposition between the cost of food, wages and parish relief came in February 1801, when 300 country people from four Wealden parishes attempted to force the Lewes Bench into several concessions. Those from Buxted wanted lower prices, while those from Framfield threatened to strike 'if they didn't live better', and those from Chiddingly and East Hoathly wanted more generous poor relief.[61]

The nature of the Chiddingly and East Hoathly men's claims are easily understood, given the ways in which parishes had started to systematically support the wages of poor rural workers in the early 1790s. Not only had some parishes started to experiment with roundsman schemes but also, and most notoriously, *de facto* wage subsidy schemes, a.k.a. the Speenhamland plan.

On 6 May 1795, at the Pelican Inn in the Berkshire hamlet of Speenhamland, the Newbury Bench of magistrates met to consider labourers' wages and the price of corn. While we now know that their decision to adopt a sliding scale of cash payments in correlation to the price of corn delivered by the parish and paid out of the poor rates was not novel, a similar scheme having been agreed at the Dorset Quarter Sessions in 1792, the system proved hugely influential.[62] If claims to their universal importance have been over-played, such payments became, as Wells puts it, 'embedded in the principal cornlands'. Most counties enacting Speenhamland-style schemes did so through the adoption of allowances in aid-of-wages as dependent on family size, effectively *de facto* child allowances.[63] In parishes where such allowances were paid, all labourers' wages were effectively subsidised by the parish. If one farmer lowered the wages paid to his labourers, then the parish would have to increase the subsidy to maintain the policy, prompting other farmers to follow suit. The labour market so manipulated, agricultural wages were placed in a downward spiral, 'free labour', as Snell puts it, '[having] to become pauperized to find employment'.[64] The logical extension of this system was for the parish to act *as* the labour market: determining how many labourers each occupier should employ – and then subsiding each and every labourer through roundsmen and labour-allocation schemes.

In the south and east, as well as large parts of the west and north, un- and under-employment became an overwhelming problem following the cessation of hostilities between Britain and France. Measuring the depth of this problem, though, has hitherto eluded historians. Indeed, Hobsbawm and Rudé's 40-year-old contention that while we know that unemployment increased post-Waterloo, 'we have no general figures to measure its progress and fluctuations year by year' still holds.[65] We are therefore reliant on individual case studies to highlight the scale of unemployment. At Eling near Southampton by July 1816 – usually a highpoint for agricultural *employment* – there were sixty labouring men out of employ out of a total population of some 3,798 individuals and 756 families. Of these families 407 were primarily engaged in agriculture, thus approximately 14.7 per cent of agricultural families were afflicted by outright unemployment.[66] In early 1817 it was stated that out of a total population of 2,000 at Hindon, Wiltshire, 40 'strong, able-bodied men' were employed on the roads at four shillings a week. Three-quarters of all labouring families were supposed to be on wages – between seven and eight shillings a week – deemed inadequate to their support. However, even if they were paid five shillings a week, Squire Bennett thought that 'they would not leave me; they could not get work'. The chronic situation in the south and east meant that many labourers moved to the cities in search of work. At Islington, then on the northern fringe of a rapidly expanding London, it was related that the number of poor had greatly increased, in large part due to 'persons who could not get work in the country, have come to town, and that has brought fifty or a hundred persons'.[67] This was not necessarily the case everywhere in the south, especially on the London fringe, where opportunities for market gardening and the labour demands of the capital led to markedly lower poverty levels. For instance, at Harmondsworth, a 'principally agricultural' and recently enclosed Middlesex parish to the north-west of London, no one had been out of work in the winter of 1816–17.[68]

The agricultural worker in the northern counties was, as Armstrong has suggested, in a better condition, even in areas without many alternative forms of employment to labouring in the fields. According to a witness testifying before the 1828 Select Committee on 'the employment

or relief of able-bodied persons from the poor rate', in the 'purely agricultural' neighbourhood of Carlisle there was 'never any want of employment' and those labourers that needed relief were offered employment
on the roads or in doing other jobs for the parish. Invariably, such work
was refused, the labourer finding some alternative means of support.[69]

As the agrarian depression deepened, so the problem became more
acute and the division between the cornland economies of the south
and east and the economically more diverse, pastoral economies of the
north and (parts of) the west became more marked. This was a tacit
acknowledgement that the failure of households to get by was not simply
a function of the fortune of male wage labourers. A survey of Norfolk
and Suffolk labouring families in the mid- to late 1830s found that only
half the income of an average household derived from the oldest male's
daily earnings. A further third came from the labour of women and children, including from gleaning, while 15 per cent came from the harvest
earnings of all members of the family.[70] From this we can deduce some
important implications. First, as Joyce Burnette has asserted, unemployment among men meant that women were not hired, and during the
harvest such circumstances tended to depress female wages.[71] Hence,
male unemployment tended, in turn, to create female unemployment.
Second, the importance of female earnings and hence the problem
of female unemployment meant that in some parishes schemes were
devised to create – and regulate – work for women. A roundsman scheme
at Fisherton Anger (Wiltshire) in June 1817 included women who were
to be employed at six pence a day, the same rate to be received by 'all
the women put out to work', topped up by an extra shilling a week from
the parish, as agreed to at Amport (Hampshire) in April 1817. Three
years later, Amport Vestry devised a roundsman – or rather a rounds-
woman – scheme for the girls in the parish, all of whom were 'to be taken
to the different farms and employed 'till harvest in proportion to the
different rents' at three shillings a week. More typical though, 'for the
sake of morality, cleanliness, & œconomy' in the words of the Minstead
(Hampshire) vestry, were parish interventions in attempting to provide
work for women and girls in workhouse-based schemes. For instance, the
appointment of 'a woman' to instruct the 'young women applying for
relief' in spinning was part of a complex, multifaceted make-work policy
implemented at High Halden (Kent) in April 1823.[72]

Where work for rural workers was scarce, parishes adopted a wide
variety of schemes to employ those out of work – and make the workless
do something for their poor relief. Vestry books of cornland parishes
are especially replete with examples of the adoption of roundsmen
schemes, but this system was controversial and structurally flawed.

For instance, farmers were not bound to employ those men sent to them 'on the round', and besides might not need heavily parish-subsidised labour. According to Henry Boyce, the overseer of Walderslade (Kent), whilst he believed in the Smithian notion that if wages were lower more labourers would be employed, he saw that in practice those currently not employing any labourers would still not be in any position to be employers while those with the necessary capital would be 'overburdened with labourers'. In the neighbouring parish of Ash-next-Sandwich, every Thursday there was an auction for the unemployed labourers. However, frequently there were no bids at any price, even though a nominal bid of a penny would secure the services of a labourer for a week.[73]

There were, of course, other alternatives for rural parishes to find employ for those out of work. Some places simply, in the words of Rev. Collett of Haevingham in Suffolk where such a practice occurred, were relieved 'without any employment, receiving that money as the wages of idleness'.[74] As noted above, some parishes turned to road working, a non-controversial policy for the costs were low and every ratepayer benefited, however nominally. Some parishes tried to rigidly apply the workhouse test, this policy invariably soon collapsing due to either a lack of capacity or the cost of institutional relief for non-unionised parishes, while others tried parish-supported emigration of 'paupers', a policy predicated on the Malthusian belief that there were 'surplus' labourers.[75] Arguably a more influential critique of workhouse-based employment for those otherwise out of work was the belief that labourers should be employed on the land. This belief was instrumental to the formation of 'parish farms', pre-existing farms or fields hired by the parish and commercially farmed using the labour of those who would otherwise be out of work. This policy, originating at Cranbrook in the Weald of Kent in 1794, appears to have proved particularly popular in the Weald as well as parts of south Hampshire, Berkshire and Wiltshire, taking advantage of land that would otherwise remain untenanted. Parish farms also offered the possibility that they would make a profit, or at least in part cover the cost of labour, thus reducing the poor rates.[76]

Another option was to try and get farmers in the parish to throw off any employees not legally settled in the parish, thus getting – or rather recommending – farmers to employ only those who would otherwise be a liability to the poor funds. When one parish adopted the policy, neighbouring parishes would, economic logic suggested, need to follow suit. As the Fawley (Hampshire) Vestry lamented in the aftermath of Swing, 'it is the prevalent custom in other parishes' to send home labourers 'that do not belong to them'. From this circumstance, they continued, 'we have so many sent to us, that we have not houses to put them in, and it have [*sic*] increased the surplus labourers to that extent which with the present <u>high price of labour</u> it is utterly impossible the parish can maintain it'. The policy response of the vestry was to recommend that non-parishioners should no longer be employed by the farmers.[77] These dynamics helped to foster what Snell has termed a 'culture of xenophobia' that served to legitimise attacks on both non-indigent and migrant workers and those who sought to employ such workers.[78] Such attacks were most commonly targeted at Irish migrant harvest workers, increasing with frequency and ferocity in the late 1820s.[79]

It is worth noting that farmers and other employers were not entirely at fault for this state of affairs. After all, the cost of poor relief in England and Wales had rocketed from £1.5 million/£0.21 per capita in 1776 to £6.6 million/£0.63 per capita in 1813,[80] this being in part a function of population growth and the humane principles that underpinned the first Speenhamland type schemes. Against decimated farm-gate prices post- 1815, farmers, quite understandably, attempted to effect savings in all aspects of their operations, with both hired labour and the relative generosity of poor relief inevitably being squeezed. But it was a direct consequence of this retrenchment – and the way in which it was operated – that arguably became *the* key driver of rural protest in the cornland communities of the south and east, the combined effect of a lack of meaningful employment, stingy poor relief, degrading parish work, and often humiliating treatment at the hands of poor law officers acting to further politicise the poor law. If physical attacks on the institutions of the poor law in the period appear to have been few, with no organised attempts to destroy workhouses, as was seen in East Anglia in the 1760s and 1770s, or in the protests that followed in the early 1830s workhouses, and with only the occasional incendiary attack.[81] More important were vestry 'riots', attacks on the property of parish officers, and bodily assaults on overseers. The archive of vestry affrays is, as Wells has suggested, defective, but is clear that in the 1820s the judicial system was often relied upon to punish groups of male paupers who combined to use physical force and intimidation in an attempt to force more generous relief or parish pay.[82] Assaults on parish officers were arguably more common, and often took a more sinister tone. If workhouse masters were necessarily obvious and easy targets to aggrieved inmates, it was overseers who were especially subject to both violent threats and violent, premeditated attacks – especially so from the 1820s. The Bethersden (Kent) overseer, for instance, received several menacing letters before narrowly surviving an assassination attempt, while the Warborough (Oxfordshire) overseer was threatened with poisoning.[83]

An interview with a Sussex labourer, undertaken by Edwin Chadwick as part of the post-Swing Commission into the operation of the poor laws, perfectly details how this experience fundamentally altered rural social relations and spawned all protests. According to Chadwick's respondent, the talk among the Sussex labourers was that the 'land is not half-cultivated; they often say "There's no use going to America, there's America enough at home if the farmers would but let them cultivate the land"'. They did not want parish work, instead

> what they want is regular husbandry work at fair wages, they do not like the parish work, which is one great cause off [sic] their discontent. In Hailsham parish last winter, the men who are made to drag the parish carts got four of the horses' hoops of bells placed on their heads, and dragged the parish cart from Eastbourne to Hailsham market; when they were in the market one of them went with his hat to beg, and they got a good many shillings from people out of the parish. Their own farmers would not give them any thing, but looked another way; they could not bear to see it, they were ashamed of it.

The situation was almost as bad for the tradesmen as the 'poor people', both 'pray[ed] for the cheap loaf in every parish'.[84] Whatever the initial intentions of parish schemes to put the jobless to work, the effects, as Chapter 6 explores, of persistently low wages, a lack of meaningful employment and frequently inhumane treatment by parish officers were the reasons that Swing became a broad-based movement that diffused throughout southern and eastern England.

New Poor Law Protests

The situation in the early 1830s was little different. The Swing-insurrection acted to increase wages temporarily in the southern and eastern counties, but as the problem of unemployment persisted, so parishes continued to grapple with the limited number of policies they could adopt to provide work to the workless. One statutory 'innovation' – albeit an innovation that built upon a long-established variation of the roundsman scheme – was the labour rate. Made legally enforceable under the Agricultural Labourers Act enacted in 1832, the labour rate was a notional rate (like the poor rate or the county rate, charged against the rateable property value) that would only be levied if the ratepayer did not employ additional otherwise unemployed labour to the value of the rate. A year after the Act's passing, a request by the newly established Poor Law Commissioners for accounts of its adoption, only brought forth responses from the counties of Bedfordshire, Buckinghamshire, Cambridgeshire,

Essex, Hampshire, Huntingdonshire, Kent, Lincolnshire, Oxfordshire, Suffolk, Surrey, Sussex, Warwickshire and Wiltshire. Northern and western counties were not represented.[85] While its effects were not as demeaning as some forms of parish organised employment, it was not without its plebeian critics. At Brinningham in Norfolk, the adoption of a labour rate provoked two incendiary attacks and a plethora of threatening letters. As one letter, written by pauper blacksmith Josiah Turner, put it:

> You termed yourself to be a friend to the poor of this parish and to those that come to your doors in distress, how can you behave in this shameful way whereby you go in danger every day and all you farmers around, your houses and you must leave them for they shall be in flames but you G.F. shall be a dade man, prepear yourself to die for a mess of lade is got fit for you moore and moore beside you, you may call your westry meetings and your labour rate meetings for the safety of the poor to keep thear eyes shet these meetings ear no goes they bring on fires robrey murders and such like you shall be shot like a dorg before long.

The replies to the 'Rural Queries' of the 1834 Poor Law Report though perhaps offer a more nuanced, if stilted, account of the geographies of unemployment. Beyond the cornland counties of the south and east, snapshots of the extent of unemployment elsewhere come through. The responses can be classified into two categories: primarily agrarian communities, and industrial communities. At Castle Donnington, Leicestershire, it was related that there were 'not many unemployed, [and] those set to work on the roads'; the '2–6' out of work in the winter at Anderby, Lincolnshire, were supported by the poor rates and put on the roads or employed by the 'dike-reve'. The correspondent from Alcester in west Warwickshire noted that the men were 'seldom unemployed, while at Napton on the eastern side of the county, 20 to 30 men were unemployed in the winter. Patrington in East Yorkshire had up to 20 men out of work in the spring and put to work on the roads or in collecting material from the beach. Landewedack in Cornwall had six men out of work in the winter – two agricultural labourers and four fishermen – who were either put on the roads or 'work by turns as roundsmen'. Industrial communities offered a different picture. At Whickham in Durham, no agricultural labourers were 'ever out of employment', though keelmen and smiths' strikers sometimes were workless when their masters had no contracts to fulfil. Similarly at Kirkham, Lancashire, 'the working class in the hundred of Amounderness needs never to be unemployed, as weaving is carried on throughout the hundred'. At Madeley in

Shropshire, there 'being iron and coal-work in the parish', it was related that 'few are unemployed', while only the infirm were unemployed in Clifton Campville in Staffordshire.[86]

The situation under which the workhouse-based New Poor Law was imposed from the spring of 1835 was therefore underwritten by precisely the same dynamics as pertained in the late 1810s and 1820s, with the same regional disparities in the nature and depth of rural poverty. But the New Poor Law was a national system, albeit one that created unions of geographically contiguous parishes. That it was designed to counter the 'pauperism' of the south and east is well known, and that it was imposed on industrial(ising) northern communities against considerable opposition from the poor and ratepayers alike is also well understood. If the extent of poverty in the south and east was essentially driven by structural factors (long-term declining agricultural profitability and population growth), in the north the nature of the industrial business cycle created relatively short-lived but massive peaks in unemployment. Hence, to properly impose the system of less eligibility – only those in absolute need would enter the workhouse – in industrial communities would require the construction of vast, expensive workhouses that for much of the time would be more-or-less empty.[87]

Opposition to the New Poor Law was notoriously most vehement, violent and long-lived in the north. The arrival of the Assistant Poor Law Commissioners in the northern counties in the autumn of 1836 having largely completed the task of creating poor law unions in the south coincided with a steep downturn in the manufacturing economy. If cotton spinning initially continued to flourish, the textile industries slumped. While the movement assumed a largely urban focus, with most protests occurring in the industrial towns that formed the centre of most new northern unions, it was the often rurally-located outworking trades that had been most severely affected by the downturn that proved to be, in the words of John Knott, ' the mainstay of the anti-poor law movement in the north'.[88] Unlike earlier southern and eastern protests, organised opposition to the New Poor Law in the north was not based purely on workers, artisans and shopkeepers but drew considerable 'respectable' leadership involvement from Tories and political radicals alike, united in their concern for the plight of factory workers.

Notwithstanding that inspiring speeches did much to garner publicity for the cause and helped to fuse local support, it was the actions of working people that provided the most forceful opposition. While it is impossible to discern how many of those individuals who peopled the crowds and acted as ringleaders in the demonstrations were actually rural residents, it is probable that in protests which took place in the smaller towns – such as a series of notorious demonstrations at Keighley in March 1837 – rural-based workers took an active role. Some demonstrations were also organised on the rural–urban fringe, building upon the long-established tradition for Luddites and political radicals to meet on the moors and open greens.[89] For instance, the campaign in the West Riding of Yorkshire reached its climax when, on 16 May 1837, a huge demonstration was held at Peep Green near Dewsbury. That Whitsuntide morning 'the towns and villages of the West Riding of Yorkshire echoed to the sounds of bands parading the streets, calling together the marchers'. Carrying banners and flags – one from Lepton graphically depicting three figures hanging from a gibbet with the inscription, 'The three Poor Law Commissoners drawing their wages' – the protest drew from customary and symbolic ritual. But the size of the gathering, estimated at between 200,000 and 260,000, was defiantly far from the form of earlier rural protests. To the vast majority of those present the speeches and complex arguments about violence and universal suffrage would have counted for little for the simple reason that beyond the first few thousand people it would have been impossible to hear the speakers. Instead, the opposition provided undeniable evidence that town and country were united in the face of the New Poor Law. This was, in the words of the *Leeds Times*, 'a momentous meeting ... the most important ever seen in England'. More representative of sustained protest in the region, though, was the non-compliance of parish officers and vestries and smaller, localised collective actions focused on workhouses and meetings of Boards of Guardians. These were not, as is typically represented, the exclusive protests of an urban, industrial proletariat. Rather, they were the combined efforts of industrial workers, some of whom led their lives in the towns alone while many others lived lives that made no distinction between town and country, whether living on the urban fringe or working in small communities and in mills surrounded by their agricultural comrades at work in the fields.[90]

In 1838, when reviewing 'the progress of that skulking pestilence', the New Poor Law, Chartist Bronterre O'Brien suggested that only 'the men of the North' had shown any mettle in opposing the Act. All others had been guilty of either 'a cowardly acquiescence ... or a reckless disregard of the evil consequences which menace their order'.[91] But rural workers in the south and east were neither cowardly nor reckless in the face of the radical reworking of the relief system, being quick to resist any changes that imposed upon their established 'right' to relief. Southern protests against the New Poor Law even pre-empted the creation of the first poor law unions. Receiving Royal Assent on 17 August 1834, the Poor Law Commission was quick to circulate the Act to all magistrates requesting their support in attempting to put the principles of the Act into operation. Before the onset of winter, Assistant Commissioners were despatched to parts of the south in an attempt to force rural vestries into restricting their relief provision, especially to the able-bodied male labourer. While some rural vestries stubbornly refused to have anything to do with the New Poor Law until they were compelled to – the Gilbert's Union comprised of the parishes of Orlestone, Ruckinge and Warehorne on the fringe of Romney Marsh initially even refused to listen to Assistant Commissioner Sir Francis Head[92] – other vestries responded to this early call and reformed their relief regimes. Protests duly followed. At Christian Malford (Wiltshire) on 6 November 1834, 100 men, women and children occupied the church and refused entry to the overseer on it becoming known that the vestry was to discuss the introduction of some provisions of the Act. At nearby Calne an announcement made by the assistant overseer on 12 January 1835 that allowances would henceforth be made half in kind and half in money provoked extensive rioting, the sending of a threatening letter to a magistrate who put down the riot, and two incendiary attacks.[93] The application of the 'spirit' of the New Poor Law in the South-East was also generative of immediate protest, something that coincident wage cuts helped to fan. The insistence of Assistant Commissioner Hawley that Battle's parish officers should 'ensure that claimants had legitimately expended all their peak harvest earnings before receiving unemployment benefit' prompted a 'street protest' by claimants and a formal protest from the vestry to the Poor Law Commission, while overseers were among those targeted by an upturn in incendiarism that winter.[94]

The creation of unions similarly provoked immediate protests. The first recorded anti-New Poor Law protest occurred in the Milton Union in north Kent at Bapchild on 30 April 1835, 'mobbings' against relieving officers and guardians also occurring in other parishes in the union over the ensuing days, prompted by attempts to give relief partly in kind and partly in cash. This pattern of disturbance, as Knott notes, 'was repeated, with minor variations, through south-east England'. Indeed, the archive is replete with examples of attempts to resist payments in kind, for instance in the Ampthill Union (Bedfordshire) and the Docking Union (Norfolk). Anti-workhouse protests were also a noticeable feature of cornland protests, workhouses being set on fire – at Heckingham (Norfolk) a 1760s House of Industry was burnt to the ground in April 1836, when attempts were made to separate the male and female paupers[95] – and pulled down, the works of new workhouses at Chiddingstone (Kent) being disrupted in May 1835, while the works in the Depward Union (Norfolk) were reportedly being demolished by night as fast it was being constructed by day. At Stratton in Cornwall, the workhouse was not even built due to pauper protests. A large body of men, armed and 'in Military array', interupted an inspection of the site of the proposed new workhouse and then proceeded to barricade the guardians, magistrates and relieving officer into the chairman of the board's home before extracting a promise that the workhouse would not be built.[96]

Collective protests in most places, though, were easily met by the swift intervention of the magistrates and the military, the example of Swing being fresh in the minds of the local authorities. Protests, though, did not cease. Instead, incendiarism against the property of guardians, relieving officers, overseers and those who publicly supported the workings of the Act terrorised the countryside throughout the late 1830s and into the 1840s. Property crimes also soared as individuals sought alternative ways of getting by outside of the workhouse, while more subtle forms of resistance, such as refusing to perform work in the workhouse and window-breaking, helped to undermine the everyday workings of the Act. In common with the north, sustained campaigns in parts of the press – most notably in *The Times* and the Chartist *Northern Star* – highlighting abuses in poor unions were important in bringing scandals to the attention of the public and politicians. Arguably the most famous one of all, the Andover scandal where starving workhouse inmates were reported to have been gnawing at fetid bones they were supposed to be crushing to make fertiliser, prompting stricter controls of minimum workhouse dietaries and restrictions on the nature of work that inmates were engaged in. Of arguably even greater importance, though, was the fact that the New Poor Law fed southern radicalism, which in turn facilitated the penetration of the Chartist mission to the south, and led to the formation of (short-lived) rural trades unions, something examined in detail in Chapter 7.[97]

Ironically, the reduction in poor rates (by between 25 per cent and 35 per cent) attributed to the workings of the New Poor Law, was instrumental in briefly reviving the fortunes of the rural economy, though arguably the stemming of the long-term decline in prices from 1838 was a yet greater factor. As such, while there is evidence to suggest that wages increased, the stopping of outdoor relief in all but a small number of locales – invariably where Boards of Guardians either refused to stop paying outdoor relief or had yet to construct adequate workhouse accommodation – meant that in the south real incomes remained desperately inadequate. Even the boom in railway construction offered, in totality, few opportunities. The New Poor Law did not solve the problem of rural unemployment, the situation being particularly bad for lads and young men who were often over looked in favour of married men by farmers keen to keep families out of the workhouse.[98] The Act of 1834 allowed boards of guardians to raise funds to assist the emigration of claimant families – the spirit of Malthus running through the Act – but this had virtually no effect. Far more important were the actions of the thousands of artisans and small farmers who decided to migrate under their own steam, some 127,000 mostly rural dwellers leaving for Australia in the 1830s and 1840s.[99]

The concurrent slump in the agricultural and industrial economies in the early 1840s certainly created the ideal conditions encouraging out-migration, the farmers and putting-out contractors being quick to throw off labour and decline offers of new work, respectively. The agricultural slump was made worse still by the opening of corn markets after the repeal of the Corn Laws in 1847, falling agricultural commodity prices acting to drag wages in the final years of the decade down to 1820s levels. The 1840s have been labelled as the 'hungry 40s' with good reason. If unemployment remained defiantly worse in the south and east, rural 'industrial' workers in the north suffered dreadfully from short-time employment and desperately inadequate relief, with R.N. Thompson suggesting that many workers in Cumbria were close to starvation.[100] Those engaged in the mining trades of Durham and Northumberland were perhaps better protected against such trade fluctuations than other northern workers, while farm servants – a sector that accounted for a high proportion of all agricultural workers in the north, West Midlands, Cornwall, Devon and even parts of the southern cornlands – were shielded from the worst effects.[101]

Much has been made about the continuities and discontinuities of relief policies between the old and new poor laws. While it is foolhardy to deny the dramatic transformation in the provision of institutional relief – especially outside of Lancashire and Yorkshire – some dynamics did persist. Per capita, relief remained higher in the south than the north, and during the winters of the crisis years of the 1840s, the Poor Law Commission – and its successor from 1847, the Poor Law Board – often had to relax its rules regarding outrelief due to a lack of workhouse capacity.[102] The extent of the problem was perhaps best exemplified by the fact that, as the *Brighton Herald* put it, even 'respectable families' had been 'forced to flee into the workhouse due to a want of employment'.[103] In some locales, mass unemployment stimulated the gentry to employ those out of work in make-work schemes, for instance at Lenham in mid-Kent, T. Pemberton-Leigh was reported to have employed nearly all the 'surplus' labourers during the winters of the early 1840s on his newly created estate.[104] Schemes to till uncultivated land, to employ men on the roads, and even to revive labour rates, albeit in a legally non-enforceable way, were implemented.[105] The crisis also gave further impetus to the 'movement' to provide allotments for labourers, something that started in the post-1815 depression and gained momentum after Swing.[106] The 'scarcity of employment' and stagnation in trade fuelled a crime wave in the countryside, the Brighton press warning farmers in December 1849 against 'acting very inconsiderately, and invoking themselves in serious responsibilities'.[107] The reaction then, as throughout the 1840s, was not only a rise in theft but also, as Chapter 4 explores, an unprecedented wave of incendiarism.

If the New Poor Law was a reaction to the crisis in rural social relations so dramatically exposed by Swing, the evidence of social dislocations in the 1840s suggests it singularly failed to reform matters for the better. As during the autumn and winter of 1830, labouring under- and unemployment fuelled rural terror.[108] Ultimately, though, what explains the depth and persistence of popular hostility to the New Poor Law, especially in the cornland communities, was the sense that a long-held right of the poor to relief from their parish had been eliminated. What made matters worse was that attempts to protect this right had been the major driver of protest in the countryside since at least the start of the nineteenth century, and had been central to the Swing rising. The great rebellion of 1830 – analysed in Chapter 6 – had ultimately failed.

Chapter 2: Rural Workers, Custom and the State

To understand protest, we need to understand law. For, as Andy Wood has suggested, law framed what was 'allowed', determined what bore judicial consequence, and even opened up spaces of possibility. Under the terms of the 1715 Riot Act, for instance, if fewer than twelve people were gathered, then their protest was not a 'riot'.[1] Some practices, such as complaining deferentially to magistrates over the stinginess of parish doles, were deliberately framed so as to remain inside the law. Such was the hegemonic power of the law that it was even used by the poorest members of society to protect and secure *their* rights and property against the rich. Law was everywhere and everything related to it. Indeed, beyond the levying of taxation, the poor laws were the key way in which rural workers and the central state interacted. But while relief claimants knew how the poor laws operated – asserting their *rights* as enshrined in law through 'pauper letters' (letters sent by those residing outside of their parish of settlement in an attempt to claim poor relief) and in making complaints before magistrates – there is no sense that rural workers ever believed they were interacting with something beyond the parish state. This chapter then shifts the scale from these profoundly local engagements with centrally devised law (and social policy) to consider a series of rather less mediated interactions between the emergent central state, its laws, and rural workers. Specifically, it examines these tensions through three interrelated foci: extensions of the criminal code to protect political interests; extensions of the criminal code to outlaw customary practice and define private property; and, finally, to gather revenues. It then concludes with a brief consideration of other ways in which rural workers directly critiqued forms and practices of state-making in eighteenth-century England.

As E.P. Thompson, in *Whigs and Hunters*, his seminal study of the passing of the Black Act, put it: 'The British state, all legislators agreed, existed to preserve the property and, incidentally the lives and liberties, of the propertied.'[2] All three examples analyse different applications of this principle, examining how rural workers responded to attempts by the central state to defend and (re)define private property. The case studies also represent different articulations of the ways in which rural workers – often in league with small and tenant farmers – believed how the state should operate and how social relations should function. Furthermore, in the examples of early eighteenth-century smuggling and the practices of the 'Blacks' of the forests of southern England, we see something more complex. Here, a form of radical Jacobite politics – that is to say anti-Whig and pro the deposed House of Stuart (see Chapter 7) – both acted as motivation and as the goal of their actions. It was the justification and the end game. The following examples, though, do not work from the foundational assumption that all poachers and smugglers were directly aiming their actions at the government as a form of explicit critique of the polity. Most were not. Rather, it articulates the ways in which rural workers resisted the policies of the emergence of a particularly modern form of statecraft concerned with the definition and protection of private property. In all three cases, custom was the principle wellspring of resistance. It was the regulator of social and political interactions and was thus invoked as that which should guide the relationship between manifestations of the modern state and the rural worker.

The 'Blacks' and the Black Act

The recent resurgence of interest in the history of forests has reminded us that in the mid-medieval period it could be claimed that forest history truly represented 'half our history', so extensive was the network of royal forests created by the Normans and early Plantagenets as personal hunting grounds.[3] In law, forests were defined as 'territor[ies] of woody grounds and fruitful pastures, privileged for wild beasts and fowls of forest, chase and warren, to rest and abide there in the safe protection of the King, for his delight and pleasure'. Protecting the monarch's 'vert' (the trees and plants) and 'venison' (the animals) was forest law, an alternative legal system codified in the 1217 Charter of the Forests, which took precedence over common law in forests.[4] By the turn of the eighteenth century, this system was in a state of near collapse. Disafforestation (technically removing an area from the strictures of forest law) through 'assarting' to create arable land, from the early fourteenth century, and the selling off of forest land to raise revenues, combined with the struggle to re-establish royal forests post-Restoration, having been abolished by Oliver Cromwell, meant that the area covered by forests had massively declined. What was left, though, represented a significant state resource, albeit one that was being abused systematically by both forest officers appointed by the lord wardens (responsible for the protection of the vert and venison) and by the exchequer (representing the crown's forest-bound revenue generation) and by local people with and without rights of common in the forest.[5]

In the decades following the Restoration, five separate nationwide commissions of enquiry into the 'waste' of timber in English (and Welsh) forests, with a further House of Lords Committee in 1698 into abuses in the largest royal forests, attests to successive governments' desire to limit abuse and make forests fiscally productive. However, the granting of forest offices, with all the privileges and sinecures that came with such office, to political appointees potentially undermined this desire, especially so if those appointed used their office for wholesale plunder of forest resources and used their new powers arbitrarily. This was the situation in the early eighteenth century. Against Jacobite plots attempting to overthrow the fledging Hanoverian succession, and in the context of the financial and political crisis brought about by the collapse of the South Sea Bubble, England's *de facto* first prime minister, Robert Walpole, needed to secure the Whig ascendancy. A combination of using government office as a system of patronage and the forces of state to inculcate terror was his response. So much for the libertarian rhetoric of the settlement of 1688 that the Whigs piously proclaimed to uphold. Instead, as Thompson put it, in the true style of a banana republic, the Whigs and their appointees duly proceeded without adhering to 'rational or bureaucratic rules and forms' to fight for the spoils of power. Even Walpole himself had interests in 'privatising' Windsor Forest, the very forest in which Queen Anne and then George I revived the long-since dormant obsession of the monarch to hunt. Thus, rich, time-serving men of the Protestant succession in many cases literally appropriated forests as huge extensions of their deer parks – and became yet richer, and more arbitrary in their exercise of power.[6]

The battle between those with hunting privileges, forest officers and the agrarian communities that lived in and around forests was as old as the forests themselves. But early in 1720 a seemingly more determined set of gangs in Windsor Forest and the forests of south Hampshire and the Hampshire–Surrey borders began a systematic campaign of deer-stealing, blackmailing, and directing threats and violence against the forest officers. Following years of alternately lax and vigorous application of forest law, the reign of Queen Anne brought the situation of forest governance to a head. Broken fences in Windsor Forest meant the deer were free to wander as they pleased, while the overgrazing of sheep, the digging of heath, turves and peat, the grubbing and assarting of woods, and the systematic taking of wood for commercial sale meant that the deer were forced into the woods on the forest edge and the surrounding country to find food. Furthermore, during the Commonwealth and since the Restoration, the population of the forest and settlements on the forest fringes had exploded, putting further pressure on forest resources. Deer, in short, became easy game for country people.

Against these problems, from 1716 new Whig forest officials were appointed, and on George I's first visit to Windsor in 1717, the Swanimote Court, the forest court at which all offences and offenders were to be presented, was revived for, in Thompson's words, 'a campaign of harassment'. Contrary to received opinion, forest law was far from being toothless in the early eighteenth century. At the same time as deer-stealers, wood-takers and turf-cutters were being hounded, it was decided to restock the forest's New Lodge Walk with red deer, large animals with huge appetites, especially for the soft arable crops that grew on the edge of the walk. The nobility and local gentry also continued to expand their deer parks, privatise the ponds, and lay exclusive claims to rights over the manorial soils of the forest.[7]

In this context of the irresolvable tensions between the exercise of customary rights and customary practices, and between the forest officers and their keepers, on 22 February 1720:

[F]ourteen Men in Horseback, all armed with Guns, and some with Pistols, and two Footmen with a Greyhound, did, in a violent and outragious Manner … at Four of the Clock in the Afternoon, come into Bigshot-walk in Finchamsted Bailiwick in the Forest of Windsor, with their Faces blacked and disguised, some with Straw Hats and other deformed Habits, and did there pursue and shoot at our Red Deer, and did continue Hunting there till after Six o Clock, in which time they did kill four Deer there, three of which they carried away while, and did cut off the Haunches of the fourth, and left the rest of the Carcase, and did terrorise and threaten the Keeper of our said Walk to shoot him.[8]

So started, at least by record, the activities of the Blacks, or specifically the Windsor Blacks as opposed to the related Waltham Blacks active in east Hampshire, so named because of their chosen method of disguise. Concerned more with the symbolic value of deer rather than the value of venison, the Blacks meted out a form of retribution against the heightened exercise of authority in the forests. Their protests, for such they were, went beyond armed, organised deer-stealing. Keepers were subjected to violent attacks, blackmail, and threats that their property and animals – especially their dogs – would be destroyed. Keeper and Deputy Steward Nunn's house was the subject of numerous threats and was even occasionally the night-time target of Windsor Black gunmen. It was, so it seemed, open season for keepers as much as it was for deer.

In the Hampshire forests, the Waltham Blacks adopted a similar strategy. Here, though, the authority of the crown was weaker than in Windsor. Instead, the Bishop of Winchester – owner of two of the eighteen 'purlieus' in Bere Forest and a substantial park on the fringe of Alice Holt Forest – was the key antagonist in the minds of the Blacks, a tension that had existed for decades. Sir Jonathan Trelawny, Bishop from 1707 until his death in 1721, was an 'ardent Hanoverian', constantly in fear of Jacobite plots, and ruthless in exposing what he perceived to be the abuses of the customary tenants on his land, and those committed by some of his lesser officers. Timber rights were a particular bugbear, being used as an excuse to revoke the leases of many of his customary tenants and in place create new commercial leases. Through such manoeuvrings, common rights in Farnham Old Park were all but eradicated. Still, the Bishop's tenants frequently raided Alice Holt and the Farnham parks for both wood and deer by night and even more brazenly by day. By the late 1710s, the raiders were increasingly armed, leading Trelawny in 1718 to consider placing a notice in the *London Gazette* (the official communication of government) offering a reward for any information leading to the successful conviction of the armed poachers. It was over such issues that the Waltham Blacks waged their campaign.

Initially, the Hampshire protests centred on Farnham Park and focused on organised deer-stealing. Indeed, they were highly organised in comparison to the Windsor Blacks. Their leader went by the name of King John, 'elected' as part of a 'mock kingly government' in response to two deer-stealers having been imprisoned following a 16-man raid on Farnham Park in October 1721 in which a keeper was shot and wounded. Their next raid was more audacious still. An even larger group than before broke into the park and stole eleven deer, leaving as many dead in the park, before riding through Farnham that market-day morning in triumphant defiance. Having repeatedly targeted the deer, they duly turned their hand to burning the Bishop's lodges, destroying the timber and shooting at his cattle, before focusing their protests on Waltham

Chase, some 25 miles to the south-west. Raids on the deer in the Chase were followed by a campaign of intimidation against informers and forest officers, and, in due course, on those members of the local gentry who had offended the sensibilities of the Blacks. Attempts to restrict the timber rights in Alice Holt continued to generate hostility – and protest, including stripping the bark off the standing trees on the estate of farmer Wingfield. As Thompson put it, 'the resentments of decades sheltered [King John] and his band, as he rode openly about administering folk justice'.

Together, the action of the Waltham and Windsor Blacks constituted a crisis – or, at least in the feverish political climate of the time, what could be *presented* as a crisis. On 2 February a royal proclamation was duly issued. Invoking the 1485 Hunting in Forests Act (1 Henry VII, c.7), the proclamation offered a reward of £100 to any individual 'discovering or apprehending' any of the offenders or their accomplices.[9] Cases were swiftly brought to trial at the Berkshire assizes, and Blacking ceased beyond seemingly isolated cases, even King John announcing to his followers after a deer-stealing episode in Waltham Chase in late March that he would 'not concern himself with publick affairs' for some time. Still, in a mere four weeks an act was drafted, debated and passed by parliament in response to the actions of the Blacks. From being armed and 'blacked' in a 'forest, chase, park or enclosed ground ... wherein any deer have been or shall usually be kept', to hunting deer, sending threatening letters, maiming cattle, cutting down trees, setting fire to haystacks, breaking down the heads of fish ponds, among many other of the Blacks' protest practices, all offences were now punishable by death.

So a series of intense but localised protests in the forests of Berkshire and Hampshire were used to justify an act which, to paraphrase Leon Radzinowicz, contained more capital statutes than any other country possessed in their entire criminal codes.[10] And as with all general acts, it applied throughout the realm. In short, the response to the protests of the forest residents of a small area of southern England – or rather the acts of statecraft which were justified on the basis of the actions of the Blacks – had implications for the regulation of social relations from Cornwall to Cumberland, whatever the community context. It was ultimately motivated by a desire to protect capital, to protect the interests of landlords in making money from what was previously of little value to them: commons, woodlands, even ponds. Thus the Black Act can be read as a defining moment in the history of agrarian capitalism, the point at which the British state announced its intention to defend property through attaching the ultimate sanction to those who denied the primacy of property rights. The majority of the 50 capital offences detailed in the Act related to offences against property, the Black Act thereby doing more, according to Thompson, to 'habituate men's minds to this recipe of state' than other event or legislation.[11] In itself, it was 'an overarching capital statute covering almost every conceivable criminal activity'.[12]

As Peter King has noted, though, in the eighteenth century there was a growing gap between law as created and law as practised.[13] That the Black Act was, to quote Adrian Randall, a 'sledgehammer, created to crack the nut of determined local resistance' might act to limit its possible application.[14] What, one might reasonably ask, were the consequences of the Act? How was it used, if at all? Protests persisted in the forests of Hampshire and Berkshire and around Farnham, albeit with less frequency. Farnham Park also continued to be raided by deer-stealers into the 1730s. However, these were not remnant protests but rather either, as in the case of deer-stealing, a deeper persistence, or, as in the case of arson and the maiming of trees and stock, evidence of a breakdown in local social relations. Keepers continued to be targets, especially so if they were perceived to have carried out their work over-enthusiastically. In some such cases the Black Act was invoked in proclamations against those practising these forms of counter-terror, but in many others it was not. That the passing of the Act had failed to quiet these forest-bound communities is highly suggestive that very quickly it came to be viewed as too blunt, too severe an instrument. It is especially telling, then, that while the Black Act was invoked against keeper-cum-gang-leader Lewis Gunner in 1729 for shooting a local farmer in an alehouse at Alton, a 1733 proclamation against deer-stealers made no mention of the Act at all.[15]

Beyond this initial context, the Black Act was deployed even less frequently. According to Frank McLynn, it was soon 'a dead letter' regarding poaching as it was 'far too blunt a weapon'.[16] The same was true in relation to other offences. While the cutting down and destroying of trees was arguably the offence for which the Black Act was most frequently invoked in the early and mid-eighteenth century, the practice was typically prosecuted through earlier, less draconian statutes.[17] Moreover, so loosely drafted was the Act that it became a spawning ground for subsequent legal judgments that added further capital offences. Cutting hop bines was added in 1731, while the practice of 'blacking' one's face was detached from going armed to form a separate offence. This led to a farcical situation when in 1736 two Herefordshire colliers were sentenced to death for taking part in an anti-turnpike protest by virtue of having faces blackened by coal dust. Inadequacies with the Black Act saw that separate laws against arson were enacted in 1737 (against arson in pits and mines) and in 1758. Similarly, a new law was passed in 1754 making the sending of any threatening letter a capital offence, it being perceived that the Black Act referred only to extortion.[18]

Revisions to the Black Act and subsequent separate laws attest to the persistence of incendiarism, sending threatening letters, breaking fish ponds, maiming animals and plants, and the continued use of disguise in carrying out covert protests or poaching and smuggling in rural England. Indeed, in the upturn of covert protest that followed the end of the Napoleonic Wars there was a marked increase in the use of the Black Act itself, notably in the forest communities of Hampshire, from where the Act developed.[19] It was even used in the prosecution of Swing protestors in 1830. By this time, though, the tide had already turned against the 'bloody code' of the eighteenth century. Legal reform was driven partly by moral sentiment, and partly by a desire to rationalise the law relating to felony. There were, so Home Secretary Peel noted in 1826, some 20 statutes relating to the theft and malicious damage of trees alone. It was also a function of the fact that eighteenth-century judicial innovations such as the Black Act were responsible for fewer executions in the eighteenth and early nineteenth centuries than earlier Tudor and Stuart legislation.[20] The massive increase in felonies tried from the early 1810s also meant that, as Vic Gattrell has observed, more individuals would be sentenced to death, ergo the only way to avoid a spike in the numbers executed was increasingly to pardon those so sentenced. Post-1815, 90 per cent of those convicted for capital offences were pardoned, which made the system little more than a lottery. The result was a shift in policy. The Judgement of Death Act, passed 100 years after the Black Act, gave judges discretion in deciding whether the death penalty would be imposed or some less draconian sentence. The number of capital crimes itself was also reduced – by two-thirds – in 1832. The upswing in arson and animal maiming, the most graphic forms of rural terror, beyond 1815 meant that they remained on the statute as capital offences.

From Custom to Crime: Poaching, Wood-taking and 'Social Criminality'

Of all past rural practices, poaching has arguably left the most romantic legacy, but the image of the poacher as someone who occasionally, and opportunistically, netted a rabbit for the pot hides a far more complex reality. Beyond snatching an injured bird or animal, poaching necessarily required some planning and equipment: shooting and laying snares and nets were all premeditated acts. Even if an individual came across a hare's nest or a pheasant's roost they would still need equipment to catch their quarry. If the purely opportunistic poacher is a distorted fiction,[21] then we also need to dispel the myth that poaching was something only undertaken by those seeking to feed their families. For while game, as Joan Thirsk has shown, did increasingly represent an important source of nutrition in rural diets otherwise deprived of protein,[22] much poaching was carried out by organised, and often violent, gangs.

Poaching has been represented not only as the archetypal rural crime but also as a special sort of crime, a practice that while illegal by statute was regarded by rural workers as not being 'criminal'. This distinction between acts universally accepted as crimes and those whose criminal status were questioned was first delineated in a landmark essay by Eric Hobsbawm in which he gave the name 'social crimes' to the latter category.[23] A subsequent, and influential, paper by John Rule further refined the concept, noting that a huge range of rural practices, from poaching, through wood-taking, sheep-stealing, smuggling, and coastal 'wrecking' all betrayed an element of social dissent by virtue of being carried out with the support of the working community but in defiance of the law.[24] Subsequent studies by Wells on sheep-stealing, Bushaway on wood-taking, and Freeman on deer-stealing have further explored this theme, noting both an element of social protest in these practices as well as evidence of an alternative plebeian conception of property rights. Shakesheff has also suggested that crop theft – in addition to wood-taking – was also driven by an element of protest rather than 'just' being an act of petty acquisition by hungry labourers.[25]

There are problems with this conceptualisation, though. The theft of sheep was always that – theft. For even if the taking of sheep from rich capitalist farmers' folds might gain some political support among the working community, we must remember that sheep-stealing was often a commercial enterprise, with butchers, or those working as conduits and fences for butchers, often involved.[26] The taking of deer was more problematic. Outside of areas that fell under forest law, deer that had not wandered from forests and chases belonged to the landowner. Within chases, the right to shoot deer was more complex, and, as Caroline Cheeseman has shown, subject to repeated challenge in the higher courts.[27] To many tenant farmers deer were a nuisance, damaging fences and eating crops. To them, shooting deer might contain some element of resistance against landowners failing to restrict the movements of deer, but ultimately their actions were pragmatic rather than protests. Many rural workers viewed deer as 'fair game', a way of making money when sold on illicitly to higglers and dealers for the major urban markets. Such acts contain little in the way of explicit protest but, perhaps more profoundly, questioned the very notion of property rights under agrarian capitalism. Their 'right' was clear. It was a custom not vested in manorial records or deeds but in what

Hudson in his classic account of the lives of Wiltshire shepherds labelled 'moral law ... written in the heart of the peasant'. Wounded game 'is his by a natural right'.[28] Or as George Crabbe put it: 'The poacher questions with perverted mind, / Were not the gifts of heaven for all design'd?'.[29] And in relation to deer, farmers were more than happy to turn a blind eye. As Chapman noted of the farmers of Cranborne Chase, 'the deer-stealers are their best friends; for if it was not for them, they should be overrun with deer, and not able to live on their farms'.[30]

Moreover, for all its conceptual neatness and its attractiveness to historians attempting to discern voices of dissent in the archive beyond riot, as a concept, 'social crime' obscures a deeper, more complex history. Such acts had particular histories in which the juxtaposition between use and customary rights and ownership created legal ambiguity. The British state attempted to remove these ambiguities through ever more specific and tightly worded judicial legislation. The classic example of this new role of the state was an act passed in 1663 in response to earlier protests, attempting to establish the right of access to woodlands for fuel, pannage and cattle grazing.[31] Those *suspected* of stealing wood – and fences – could be summarily fined ten shillings by a lone magistrate, a second offence being punishable by one months' imprisonment.[32] So much might appear to be mere expedience, the Act offering prosecutors a method by which alleged wood-takers could be swiftly, and inexpensively, tried. But beyond convenience, the Act was a deliberate attempt to underline the primacy of private property, carefully specifying what counted as wood and timber. The protection of capital was imperative. Contemporaneously, in 1671 the first major challenge to the customary idea that game belonged to all came in the form of the Game Act, an Act that remained in force until the 1831 Game Act, which proscribed 'ownership' even more tightly and established a 'close season' in which game birds could not be caught. Even tenant farmers were not allowed to catch game on their farms. This was, as John Fisher has suggested, arguably the greatest of all tensions between farmers and their landlords.[33]

The privatisation of once common goods through enclosure and allied attempts to eliminate forms of customary tenure – notably life-hold and copyhold – were also an important component in this shift from custom to crime. In the face of such threats, commoners appealed to local custom not as a 'vague body of tradition' but instead as a regulator of community tension given legitimacy as 'a rigorous, detailed, and precise *corpus* of local law'.[34] The taking of wood and game was thus carried out, as the practitioners perceived it, not against the law but within the corpus of the law. Moreover, even unambiguously criminalising an existing practice does not necessarily mean that the law is necessarily upheld. Studies of wood-taking obtained from magistrates' notebooks have shown that ostensibly similar criminal charges could result in a wide range of outcomes: from cases being indicted in higher courts, through small fines, admonitions and even cases being dropped on the accused confessing their guilt and apologising to the prosecutor.[35] In this context, gentlemen and farmers founded prosecution associations to encourage, promote and financially support the arrest and prosecution of those suspected of the theft and destruction of their members' property. First emerging in the late seventeenth century but increasing markedly after 1780, a central focus of such rural associations was the prosecution of, in the words of the Wiltshire Association, 'cutting, cropping, lopping, or damaging any trees, or stealing wood, underwood of fruit'. Whatever their success in deterring and prosecuting all such acts – something essentially unknowable – the existence of such societies served as a reminder to magistrates that agrarian capitalists expected the primacy of private property to be upheld.[36]

There was, of course, a world of difference between taking wood for the domestic fire and removing it for commercial sale, a particular problem in the crown forests. Attempts to suppress such manipulative practices even led to a series of 'timber-stealing riots' in the Northamptonshire forests of Whittlebury and Salcey in the late 1720s. The Duke of Grafton's bailiff – extensive common rights having been granted to the Fitzroy family by Charles II in 1673 – reporting that: 'We are in the Forest nothing but confusion and disorder, by ye whole country's coming in, in a violent manner, and carrying away ye best of ye timber, 20 or 30 pounds worth to some towns, and there is no resisting them.' But resist them bailiff Herbert tried. Before the end of 1728 he was dead, poisoning being popularly assumed to be the cause of death.[37]

Similarly, other rural crimes such as deer-stealing and other forms of poaching were often the practice of highly organised criminal gangs.[38] Indeed, Osborne's analysis of the seasonality of poaching in Cumberland, Westmorland and Suffolk has suggested that poaching peaked when game was in the best possible condition to sell on to higglers and dealers.[39] Archer's analysis of poaching in nineteenth-century Lancashire has also highlighted the fact that many poachers were not only part of organised and armed gangs but also that they were often not rural workers at all, instead living and working in towns to which many of the large game estates adjoined. Wells' study of criminal gangs in the south in the early decades of the nineteenth century has likewise shown that systematic poaching was often part of a wider range of arguably more straightforward criminal acts such as sheep-stealing, and even burglary. Some of these gangs operated in tightly defined local areas, while others were more mobile, moving between the countryside and urban fences, even from county to county.[40]

That the turn to organised, violent poaching coincided with the post-Napoleonic slump is no coincidence. Poaching, as Doug Hay's studies of Staffordshire have shown, had a long history of rising and falling with unemployment and price levels.[41] When, post-1815, unemployment reached unprecedented levels in the cornlands, there was a marked increase in poaching, something evidenced not only through lengthening indictment rolls but also by the increased frequency of reports in the provincial press. Improved, and relatively low-cost, firearms also increased the potential for poaching in game roosts – and the possibilities of violent encounters with similarly armed keepers.[42] This resort to violence was in part a function of increased attempts by landowners to protect and profit from their game reserves, the planting of new covers being a major change in many rural landscapes in the first half of the nineteenth century. The gentry and nobility's developing obsession with pheasants in particular drove this expansion. As William Cobbett remarked, the nobility appeared to think more of their pheasants than the corn growing on their estates.[43] Increasing numbers of game birds thus led to greater potential rewards for poachers, but larger reserves required more keepers, which in turn also increased the chance of violent confrontation. As noted in the previous section, that gamekeepers were viewed as the henchmen of the landed, as living both on the physical and figurative fringe of communities, they also acted to popularly justify violence: they were subjects to whom beatings could be handed out with impunity.[44]

Beyond conceiving of poaching and other once customary rights as a form of social crime, we do well to remember that petty acts of resistance often went hand-in-hand with much more explicit – and bloody – forms of social conflict. As Hobsbawm and Rudé noted, the level of poaching was a good barometer of the state of rural social relations.[45] But it was the resort to violence against keepers that was arguably a more accurate measure. The passing of the Black Act brought hatred and resentment of keepers to the boil, and the deep post-1815 depression led to a renewed ferocity in wood-bound relations in England. As Harry Hopkins suggested in his excellent study of poaching from the 1760s through to the start of the First World War, this was a 'long affray', an attritional battle between the landed and the landless that assumed an almost war-like aspect. That many keepers were slain at the hands of poachers, while countless poachers died either in the heat of battle or on the gallows tends to suggest Hopkins' words were well-chosen.[46]

If the 'battle' by the landed to preserve what in law was judged to be their game had an unusual ferocity, it is worth remembering that poaching assumed a deeper cultural symbolism to both the hunter and the landed classes. Indeed, such was the landed's obsession with the protection of game and the punishment of their demotic foe, that game legislation was responsible for spilling more blood and for more published words than parliamentary reform in the eighteenth century and the early decades of the nineteenth century.[47] As Roger Manning notes, deer poaching 'was a symbolic substitute for war … a symbolic enactment of rebellion' following the suppression of the mid-Tudor rebellions.[48] To eighteenth-century naturalist Gilbert White, hunting was innate to the forest dwellers of east Hampshire. 'The temptation is irresistible,' he suggested, 'for most men are sportsmen by constitution: and there is such an inherent spirit for hunting in human nature, as scarce any inhibitions can restrain.' To hunt was a rite of passage for the young men of Woolmer and Alice Holt forests. It was integral to becoming a man, to asserting one's masculinity. In White's writings there is even a qualified respect for the poacher's knowledge of the natural world. As Donna Landry has put it, '[t]he greatest field naturalists were often poachers'.[49]

Smuggling

The centralised levying of customs to fill the coffers of the treasury is a practice that dates back to the early thirteenth century, the first customs officers being appointed at the end of the same century. The creation of this fledging customs collection service, systematised in 1643 with the creation of the Board of Customs, acted to encourage the smuggling of goods on which high levels of customs (levied on exported or imported goods) were charged. Typically, wool was exported, a product for which there was a huge demand in continental Europe. On the return journey, smugglers either imported cargoes legitimately, or clandestinely imported goods on which high excise duties were normally levied. The outlawed export of grain during times of dearth was also a potentially highly lucrative business. In the eighteenth century, tea and spirits became the smugglers goods of choice, both being of high value, relatively easy to transport, and, critically, in demand. Indeed, smuggling facilitated the adoption by the middle classes of tea and brandy drinking forms of consumption that had hitherto been the preserve of the elites.[50]

All of this required capital, both to obtain the goods to export (though farmers were often involved) and to secure boats. As with poaching, the popular romanticised idea that all smugglers were the poorest members of rural society attempting to make a living is not true. Many smugglers were – and many others became – men of considerable property. A group of smugglers based at Seasalter on the north Kent coast were led by a surgeon, Dr Isaac Rutton, while William Baldock, one of the leading associates, rose from being a cow lad to living, by 1792, in considerable style in Canterbury, owning a brewery and sitting on the Canterbury Bench. On his death in 1812, he was reported to have amassed a huge fortune, in excess of £1,000,000.[51] The owners and part-owners of smuggling vessels were often merchants and shopkeepers, though the export of guineas was funded by even wealthier speculators: London bankers and larger merchants.[52] Other wealthy individuals allowed the trade to continue as they personally stood to profit. We know, for instance, that Parson Woodforde of Weston Longeville in Norfolk wittingly purchased smuggled rum and brandy.[53] It was the men who crewed the boats, and landed and 'ran' the cargoes that were drawn from the ranks of rural workers.

Unlike poaching, smuggling in the eighteenth and early nineteenth centuries has not attracted much systematic analysis, notwithstanding a huge 'popular' fascination evidenced by the excellent series of regional histories published by Countryside Books.[54] As Cal Winslow noted in his landmark 1975 study of Sussex smugglers, 'smuggling has generally been left out of social history, and, unfortunately, out of the traditions of resistance'.[55] More recently, Gavin Daly has reiterated Winslow's claim, stating that 'Channel smuggling ... remains a neglected subject of historical investigation'.[56] What we do know focuses earlier on the importance of smuggling in the development of overseas trade, or on particular episodes of conflict, Monod's study of early eighteenth-century smuggling being a notable long(er) durée exception.[57]

From these few studies, it is apparent that smuggling was an ever-present practice, but one that fluctuated in intensity and extent in relation to economic fortunes and changes in excise policy, and the effort expended by local and central government in repressing the illicit activity. At the turn of the eighteenth century a complex system of revenue protection was already in existence. Customs officers were stationed at all ports, while 'revenue cruisers' patrolled the seas of the eastern and southern coasts, a duty expanded to all coasts by the end of the eighteenth century. The key smuggling coasts of Kent and Sussex were further 'protected' by 'riding officers' whose job it was to prevent the running of smuggled goods inland. The board of excise also had a parallel force of revenue cruisers and riding officers. Further additions were made by the creation of the Preventive Water Guard – essentially a deep-water force – from 1809, the dedicated anti-smuggling Coastal Blockade force that operated on the Kent and Sussex coasts from 1816 to 1831, and, finally, the Coast

Guard in 1821. Notable peaks in smuggling activity in the 1740s, the late 1770s, and on the immediate cessation of the Napoleonic Wars were in part responsible for not only driving these changes but also legal innovations. In 1746 the Smuggling Act was passed which made 'running' smuggled goods a capital offence, while in 1779 a revised and even more draconian Smuggling Act was passed.[58]

The 1740s in particular represented a high point in smuggling fortunes. By 1744 it was noted that '[t]he smugglers are got to an amazing height on the Kentish and Sussex coasts ... vast quantities of goods [are] clandestinely imported'. The success of the smugglers, it was asserted, was a factor of their having intimidated both officers of the revenue and local magistrates who 'fully decline putting the laws in execution against them'.[59] Beyond the popular belief that smuggling was 'no crime' but instead a rightful practice of the rural poor in the fight to maintain themselves, the success of smuggling gangs in the 1740s is evidence of a broad-based fraternity in which all but the richest members of rural society were involved. Smuggled goods passed through an elaborate network of provincial shopkeepers, innkeepers, and dealers and merchants – increasingly located in London – who in turn sold their goods to all consumers. For instance, three-quarters of all tea consumed in Britain in the 1740s was thought to be smuggled, suggesting the likelihood that even the tea drunk in the houses of noblemen was illicit. Many farmers were involved indirectly, allowing their horses to be taken by night and their barns to hide cargoes in return for a small share of the booty: a pack of tea, a cask of gin. There is a sense, though, that the actual smugglers, drawn predominantly in the 1740s from the ranks of the artisan and the labourer, thought of themselves as 'rebels' against the existing social and political order. This is evinced in part by the smugglers' almost total defiance of customary forms of deference – examples of smugglers openly and victoriously parading their cargoes through the streets of provincial towns being legion – but also in the suggestion that some smugglers had Jacobite sympathies.

It was the rising tide of violence against officers and informers, in defiance of both the law and community sanction, that proved the smuggling gangs' undoing. Following an investigation into the attack in October 1747 on the Custom House at Poole by the Hawkhurst and west Sussex smuggling gangs to reclaim a large seizure of tea, informant Daniel Chater, accompanied by riding officer William Galley, was to be examined by Surveyor of the Customs and magistrate Major Battine at Stansted near Chichester. The examination never took place. Instead, Galley and Chater were captured by the smugglers at Rowland's Castle, on the Hampshire–Sussex border, and eventually tortured to death.

To the Sussex grandee and staunch Whig the Duke of Richmond this was too much, and he made it his personal mission to rid his domain of smuggling and to make sure that the murderers were punished. Through force of will and the absolute execution of the law, he was ultimately successful. A Special Commission was held at Chichester in January 1749 at which five smugglers were found guilty of murder and two of being accessories to murder. All seven men were executed on 19 January. Subsequent trials at the Old Bailey, and the Kent and Sussex assizes resulted in the transportation of one further smuggler and the execution of a further 20.[60]

The example was thus brutally made and the major smuggling gangs broken up, but it did not stop smuggling altogether. Greater restrictions imposed on the gin and tobacco trades in 1751 and an increase in tea duties in 1759 offered renewed encouragement. Far more important, though, was the outbreak of the War of American Independence. England being duly 'denuded of fighting men' gave smugglers greater opportunities to land their cargoes.[61] This huge upturn in smuggling in the 1770s and 1780s was not confined to the south coast but was true also of the Bristol Channel and the whole east coast. Smugglers invested in large cutters able to carry huge cargoes. They were also often so well-armed that the revenue vessels were totally inadequate to the task. Such was the mismatch on the Hampshire and west Sussex coasts that naval warships from the dockyard at Portsmouth were occasionally called on to take smuggling cutters. Given the investment of smuggling networks, the increasing cargo of contraband was also mirrored, again, by a rising tide of violence in defiance of the revenue forces.[62]

The slashing of tea duties by Pitt the Younger in 1784 – from 127 per cent to 12.5 per cent – acted to check this renewed vigour, historians of eighteenth-century smuggling even going as far as to say that this shift in government policy brought to an end the golden age of English smuggling.[63] But smuggling did not suddenly cease. Indeed, notwithstanding the restrictions of the highly fortified coast in the Napoleonic epoch, the Napoleonic state supported smugglers both as a way of securing guineas and as a means to traffick escaped French prisoners of war. As Daly notes, smugglers were used as a 'weapon of war' against the British state and as a way of supporting French industry, while hitting the fiscal fortunes of the British government by continuing to flood the British market with tobacco and spirits. The small French port of Gravelines, between Calais and Dunkirk, in 1811 became the officially sanctioned – by the French government – entry point for English smugglers. Indeed, Gravelines became known as the 'city of smugglers'. It was the Kent and Sussex smugglers who took advantage of this opportunity, albeit operating in a much-altered form from the high point of the 1770s and early 1780s. Instead of using expensive cutters, this new generation of 'free traders' favoured the traditional Kentish galley, a smaller, nimble, cheap to construct and fast boat. Their trade was vibrant: in 1813 alone smuggling vessels docked in Gravelines on 606 occasions and offered an important lifeline to rural workers for whom the war had led to a deterioration in their real wages. Even a small galley, crewed usually by five or six men, required a sizeable force to land the cargo and 'run' it, the commissioners of excise reckoning that as many as 200 men were employed per mission. According to Arthur Young in 1813, Sussex field workers could supplement their usual daily wages of one shilling and sixpence by as much as seven shillings a night for helping land the contraband.[64]

This unusual arrangement was short-lived, with Napoleon's fall from power ending this unique phase in the history of smuggling. The effective and swift demilitarisation of the south and east coasts meant that landing smuggled goods became, albeit temporarily, relatively more straightforward. Moreover, the agrarian depression meant that smuggling was an increasingly important way of supplementing low wages or even completely supplanting labouring. This state of affairs was temporary, the creation of the Coastal Blockade and Coast Guard heralding a new, more systematic approach to the suppression of smuggling. Located at strategic intervals along the coastline, Coastal Blockade stations allowed a far closer eye to be kept on smuggling activities than hitherto had been the case. If previously customs officers were alert to the many acts of subterfuge adopted by smugglers – hiding a few tubs of brandy or casks of gin under 'legitimate' cargoes – now other practices came to light. A log kept by a 'supernumerary lieutenant' of the Blockade stationed near New Romney on the coast of the notorious smuggling area of Romney Marsh – sparsely populated and with flat, accessible beaches making it ideal to land cargoes – provides telling testimony of the range of smuggling practices. The following is a set of edited entries from September and October 1820:

15 September: Picked up a tub of brandy and observed several men about the shores.

16 September: Observed a lugger stand close in off Little Stone and a man throw a line overboard: at low water found four half ankers (2 of gin, 2 of brandy) laying on the sand.

23 September: The Providence fishing smack under Loudon James Johnson delivered up to me six half ankers of foreign spirits which he picked up at sea: sent them to the Custom Store House at New Romney.

26 September: Observed two men laying on the beach between No 1 Battery and the Lighthouse. Saw several lights, supposed to be signals in the windows of a fisherman's cottage close to them.

29 September: Mr. Gibson of the Gd. Redoubt picked up in the boat (a fishing smack from Dartmouth that had run aground near Dungeness lighthouse) 4 half ankers of gin. Observed a fishing smack pick up six others and made sail out to sea.

8 October: A large party of smugglers was seen between the Lighthouse and No. 27 Tower.

10 October: At 1 o'clock observed a great firing between Little Stone and No. 27 tower which proved to be a galley attempting to work a cargo by a gang of armed smugglers which made resistance was beaten off and prevented by Mr. Comboule, mids[hipman] of his party.

31 October: Between 7 and 12 whilst visiting Port Suthersland and Monerial Towers 22, 23, 26 and 27 observed many lights made by smugglers as signals amongst the Marsh.[65]

Smuggling clearly took many forms, from highly organised and quick to violence, to reliance on hiding small numbers of casks in the sea awaiting collection by only a small group of runners.

While being involved in a smuggling gang instantly labelled an individual as a smuggler as opposed to, for example, a labourer or a shoe maker – during Swing magistrates were quick to claim that mobilisations were the work of smugglers[66] – most individuals involved in smuggling combined the practice with other work. Indeed, depositions of smugglers acting as informants show that it was through their agricultural work that they first made contact with smugglers and were drawn into the practice. Other smugglers also used their farm work to mask their illicit activities. On being tried at the Old Bailey in April 1821 for his involvement in the so-called Battle of Brookland, the last major pitched battle between smugglers and the preventative services in England, Richard Wraight claimed that he was a 'labouring husbandman' who attended the markets to sell the crops and purchase seed for his mother's small farm at Pedlinge near Hythe in Kent. Through this work, Wraight claimed, he had developed substantial networks that necessitated his constantly moving from farm to farm on Romney Marsh. He was on his way to Rye when having fallen in with a group of men he was taken into custody. His pockets contained gunpowder and shot and his face was blackened with gunpowder for the simple reason, so he claimed, because: 'I am in the constant habit of going out with a gun on my mother's farm, for the purpose of shooting rooks and other birds, that destroy the seed corn, for which purpose I am very seldom without a little powder and shot in my pockets.' Wraight, unlike his co-accused and Aldington Gang leader, Cephas Quested, was found not guilty.[67] This gang, under the new leadership of labourer-turned-waggoner-turned smuggler and unlicensed publican George Ransley, started to branch out into broader criminal activities, including burglary.[68] However, their increased resort to violence, including the shooting dead at close range of a quartermaster in the Blockade in July 1826, was their undoing. The subsequent government-sponsored repression led to fourteen members being transported for life and for large-scale smuggling in East Kent to cease. The rump of the gang attempted some desultory smuggling missions but turned most of their efforts towards armed poaching, something that combined their knowledge of the networks through which illicit goods could be fenced with their violent tenacity. But a combination of armed raids and attacks on keepers proved their undoing when in 1829 several of the gang were successfully prosecuted for poaching on East Kent Quarter Sessions' chairman and local MP Sir Edward Knatchbull's Mersham estate.[69]

Some smugglers may have been simple opportunists but many were rebels with a different worldview to that expected of rural workers. Not only was violence and intimidation endemic, but, as the above example illustrates, smuggling was often linked to wider forms of criminality and other forms of protest practice. We have noted that the authorities in the early eighteenth century believed that smugglers were Jacobites, or at least acted as a form of connection and communication between James II's exiled court in France and those Jacobites who remained in England. In an important intervention in the history of the Black Act, Cruickshanks and Erskine-Hill have shown that the Waltham Blacks not only started off as an early smuggling gang but were also involved in the Atterbury Plot, by which the royal family were to be captured and the 'Pretender' instated as king. The connection was Sir Henry Goring, a Tory loyal to the Stuarts who, being deprived of his regiment on the Hanoverian succession, turned his military experience into a way of money-making through organised smuggling, and who was heavily implicated in the plot.[70] Other early smuggling gangs, again often in league with Stuart-supporting landowners, who saw smuggling to be a good way of making money as well as transporting Jacobite agents and supporting communication, were active Jacobite propagandists. In 1716 – the year after the Jacobite rising – the surveyor general of riding officers in Kent complained that the smuggling gangs were distributing copies of the Pretender's declaration. Five years later, when the Mayfield Gang mounted an armed rescue at Lydd, the captain of the Rye revenue cutter reported that the gang was 'not less then 200 & every man of them for ye Pretender'. Members of the same gang tellingly also claimed that they were the 'ffarnham Blacks'. Another gang centred on Hawkhurst similarly met and drank the Pretender's health at the Oak and Ivy Inn, the pub being named after the Jacobite symbol.[71]

The cosmopolitanism of smugglers was thought to mark them out as natural rebels. Many smugglers spent significant amounts of time in foreign ports, building networks that not only crossed national boundaries but also political divides. This meant that they were viewed as being more open to treasonous influence. In commenting on the early Swing protests, a Mr Pilcher of Sandwich claimed that 'many thousands of countrymen' were employed in gangs whose 'nightly visits' to the shores of the continent invested them with 'French tastes and inclinations'.[72] Perhaps of greater importance, though, was that being a member of a smuggling gang taught discipline and organisation, located individuals in widespread networks and thus made them more mobile subjects, and gave them access to guns. Being in a smuggling gang thereby not only taught the importance and techniques of solidarity but also equipped members with the skills necessary to resist. It is particularly striking then that the first Swing mobilisations in Kent and Sussex, respectively, occurred in the smuggling centres of Elham and Brede. Both sets of protests involved men armed with pistols – the runners' weapon of choice – strong internal discipline, and in the former place an ability to cover huge distances in a single night.[73] Arguably the best example of this connection came at Alfriston, a veritable hornet's nest of criminality and dissent. It was to here that a Swing activist who had evaded arrest at the smuggling centre of Ninfield fled. When the constables finally caught up with him, he was 'rescued on the road' in the time-honoured style by a group of local smugglers with blackened faces. The whole population was reportedly 'cognizant, but no information [could] be gained'.[74]

Beyond Custom

Together, the actions of the Blacks, wood-takers, poachers, and smugglers represented a total systematic challenge to the state's primary motivation of defining and defending the interests of private property, their actions occasionally even assuming wider political ambitions, too. If to claim that, outside of Jacobitism, their actions represented a genuine threat to the landed elites and to the state, was absurd, we do well to remember that it was as much the perception of landed elites as opposed to lived realities that drove judicial practice.[75] As David Rollison's study of the Gloucestershire community of Westonbirt in the early eighteenth century so vividly demonstrates, absentee Whig landowners readily interpreted the playing out of a muscular, independent culture as evidence of Jacobitism. Moreover, this reading was used to justify 'keeping sinecures in the hands of reliable dependants ... [as] part of the Whig state's attempt to "colonize" a potentially Jacobite society' to inculcate Whig values and to relay evidence of anti-Whig sentiment back to London.[76]

We might therefore read the actions of the Blacks, poachers, smugglers and wood-takers as evidence of the persistence and tenacity of truly demotic cultural forms and beliefs shared between rural communities that refused to be bent to the will of the state. Taking wood to fire the stove may not have been a revolutionary act but it was an important act of rebellion, an assertion of independence and a right to self-determination in the same way that the Blacks and organised smugglers protested the seemingly arbitrary imposition of state power. Understanding the role of organised poaching and criminal gangs from this perspective is necessarily harder. Indeed, it could reasonably be argued that their acts bore no relation to the acts of rural workers attempting to take what was 'theirs'. However, such organisation (and violence) can also be read as a response to the increased securitisation of property – estates 'protected' by mantraps, spring guns and armed keepers – and the increasing desperation of rural life after the Napoleonic Wars. It was evidence of a breakdown in social relations.

The defence of custom and customary practice may have been the most significant interface between rural workers and the eighteenth-century British state but there was a more immediate way in which the form and function of the state was challenged: opposition to enforced military enlistment. The British state was increasingly organised according to militarist-expansionist principles, in relation to both the expansion of the standing army to support foreign military campaigns with its attendant fiscal demands, and the increasing militarisation of society.[77] While the impacts of this latter dynamic were most pronounced during the Napoleonic Wars – explored in depth in Chapters 6 and 7 – it also had profound impacts earlier in the eighteenth century through the compulsory muster of militia. The received belief among the rulers of rural England was that the best form of defence was that offered by those whose liberty and property was in danger. The creation of organised citizen militias were, therefore, considered an ideal solution, encouraging the people to 'recognize that they must be prepared to bear arms and to take risks themselves if they were to preserve their liberty and their property'.[78] That the Jacobite Rebellion of 1745 (the '45') had eased its way as far south as Derby without encountering any effective resistance, while the Seven Years War had put a huge strain on military resources, shifted government opinion in favour of raising a new militia. Receiving royal assent in 1757, the Militia Act allowed for a national militia organised on a county basis, officered by the gentry, with the rank and file chosen by lot from all otherwise exempt, able-bodied men between the ages of 18 and 50. In terms of pure numbers, the Act therefore shifted the burden from the landowners under the old militia of 1662 to workers and farmers. As Randall notes, the ensuing protests reflected this balance, with the 'worst conflicts' occurring not in manufacturing but in agrarian districts.[79]

Perceived as a clear case of class self-interest, attempts to enrol the militia in the summer of 1757 generated considerable protest. That it coincided with a wave of food rioting only served to intensify the alarm. As protestors at Lincoln proclaimed: 'We will not fight for what does not concern us, and belongs to our landlords; let the worst happen; we can but be tenants and labourers as we are at present.'[80] The protests started at Washingborough in Lincolnshire on 23 August when lists of eligible men were returned to the chief constables. Under threats that the gathered mob would pull down and set fire to their houses if further lists were made, the protestors were complied with, which, in turn, encouraged others elsewhere in Lincolnshire to protest.[81]

Protests of a similar form – lists being seized and destroyed; money and beer demanded; and the property of the gentry damaged in acts of intimidation – soon spread to Nottinghamshire and Bedfordshire. By mid-September, the protests had diffused throughout eastern England as well as in Lancashire, Middlesex, Northamptonshire, and Yorkshire. The following month riots also occurred in Derbyshire, Norfolk, Surrey and as far west as Gloucestershire.[82] Renewed attempts in Kent during the summer of 1759 to enrol a militia provoked yet more protests,[83] while further unrest occurred between 1759 and 1761 in Buckinghamshire, Huntingdonshire and Warwickshire.[84]

Far more serious, though, were a series of riots in the North-East. The publication in February 1761 of notices that the constables of Northumberland and Durham were to draw up lists of all men eligible to serve in the militia prompted opposition, as had been expected. Starting in Gateshead on 28 February, the protests soon spread to Morpeth and Belford, while ballots were abandoned elsewhere on the *expectation* of opposition. The most dramatic protest occurred, though, at Hexham, where a reported 5,000 individuals from along the Tyne Valley filled the market place at Hexham on 8 March. It would appear that by 1pm the ballot had been drawn and parts of the crowd were issuing 'murderous threats', prompting the magistrates to read the Riot Act. The huge crowd refusing to disperse, the North Yorkshire Militia – stationed to protect those issuing the ballot – formed a line to prevent the crowd from entering the Sessions house, which, in turn, led to some of the armed members of the crowd attempting to seize the bayonets and muskets of the militia. In the ensuing melee, one militiaman was shot dead by his own musket, while one ensign was mortally wounded in the stomach. The line breaking, an order was given for the militia to fire. What followed was the biggest massacre on English soil in the eighteenth century up to that time. Figures vary, but the final official figure was that 42 men were killed and a further 48 badly wounded, the actual death toll probably in excess of 50. A 74-year-old farmer was also later hanged for his involvement in the Morpeth protests.[85]

If this was the end of the protests of the 1750s and 1760s, the Hexham bloodbath was not the end of anti-militia riots. While further systematic research is needed, we do know that anti-enrolment and embodiment protests occurred in Bedfordshire in 1769 and in mid- and west Sussex in 1778, where protests by 'large bod[ies] of country people' were particularly sustained and robust.[86] Further protests occurred in 1795 in Lincolnshire on the renewed drawing of lists, but the greatest protests, though, were occasioned by a new act of parliament receiving royal assent on 11 November, which provided for raising a further 60,000 militiamen because of the fear of a French invasion. Outside of Scotland, where opposition was most vehement, protests again centred on the Fenland borders of Lincolnshire as well as occurring in Norfolk, Northamptonshire, the Lake District, Wing (Buckinghamshire) and Oswestry (Shropshire) and 'signs of unrest' elsewhere. Small farmers were, as Charlesworth notes, again the key instigators, many being arrested in the swift government-sponsored repression.[87] These riots appear to have been the last involving militia recruitment, though during the Napoleonic Wars different companies of militia were active in food riots – as will be detailed in Chapter 4 – and occasional riots concerning conditions, such as occurred at Devizes in Wiltshire in June 1810.[88]

Chapter 3: Land and Environmental Change

Studies of enclosure have proved to be arguably the most enduring field of rural historical enquiry – and with good reason. For without first understanding the changing structure of land ownership and land use it is impossible to grasp the complexities of the emergence of agrarian capitalism, and even the making of the landless proletariat. Yet notwithstanding this historiographical pre-eminence, and in contrast to the centrality of land disputes to agrarian change in Scotland and Wales, the role of opposition to enclosure in England has often been underplayed.[1] Indeed, while earlier rural histories, typified by Chambers and Mingay's *The Agricultural Revolution*, often acknowledged that many enclosures provoked resistance, it was not until the late 1980s that attempts to understand these oppositions went beyond considerations as to whether enclosure improved or worsened the lot of rural workers.[2] The enclosure of commons and wastes, so revisionist studies suggest, always represented a dislocation in the way of life of rural workers, and as such, on whatever scale enclosure was enacted it always generated resistance. Opposition could occur over many years, both pre- and post-enclosure; coalesced around often surprising cross-sections of rural society; and deployed across a wide variety of protest practices. What follows also contends that while studies of enclosure have been critical to the advance of a less narrowly *social* rural history, they have tended to shadow other major land use and environmental changes in the English countryside. Thus, after beginning with an analysis of opposition to enclosure, the chapter goes on to examine resistances to land use changes and the importance of technological projects as generators of conflict.

As noted in Chapter 1, between 1760 and 1820, 30 per cent of the agricultural land of England was enclosed through parliamentary enclosure, the peak periods being the 1760s and 1770s, and then again during the Napoleonic Wars. By 1850 the remaining half of the open-field systems that had persisted to 1750 had been extinguished by enclosure. The change was especially pronounced in the Midland counties, significant areas of East Anglia, Gloucestershire, and East and West Yorkshire, with counties such as Northamptonshire and Nottinghamshire becoming major exporters of grain to the London market – and frequently the sites of riots attempting to prevent the 'export' of food.[3] It is possible to overplay the national impact of enclosure, though, for counties such as Cornwall, Devon, Essex and Kent were largely already enclosed.[4] Moreover, as Leigh Shaw-Taylor has asserted, '[p]arliamentary enclosure did not … represent the last decisive stage in the development of agrarian capitalism. Capitalist farmers *and* proletarian labourers dominated English agriculture before parliamentary enclosure'.[5]

Yet such crude geography masks a more complex spatiality. Significant areas of other counties not classically associated with the parliamentary enclosure movement *were* so enclosed. Of the 7 million acres of land in England enclosed by acts of parliament, 2.3 million were lowland commons, heathlands and – critically – upland waste. For instance, Cumbria in the late eighteenth century had the highest proportion of unenclosed upland waste of any English county. By 1830, almost a quarter of the region had been enclosed by parliamentary acts, very little of which was arable land. Cumbria was not alone. Graham Roger has also shown that the eighteenth-century enclosure of wastes impacted significantly on an otherwise forgotten rural population in supposedly 'enclosed' south-west Lancashire dependent for their livelihoods on the exercise of common rights. Elsewhere in Lancashire, Henry French has shown that the town moors at Clitheroe – in an area still rich in unenclosed 'wastes' – were a key source of income to poorer townsfolk. On enclosure, agricultural systems continued to operate more-or-less unaltered, but an important 'second income stream' for labourers was now lost. Similarly the Wiltshire town of Chippenham kept its open fields until the end of the eighteenth century.[6] Enclosures of Crown forest by dedicated acts also had significant local impacts. Parts of the two largest forests – the Forest of Dean in Gloucestershire and the New Forest in Hampshire – were given over to sylviculture in 'temporary' enclosures in the period, while the smaller forests like Needwood in Staffordshire and Exmoor in Somerset were disafforested, enclosed and the land divided in the early nineteenth century.[7]

Thanks to the work of John Chapman and Sylvia Seeliger, over the past two decades our understandings of processes of enclosure in the eighteenth and early nineteenth centuries have also been revised. Specifically, the way we conceptualise the processes of enclosure, and therefore its impacts, have altered in several critical ways. Enclosure by consolidating holdings – often referred to as 'piecemeal' enclosure – and by agreement have both been shown to be more important in transforming rural landscapes and agrarian practices than previously thought. Systematic analyses of these processes suggest that it was particularly important in the chalklands, with rising cereal prices in the late eighteenth century and early years of the nineteenth century not only stimulating enclosure but also tillage. Given this dynamic, it is not too surprising, then, that the peaks in enclosure by agreement coincided with peaks in parliamentary enclosure, for both processes achieved the same end, enclosure by agreement simply being cheaper and quicker.[8] In eighteenth-century Hampshire, for instance, there was only one more parliamentary enclosure than enclosure by formal agreement: 39 and 38 cases, respectively.[9] Work by John Broad and Briony McDonagh has also highlighted the critical roles taken by estate owners as projectors of enclosure on their demesnes, both through acting as sponsors to parliamentary bills and in driving 'agreements' among their tenants. Through wielding the powerful tool of patronage, potential public opposition might well be driven underground. As Broad notes, the Verney family might have sought 'agreement and consensus whenever possible and avoided open conflict' but local opposition 'was muted because most villages had little access to the institutions and levers of power'. Bailiffs played an important role, too, in managing influence and opinion. McDonagh also reminds us that enclosure was not simply a masculine project. Female estate owners were often the leading advocates of enclosure, taking charge of major agricultural 'improvement' projects in their lands.[10]

Understanding Opposition

On the night of 8 August 1795 the gate was 'cut' to pieces and the posts and rails thrown down of a recent small enclosure of waste ground at Fleet End in the township of Newtown in the Hampshire parish of Titchfield. While the protestors adopted the age-old anti-enclosure tactic of levelling the physical enclosures, we only know of this act of anti-enclosure protest by virtue of an advert offering a £20 reward for information leading to a conviction, placed by the lord of the manor in the Portsmouth and Salisbury papers. Indeed, we only know of the

enclosure because of the adverts, for this was not one of the totemic parliamentary enclosures copiously documented in the archives, but rather
an example of enclosure by agreement, a process whereby all interested
parties agreed to enclose the open field, common or waste.[11] In understanding opposition to enclosure, we are, necessarily, in thrall to what
the archive details. Thus, long-standing accounts of oppositions – John
and Barbara Hammonds' *The Village Labourer* being the foundational
study – have tended to focus on the most dramatic events that were
reported in the national press or detailed in letters to officers of state.[12]
The low archival visibility of many enclosure protests has led to a degree
of ambivalence among rural historians as to the depth and strength of
opposition. Turner's study of Buckinghamshire, for example, concluded
that commoners in that county 'were disposed … with but little demur',
while Wells concurred that the characteristic response to enclosure in
the south was passivity.[13]

Such methodological and interpretative problems aside, as Charlesworth
delineated in his *Atlas of Rural Protest*, there appears to be a more-or-
less predictable *pattern* to the timing and spacing of dramatic anti-enclosure protests. The second half of the seventeenth century witnessed a
series of enclosure riots in the Fenlands of the east and in the forests of
Wiltshire, Dorset and Somerset, the Forest of Dean, High Peak Forest
in Derbyshire, Cannock Chase in Staffordshire, Needwood, and Enfield
to the north of London. This period of upheaval was followed by relatively low levels of enclosure in the early eighteenth century, dramatic
protests against enclosure and restrictions to common rights essentially
being confined to the forests of Northamptonshire, Dean, Charnwood
and Cannock Chase, protests in the latter two places focusing on landowners' claims to free warren. From the late 1750s to the late 1770s, the
upturn in enclosure prompted a new wave of anti-enclosure protests. In
addition to a wave of riots in the East and West Midlands, land protests
also occurred in Oxfordshire, Wiltshire, the Lincolnshire Fenlands and
the Somerset levels. A broadly similar pattern was also evident in the
period from the late 1780s through to the Napoleonic Wars, though East
Anglia also became an important locus of anti-enclosure protests, and
attempts to enclose town fields and lands adjacent to rapidly expanding
northern industrial towns also became a key feature. Riots in the 1830s
and 1840s were far fewer, a reflection of the reduced intensity of enclosure at the time, tending to focus on the urban fringe.[14]

More recently, microhistorical studies have begun to complicate this
neat picture. Engrossment – the consolidation of smaller farms into
large holdings – and allied attempts to eliminate or limit the practice
of common rights could potentially lead to protest. In Cheshire and

Shropshire, the effect of engrossment on an epic scale in the second half of the eighteenth century – effected by leases not being renewed on small 'peasant' farms – was in large part mitigated by those who were displaced migrating to secure work in new industries. Similarly, in Cumbria, those who were protests against enclosure and changes to customary agrarian systems were also, so reckons Appleby, largely avoided by increased employment opportunities beyond agriculture, especially in mining and the Irish coastal trade. Yet in locales outside the 'core' areas of protest, tensions over enclosure *did* surface in the form of protest. Pearson's study of Great Tey in Essex offers a useful counter. Here, farmer Lay had expanded his holdings aggressively in the parish through a strategy of leasing then purchasing land. In 1725 he took out a lease on the Playfield, an area customarily used by both parishioners and those from neighbouring parishes for recreation and customary ceremony, and over which the copyhold terms prohibited cultivation. The field, however, lay between two of Lay's farms, and so in the spring of 1727 he ploughed the land and planted a crop of oats. This was, so Pearson asserts, a final act of aggression, and prompted a shift from bitter dissent to overt protest. Two months later, symbolically on the day of the annual Trinity fair – when a bonfire would customarily be lit on the field and when the manor court was held – a group of men assembled on the field and, according to Lay, riotously trampled the oats, lit a bonfire and threw firebrands into one of Lay's adjoining closes. This was no conventional levelling of fences, no attempt to seize the land or to occupy space, rather it was an assertion of customary rights and a critique of the antagonistic use of a rich man's power against the interests of the poor. It was neither dramatic nor a knee-jerk response, but rather a culmination of resentments and framed through calls to moral economic values and customary law.[15]

The most important lesson from Pearson's paper is that we must be alert to the fact that formal enclosure, whether by parliamentary means or agreement, was not the only way in which land holdings were transformed. Indeed, the elimination of common and customary rights – enclosure's greatest social and economic impact – could be effected through many other means. Even in areas where customary rights were not eliminated by enclosure or undermined systematically by engrossment and riding roughshod over local custom, manipulations of customary tenures by manorial authorities generated sustained conflict. For instance, Searle's finely-grained study of custom and agrarian change in eighteenth-century Cumbria offers evidence of sustained resistance against attempts to try to squeeze ever higher manorial fines and fees from tenants on customary tenures. In 1723, tenants on the Duke of Somerset's estates even went as far to declare that they had been 'forced' to enter into a 'Strict and

Solemn Combination and Confederacy ... to stand by & Assist each other
with Mutual Contributions & all other ways and means of Assistance' to
resist an attempt to impose an 'exorbitant and unreasonable' general
fine.[16]

It is important to remember that what underpinned all this opposition
was the perception that enclosure would force the petty producers and
commoners from the land and into absolute reliance on the demand for
wage labour. Notwithstanding Shaw-Taylor's aforementioned assertion
that, before parliamentary enclosure, capitalist farmers and proletarian-
ised workers dominated agricultural production, and where enclosure
was planned it threatened to remove access to the means of production
from the poorest members of rural society. Moreover, as the work of
Martin on Warwickshire, Neeson on Northamptonshire, and Turner on
Buckinghamshire has shown, when enacted, enclosure did turn commoners and, with few exceptions, small farmers into proletarians. Enclosure
accelerated the process of consolidating agricultural holdings, and the
concurrent reduction in the number of landowners, but also, as Turner's
use of Land Tax returns shows vividly, often led to the almost immediate
sale of land by those awarded small plots post-enclosure.[17] Even more
strikingly, enclosure, as Jane Humphries, echoing the earlier arguments
of Ivy Pinchbeck, showed, increased women's reliance on male labour,
as their ability to exercise common rights in support of the household
economy was removed by enclosure. This was, Humphries asserts, no
coincidence:

> Employers' interests in the development of proletarianization, directly
> motivated by seasonal and sectoral variations in the demand for
> labor, necessarily spilled over into interests in intrafamily patterns of
> dependence and support. The dependence of whole families on wages
> ensured a sufficiently elastic labor supply to cope with an unmecha-
> nized harvest. The dependence of whole families on wage earners
> strengthened discipline and commitment: to be a good husband or
> father it became necessary to be a good wage earner.

Enclosure therefore did not just coincidentally transform the gender
politics of the English countryside and the gender relations of the working household, but was deliberately employed to effect these changes. It
is little wonder, then, that while women were rarely recorded as being
active in open, collective oppositions to enclosure, their protests took
the less dramatic but arguably more successful form of continuing to
take wood for fuel (as analysed in Chapter 2) and in the persistence of
gleaning and nutting.[18]

Resisting Enclosure

It is, of course, notorious, that the landed peasantry of England, and not without good reason, had no enthusiasm for the enclosure movement. Some well-known and very scholarly books of the left suggest that the change it involved was forced upon the countryside in the teeth of a bitterly resentful peasantry. It was quite usual, it is implied, for the opposition to exhaust all legal methods of protest. Then in despair at the extent to which the dice were loaded by the landed class in its possession of pulpit, courts, and parliament, the peasantry might well rise in revolt.[19]

So wrote W.E. Tate, the pioneering historian of enclosure, in 1948. His point was that when one consulted the archive there was little evidence of 'organized protest', this being a function of the fact, as he saw it, that the enclosure 'movement' was carried out with 'care'. Specifically, Tate charges parliament with having carefully scrutinised enclosure bills, of having listened to opposition against petitions, and having subsequently amended or dropped bills. Analysing 170 enclosure petitions – documents that required a substantial majority of the value of property concerned in favour of enclosure – for Nottinghamshire between 1743 and 1826, Tate draws two conclusions. First, parliamentary committees did not manipulate cases in favour of those proprietors supportive of enclosure, contra the argument of the Hammonds. Second, that the petitions evidence a 'marvellously small' and 'remarkably unvocal' opposition.[20]

The first conclusion has since been challenged, it having been shown that projectors of enclosure often did try to influence the make-up of parliamentary enclosure committees, calling on their parliamentary friends to ensure that the evidence was presented in such a way as to give the appearance of universal support for the measure among interested proprietors.[21] Simply put, the leverage of aristocratic and major landowner power could achieve any desired outcome and render public forms of opposition effectively impossible. The second conclusion has proved more enduring. A long line of historians of enclosure, from Gonner, through Hoskins to (in his early writings) E.P. Thompson, have assumed that the small farmers and poor commoners found that opposition to parliament was beyond them. They could, Thompson asserted:

[O]nly in the most exceptional circumstances – and with the advice of some men of education and substance – have had recourse to the costly and procrastinating procedures of an alien culture and an alien power. The fatalism of the cottager in the face of this ever-present power, and the uneven, piecemeal incidence of enclosure ... go some way towards explaining the seeming passivity of the victims.[22]

It was a pioneering study by Jeanette Neeson that offered the first decisive blow to this position. By first delineating the potential economic and cultural value of common rights to commoners, and thereby highlighting the potential size and motivations of the anti-enclosure lobby, Neeson proceeded to show that between the historic totems of counter-petitions and riot, commoners used a wide array of protest practices in defence of their livelihoods.[23] Besides, as Whyte has recently asserted in his study of the North-West, counter-petitions were often from individuals rather than local groups, thereby lacking both force and collective potency.[24]

The first possible 'stage' in any attempt to resist a proposed enclosure was a form of protest rarely recorded in the archive: grumbling. This was not, as John Stevenson has claimed, 'passive'.[25] Rather, grumbling served as both an important psychological coping strategy in the face of change and as a way in which those of like mind could come together. It was, Neeson claims, 'the first stage of more effective opposition'. At West Haddon, Northamptonshire, in the 1760s, 'grumbling' among the majority of the landowners led to a parliamentary counter-petition which, in turn, led to the first enclosure bill being withdrawn. On being interviewed as to the reason for their opposition, most said enclosure would not benefit them, while others objected on principle, farmer James stating that he 'can't answer it to his conscience'. Opposition took a slightly different course at Wellingborough. Surveyor Thomas Cowper was met by a 'warm discourse', many of the landowners and landholders refusing to sign the enclosure bill and duly drafting a counter-petition to the House of Commons on the fear that they would lose their 'small but comfortable Subsistence'. This strategy failing, a plan of the fields and the field books detailing how the enclosed lands were to be allotted were taken from the enclosure commissioner's house. The enclosure was duly delayed and the costs of enclosing increased.[26]

In both cases, initial grumbling ultimately led to some successes. The tactic of making life difficult for the surveyors did not have to take the form of theft but could instead focus on 'stubborn non-compliance, foot-dragging and mischief'. Refusing or deliberately neglecting to mark out one's lands to survey, delaying signing the enclosure bills, and removing surveyor's posts were all potentially important tools of opposition. It was not just surveyors who were intimidated. The projectors of enclosure, and those who sought to devalue common rights by restricting access, were also frequently targeted, being the recipients of threatening letters, their property set on fire, and their sheep and cattle maimed. At Flore in Northamptonshire, the gates of the squire's hall were even broken down.[27]

The holding of local protest meetings was the way in which 'grumblings' could coalesce in a public setting, and give a sheen of legitimacy to the complainants' discourses. While we are necessarily in thrall to what is recorded in the archive – the likelihood being that more ad hoc, less formalised meetings were less likely to be recorded – it would *appear* that some meetings were held speculatively to test the strength of opposition while others were intended explicitly as a show of force. For instance, contrast the advert placed in the Reading press giving a day's notice for a meeting 'of persons interested in preventing the enclosure' of Cookham Common (Berkshire), with the meetings of the Association for Opposing the Harrow Inclosure (Middlesex). However, such a reading, while seemingly sensible, ignores a deeper archival understanding, for despite the apparent contrast both meetings *were* the public product of highly organised opposition, the Cookham protests being backed by a fighting fund supported by several wealthy local residents. The Cookham protests were successful, the House of Commons rejecting the bill on its second reading, while the Harrow enclosure proceeded.[28]

If grumblings, protest pamphlets, opposition organisations, public meetings, non-compliance, and petitions were unsuccessful and parliament supported the enclosure – either through a dedicated act or after 1801 through the auspices of the General Enclosure Act – then opposition needed to take a more direct course. This was also necessarily the case for enclosures by agreement and those affected by unity of possessions. Sometimes the initial strength of opposition might waver if, as often occurred, there was a considerable time lag between parliamentary support being granted and the actual physical enclosure occurring. Initial coalitions of opposition who were prepared to take legal means might also baulk at the tactics of overt protest. But, in common with opposition to enclosure in the sixteenth and seventeenth centuries, when faced with the immediate threat to livelihoods and ways of life, small farmers, commoners and cottagers were not slow to attempt to sabotage new enclosures. The tactic usually deployed was to level the fences, quick-set hedges and banks of enclosures, to eliminate whatever acted to exclude physically. As Nick Blomley has stated, it was the fence and hedge that 'performed' property, and hence became the symbolic and material icons of enclosure.[29] This was nothing new. Indeed, the name of the mid-seventeenth-century democratic and socially egalitarian radical group the Levellers was not only an invocation of making all socially and politically even but also of making property even, of levelling barriers and divides. Of levelling hedges and fences.

The practice took two forms. First, mass invasions and occupations of enclosed space, something that was done with a strong degree of organisation to assert both the depth and strength of anti-enclosure opinion, and to offer a public display of force. Second, secretive acts performed by – as far as the archive infers – only a small number of people and often under the cover of darkness. The following examples offer a useful contrast. On 10 January 1781, the enclosures in Oakly Park in Ludlow, Shropshire, were 'totally levelled', after which, so the report ran, the 'mob ... proceed[ed] to commence further violence'. On the news reaching Birmingham, three troops of the (mounted) Scotch Greys were duly despatched to put down the protests.[30] Similarly, a group of men, reportedly nearly 300 strong, from Gillingham in north Dorset and the surrounding villages of the Dorset–Somerset–Wiltshire borders met at Mapperton Hill and Piercewood before proceeding to destroy 'long lines' of new fences of the new enclosures on the former commons of the parishes of Milton and Mere. While the troops from Dorchester arrived too late to prevent the destruction, they remained quartered in the neighbourhood for several days to prevent further protests.[31] By contrast, in December 1816, 'several' of the fences 'put up by the order of the Commissioners' of the East Downton and Hampworth enclosure on the Wiltshire fringe of the New Forest were secretively destroyed, prompting the offer of a £5 reward for information in an advert in the Salisbury press.[32] Similarly, at Swyre in west Dorset, labourer Robert Northover engaged in a one-man campaign to destroy the fences and newly planted quick-set hedges, being prosecuted in 1800 and again, at the age of 60, in 1811.[33] Even planning 'overt' protest, though, required a degree of subterfuge. For instance, when the West Haddon enclosure bill became law at the third attempt in the summer of 1765, those in opposition placed an advert for a game of football in the Northampton press. During the two-day 'game' that followed, the 'gentlemen players' pulled up and burnt posts and rails to the value of £1,500 'and did other considerable Damage'.[34]

While the sociology of anti-enclosure protestors awaits systematic study, we can piece together some initial understandings. Northover, so it would seem, was not an atypical protestor, for those who resisted enclosure were a remarkably heterogeneous group. It was the 'gentlemen' of the New Forest who opposed planned enclosures in the Forest in the 1790s, an opposition at least in part predicted by the fact that common rights attached to their properties substantially increased rental values. It was also thought that 'the most forceful difficulty' in executing the plan would be:

[S]urmounting the Prejudices, which the shortsighted Farmers in the Country will Infuse into the Proprietors of Estates having Common rights, and their agents may be incompetent to form a true opinion upon the subject; and the objections however futile which will be diffused about by certain persons who are unquestionably Interested in the Forest remaining in the present state.[35]

An analysis of the men from Gillingham committed to gaol for rioting in the aforementioned anti-enclosure protests in and around Mere shows a broad cross-section of the (male) community. Of the nine men arrested, two were farmers, one 61 years old, the other 28; five were labourers, three married, one single; one was a mason; while another was a horse dealer. Elsewhere in Dorset, on the Pimperne enclosure being effected in the autumn of 1811, gaps were made in the fences by the Cranborne Chase keepers as they, in the words of a formal notice, 'suffer [warden of the chase] Lord Rivers' interests in the Chase'. We find a similar pattern among Neeson's Northamptonshire protestors. At West Haddon, butchers, innkeepers, dual occupationist farmer-artisans, and cottagers alike united in opposition to the planned enclosure. Clearly, not just commoners and the poorest members of rural society stood to lose out from the loss of common and customary rights.[36] Indeed, it is also worth remembering that in some places it was the customary tenants who took the initiative to enclose rather than the major landowners. At Preston Patrick in Westmorland, for instance, the majority of the tenants wrote to the Earl of Lonsdale desiring an enclosure act. Similarly on the Somerset levels, concerns that the largest farmers were abusing their power by overstocking the commons were the motivating factor behind promoting enclosure.[37] As Shaw-Taylor reminds us, in some locales enclosure was less controversial and less socially divisive than in other areas.[38]

In the long run, many enclosures were forced through, and where they acted to radically alter the structure and functioning of rural societies, sustained open resistance was rendered almost impossible. Besides, the material presence of enclosure in the form of ditches, fences, quick-set hedges and new roads very quickly became so integral to local landscapes that they became impossible to erase. Indeed, it is particularly striking that the anti-enclosure tactic of 'mass ploughings' – the philosophy of the Diggers made material – uncovered by McDonagh in the sixteenth-century Yorkshire Wolds were not a feature of protests in the modern age.[39] But none of this is to deny the persistence and potency of anti-enclosure protest in the period. While there is some truth in Andy Wood's claim that by the early eighteenth century enclosure riot was 'no longer the "pre-eminent form of social protest"', 'loud clamour against agrarian change' had not totally given way to 'bitten lips and closeted complaint'. Nor was opposition confined exclusively to 'a relatively small number of regions'.[40] As the foregoing analysis demonstrates, wherever one digs into the archive of eighteenth- and early-nineteenth-century enclosure, evidence of various forms of opposition from petition and riot to the tools of rural terror can be found.

Land-use Change and the Technologies of 'Improvement'

Many enclosures, especially those by parliamentary act and by agreement, involved not only changes in ownership but also a radical shift in land use, often involving large-scale technological projects such as the draining of fen and marsh, the breaking up of downland and upland wastes, or the creation of gardens, orchards and plantations. For instance, new agricultural techniques and technologies in the eighteenth and early nineteenth centuries made the hitherto difficult tilling of chalk downlands of the south and the wolds of the north possible to profitably cultivate land, thus promoting enclosure. Technologies that allowed for the relatively inexpensive processing of lime facilitated the tillage, and hence enclosure, of much upland 'waste', from Dartmoor in the South-West through to the North Pennines. Even the perfecting of the technology of water meadows, creating higher fodder yields, allowed for one-time chalkland pasture to be given over to tillage.[41] Thus technical 'advances', when mapped on to local variations in environment, landscape and ownership were, as Chapman and Seeliger have asserted, critical determinants of the topologies of enclosure.[42] While land-use changes were not necessarily predicated on enclosure, as any landowner could decide to invest in the 'improvement' of their land in an attempt to secure higher rental income, the two often coincided as co-manifestations of the developing mania for agricultural 'improvement'. Indeed, this combination was particularly resonant in popular culture and popular politics in the spectre of the depopulating enclosure converting open arable to sheep-walks. As McDonagh and Daniels note:

> In Georgian England, the enclosure of fields and commons was a wide ranging cultural and political act, resonant with larger social narratives of exclusion and dispossession, of deserted villages and invasive powers, tales of a world we have lost. For villagers tutored in the imaginative geography of the Bible, stories of exile and oppression, of forfeited and promised lands, might have material force as a response to events in their own parish, of fenced spaces and stopped pathways.[43]

Moreover, as Nicola Whyte has powerfully asserted, we need to remember that the landscape was not simply the backdrop to everyday life but rather something that helped to structure and give meaning to the practices and customs of rural workers. Thus whatever the gap between emotional *affects* and material *effects*, land-use changes provoked resistance precisely because they necessarily disrupted the 'habitus' of rural workers, transforming the 'taskscapes' of everyday life.[44] Urban development and the changing management of agricultural land – not least in the conversion of pasture to arable, and arable to hop gardens and orchards – impacted on both the amount and gender balance of labour required and the type of work performed. Worlds of work could change as well as household incomes. The case of hop gardens, orchards and plantations is instructive.

The creation of hop gardens radically transformed the landscape from grass or tilled soil to a hybrid space of soil and inert wooden poles, but it also altered the working practices and the level of demand for labour. When the transformation was from tillage to orchards and plantations, after the initial investment in creating the orchard or plantation was made, the subsequent labour requirements were only a fraction of that required to tend arable land. Orchards required little labour other than to prune the branches and pick the fruit, a role that was often filled by female workers. Plantations, once well-established, required little labour until the timber was ready to be harvested. Those created to provide cover for game – a trend especially evident from the 1830s onwards – essentially requiring no labour beyond planting. Hop gardens were far more labour-intensive, though the labour demands were concentrated when the young hop bines needed tying to the poles and (especially) in the harvest. Both of these roles were typically the preserve of women, though men and children were also employed in the harvest. If the land was previously forest heath or waste, as was the case in many of the huge plantations created in Hampshire and on the Berkshire–Surrey borders, then the commercial planting of trees also effectively rendered common and/ or customary rights useless. Hop gardens, orchards and plantations all therefore engendered deep resentments. Indeed, outside of large-scale enclosure and drainage projects, these were arguably the most bitterly contested of all spaces in rural England.[45]

But what form did these resistances take, and how are they knowable? Unlike parliamentary enclosure and many enclosures by agreement, there was no statutory requirement or legal need to record the change. Instead, explicit evidence timing and placing land-use changes often comes from records of opposition. We cannot therefore make any meaningful judgement as to the universality – or otherwise – of popular feeling regarding land-use changes, evidence of resistance being the tip of an iceberg of unknown size. The task is made harder still by the fact that studies of land-use change – invariably heralded by the Whiggish words 'improvement' or 'reclamation' – tend to focus on the economic and technical aspects of change rather than resistance. Williams' study of the Mendip Hills in Somerset, for instance, noted that the 24,000 acres of land enclosed between 1771 and 1813 was transformed at great expense from open sheep-walks to a regular network of fields in which cereals and potatoes were grown, but not what happened to those who could no longer graze their sheep there.[46] We can, however, make some inferences regarding the strength of popular feeling.

The drainage of fens and marshes – often allied to forms of enclosure – being well-documented, has been subject to intensive study. As noted, the drainage of the Lincolnshire fens was also a major focus for unrest in the eighteenth century, centring on a series of protests at Holland Fen. Here, proposals to drain the fens had a long history dating back to the middle of the seventeenth century, the transformation into a 'prairie of waving oats and cole seed of which entrepreneurs had long dreamt' (the words are Steve Hindle's) finally being achieved in 1767. Earlier projects were ineffective because of a combination of technological failure and the sustained resistance of the 'native' fenmen, with no less a figure than Oliver Cromwell supposedly taking an early lead, before later, as Protector, actively supporting drainage. The 'breakthrough' in 1767 not only marked the end of the ancient fenland landscape but also the established community of gentry, middling farmers, large numbers of cottages and smallholders, and labourers, the cold, damp flatlands of the post-drainage landscape supporting the 'classic' agrarian capitalist tripartite social structure. But none of this happened without a fight. Riotous opposition to drainage and enclosure – sustained until the early 1770s – was mirrored by a resort to the tools of rural terror by the smallholders, cottagers and labourers. The juxtaposition between landscape change and social change perhaps best being given voice in a threatening letter sent to large farmer and several times Frampton parish overseer, John Yerburgh:

> this is to let you know that As you have used the Utmost of your power to persuade your Neighbours and knaves like your Self to Cheat the Poor of their Right Except a Reformation is heard of in the neigborhod that is but the begining of Sorow from your frind and wel wisher to Liberty & an open fen for Ever.

Ultimately, both riot and covert protest proved futile in the transformation of the fens.[47]

Wherever historians and historical geographers have dug into the archive of drainage schemes, evidence of sustained opposition has been found. Attempts to drain and enclose Otmoor to the north-east of Oxford began in 1786 but were not fully achieved until the early 1830s, fierce public opposition putting the brakes on several attempts. Here the full range of protest practices detailed in the previous section were deployed, the social bases of opposition covering both petty agriculturalists and large landowners. Their protests were not simply predicated on issues of property and loss of rights but rather on a broader conception of tradition, drainage and enclosure representing not just a reworking of the map but also of a whole way of being in the world.[48] Similarly at Croston in south-west Lancashire, the drainage of the low-lying 'mossland' in the early decades of the nineteenth century was opposed by a broad constituency of local landowners and cottagers, oppositions being intensified by the seeming inability of the drainage commissioners to undertake their work efficiently.[49]

Water was also central to other controversial technological projects, for instance, at Rye, where an expensive sluice was erected on the River Rother in an attempt to prevent 9,000 acres of Romney Marsh from flooding at high tide, a hurriedly passed act of parliament supporting the scheme. This project also, however, had the unfortunate side effect of lowering the water levels in Rye harbour to such an extent that the town's fishing fleet could not navigate the river, thereby threatening the livelihoods of most households in the town. During the night of 26 February 1830, a body of men marched to the sluice, accompanied by a band of music, and all but destroyed it, returning on the morning of 28 February to finish their task. The destruction was not only justified by an attempt to right a perceived wrong, but also, as the sluice-breakers saw it, in law, for an appeal to the Court of Chancery by the residents of Rye led to a judgment that the sluice was a 'nuisance'. Before further legal proceedings were issued, the townspeople of Rye, according to the solicitor general, took 'the law into their own hands'. Subsequent repairs were met in the ensuing months with further attacks, these being put down by the magistrates and military force, notwithstanding popular complaints about conflicts of interest, the most active magistrate being one of the projectors of the sluice.[50]

Conversely, the creation of navigations (essentially the process by which river courses were made navigable) dramatically transformed the landscapes they cut through and provoked considerable opposition. For instance, on the proposal to make the Yorkshire Derwent into a navigation, local landowners claimed that the creation of locks and dams would lead to flooding on their lands, thus reducing production and lowering rental values. Elsewhere, opposite claims were made: navigations would act to drain their meadows. Millers also objected to any innovation that reduced the flow of water to their mills, making such objections even to canal projects that ran alongside great rivers such as the Thames. The levying of tolls was also controversial, for the tidal portion of the river was always navigable, thus local users were now being asked to pay for something that was previously free. This process of making private what was once held in common – akin to enclosure and a form of 'privatisation' – also provoked sustained resistance against turnpike tolls, resentments often finding voice over decades.[51] While such opposition was manifested most notoriously in the Welsh Rebecca riots of the late 1830s and early 1840s, protests in and around Bristol against turnpike and bridge tolls drew in the colliers of Kingswood in the 1720s and 1730s, and from Gloucestershire and Somerset farmers, petty producers and labourers in the 1730s and 1740s. Opposition was equally sustained in the West Riding of Yorkshire in the 1740s and early 1750s.[52]

Resistance occurred not only on plans being made public, many navigations and canals especially failing when bills were introduced to parliament, but also during and after construction. Claims were made that the proprietors of the Derwent Navigation had neglected to dredge the channel – hence further increasing the risk of flooding – while sluices, locks and canal banks were vulnerable to occasional attack. For instance, at the Somerset Lent Assizes in 1742 a group comprised of millers, yeomen, fullers, blacksmiths and labourers were indicted for 'cutting down and destroying' three sluices at Taunton, and on 30 May 1794 the banks of the Basingstoke Canal Navigation near Ash Bottom were maliciously broken down.[53] Even the seemingly non-controversial creation of water meadows could lead to protests from millers downstream of the floated pastures, their mills now working on reduced water flows.[54]

The creation of navigations and canals, plantations and gardens, and the draining of marshes and fens, both profoundly altered the bio-physical nature of much of rural England and transformed the 'taskscapes' of rural workers, invariably excluding and making private, and displacing and changing labour demands and skills. In large parts of the country they were arguably more important in this period than even enclosure in the unsettling impact they had on rural communities. By way of conclusion, we do well also to remember that urbanisation acted to further redraw customary interactions between the land and rural workers, both through the turning of fields and woodland into suburbs and streets, and in redrawing the relationship between the rural and the urban. In the northern counties especially, many of these new spaces were of low quality and high-density housing, the new homes of recent immigrants from the villages and from Scotland and Ireland who found work in the new mills and factories also often located on the urban fringe. If there is no meaningful record of opposition to the physical processes of (sub) urban development, it is important to understand that the new communities forged therein, while often remarkably culturally heterogeneous, were far more *socially* homogeneous than those found in the surrounding countryside and in market towns. These new communities of working people were notoriously unruly, often being centres for the fencing of stolen goods, and also being at the forefront of food riots, popular radical politics, early trades unionism, and other forms of collective action.[55] As Navickas, in her study of 'Swing' protests in the north has shown, the Carlisle suburb of Caldewgate – a 'liminal periphery that was neither solely rural nor completely urban' – was both the location of many acts of protest and the inhabitants the drivers of protest in the city itself.[56] Acts of 'enclosing' took many forms beyond the loss of the open field and the common – and had consequences far beyond the elimination of common rights. Indeed, what linked all acts of enclosure, and the deep landscape and environmental changes they affected, was a shared sense of losing what helped to define the community. Not only in relation to the hard material stuff of land but also to the quotidian, the same practices in and of the land undertaken by members of the community time out of mind now irrevocably lost.[57]

Chapter 4: Community, Custom and Religion: Unsettling the Everyday

Community is a word – and a concept – that has been central to the fore-going chapters. The rate-paying community; the idea of protest as doing 'good work' for the community; the importance of community context in understanding social relations; the working community; custom as a regulator of community tensions; the role of community sanctions in condemning violence; community support for gangs; the established community: all have been mobilised to help explain protest. Clearly, in many ways, community mattered in deciding when to protest, who protested, what was protested against, and what form protest took. Protest, in short, always occurred in the context of some fracture in community relations, typically at the scale of the local community – the township, the parish, the district – or, increasingly so in relation to popular politics, at the somewhat more diffuse scale of the nation and even internationally. Shifting from the analysis in Chapters 1 to 3 of the key generators of protest, this chapter systematically explores this importance in two ways. Initially, through a study of cultures of dissent and what form dissent took, before consider-ing the importance of religion in informing and underpinning protest cultures, and, finally, the link between custom and protest.

Cultures of Dissent

As asserted in the Introduction, until the 1980s, the study of protest past tended to scrutinise the archive for evidence of insurrection, the development of class consciousness and class conflict, or the death cries of common systems in the face of the onward march of agrarian capitalism. This emphasis necessarily led to an overwhelming focus on dramatic episodes and on the period between the first French Revolution and the onset of Chartism. The riot, march and political meeting was all.[1] While Hobsbawm and Rudé's *Captain Swing* noted that incendiarism and the sending of threatening letters were an important part of the rural protestors' canon,[2] it was two parallel developments in the mid- to late 1970s that marked an important turning point in our conceptions of what it meant to protest in the English countryside. First, as delineated in Chapter 2, the conceptualisation of 'social crimes' such as smuggling, coastal wrecking and poaching as acts of resistance to the hegemonic social control of the landed elites.[3] Second, a 1979 paper by Roger Wells on the response to covert protest after the bitter repression of the 1795–6 national wave of food riots sparked a series of replies concerned with the relative resort to covert and overt protest methods.[4] As noted in the Introduction, these developments in turn stimulated work on other aspects of the 'everyday' response of rural workers to the intensification of agrarian capitalism. Such research on social criminality, the tools of covert terror (incendiarism, threatening letters, animal- and plant-maiming), and the subversive role of customary practices and ritual has usefully extended our understanding of the complexity of rural protest.[5]

To protest, so such studies suggested, was not just to make an explicit public statement of opposition. Indeed, as the previous chapters have shown, riotous forms of opposition might not necessarily be appropriate, or even possible. Instead, acts of protest could be more psychological, an attempt to instil terror in the mind of a parsimonious overseer or abusive employer. Maiming a farmer's prize bull under cover of darkness, for instance, was not only less likely to get the individual arrested and imprisoned than an 'open' demonstration, but was also far more likely to induce a sense of dread and foreboding among *all* farmers in the parish. Beyond winning a psychological skirmish in an attritional war of social relations, there is some evidence that such acts of terror could have, for labourers at least, positive effects. The morning after a deliberate fire at the neighbouring Cambridgeshire parish of Guilden Morton, the Foulmire vestry met to consider 'what they could do to put their labourers in a better state by raising their wages'.[6] Critically, such forms of protest also represented an assault on the farmers' capital. If employers were not treating their workers with respect, or remunerating them fairly for their labour, then the product of their labour was fair game.

These co-called acts of 'covert protest' were all dramatic, designed to shock, and designed to hurt. But, as the analysis in the foregoing chapters demonstrates, many other seemingly straightforward 'criminal' acts – poaching being the 'classic' example – betrayed an element of resistance to attempts to 'privatise' property. Yet reading about resistance in the archive, as Timothy Shakesheff has noted in relation to the study of wood and crop theft, is extraordinarily difficult and laced with epistemological danger.[7] Beyond acknowledging that what appears 'petty' is easily overlooked and thus rendered obscure, there is the possibility that we wrongly ascribe agency to those who had no sentient notion that they were engaging in an act of resistance. Let us take the case of a hypothetical poacher. In taking game, they were undoubtedly undermining property regimes, probably trespassing, and certainly challenging the nature of authority in rural England, but may well have had no motive beyond feeding their family. This being the case, in ascribing resistance to such practices, do we render the very concept of resistance sociologically inert? Maybe this is a moot point, because the act served to undermine private property, ignored boundaries and established authority is in itself perhaps enough. But without setting out explicitly to make these challenges – and here the archive is, again, frustratingly opaque – we cannot say that the individual(s) were protesting, that they were actively opposing the existing way of things.

We also need to be alert to the fact that acts that have traditionally been labelled as vandalism (for which read 'mindless and without motive', quite in opposition to the etymology of the term) were in actuality motivated by malice. Plant-maiming, the malicious cutting of plants as an act of protest, has until recently been ignored by scholars of protest but has now been shown to have been an important method of covert protest, especially so in areas rich with hop gardens, orchards and plantations.[8] According to a 1835 pamphlet eulogising the social worth of allotments for the Labourers' Friend Society written by a 'Gentleman residing in Wiltshire', plant-maiming was the 'usual country revenge', he having twice had his plantations 'broken down and destroyed' for 'encouraging the good and punishing the dissolute'.[9] Successive parliaments clearly thought plant-maiming important too. A clause against plant-maiming was included in the Black Act (1723), making the 'cut[ting] down or otherwise destroy[ing] any trees planted in any avenue, or growing in any garden, orchard or plantation, for ornament, shelter or profit' a capital offence,[10] while in 1732 a further clause was inserted against the malicious cutting of hops.[11]

The word resistance is, therefore, useful in making a distinction between what was defiantly an act of protest and what we can show, by reading against the archival grain, served to challenge and undermine

the existing order. The distinction is not only epistemologically necessary but also vital if we are to acknowledge that beyond riot and deploying the tools of rural terror, rural workers did not passively accept their
lot. The toolbox of rural resistance – and here I use the term to embrace
all acts and practices that served to challenge and oppose – covered a
wide spectrum spanning riot, through incendiarism and maiming, to
assault, affray and verbal threats, through 'social crime', to song and
verse, to grumbling, back-talking and foot-dragging. Even deference, as
Keith Snell has suggested, cannot be taken at face value. Quoting North
Riding of Yorkshire farmworker Arthur Tweedy, Snell has noted that
the farmhands might not readily turn to open protest or the tools of
terror in this seemingly quiescent region, but they were quick to jump
behind hedges to avoid having to doff their caps to the landlords and
farmers and call them 'Sir'. This might be a subtle act, but it was a clear
act of opposition, an attempt to undermine existing social relations and
to maintain some semblance of dignity for farmworkers. As Tweedy's
father told the young Arthur, 'Sir, my boy, is only the nickname for a
fool.' Evident before Swing and defiant post-1830, the day-to-day interactions of farmworkers with their social 'betters' betrayed what Snell has
labelled a 'deferential bitterness'.[12]

That even in supposedly quiescent areas the archive reveals evidence of
sustained resistance suggests that a culture of dissent ran deep through
rural England. Beyond grievances, which, while varying from time to
time and from parish to parish, were universal, what underpinned and
gave expression and form to resistance? Andy Wood in his survey of popular protest and politics in early modern England suggested that 'plebeian culture' was underwritten by a language of rights that in itself was
based on the 'fluid, creative relationship between custom, scripture and
local-political conflict'.[13] That is to say that religion, custom and the everyday, instrumental politics of the parish were not only the wellspring of
dissent but also helped to shape the form that resistance took. While any
attempt to offer a universal model that explained the form and discourse
of protests is necessarily totalising, these remained critical, if not exclusive, factors in the eighteenth and early nineteenth centuries.

Religion and Protest Cultures

[L]ast night some persons, commencing their operations with a loud
shot, with heavy stones destroyed in part the glass of my bedroom
windows and the shutter belonging to it. Similar mischief was done
to the windows of the parlour immediately under my bedroom. From

the direction taken by the pieces of shattered window – some of which passed over my bed and others on it – the object was to do me some bodily harm.

So wrote Reverend Jenkins JP of Axbridge, a small Somerset market town, in October 1821 to Home Secretary Lord Sidmouth. The cause of this attack, so Jenkins reckoned, was that parishioners, and those from neighbouring parishes, considered 'themselves to be exempt from all legal restraint. In the evenings, 'especially of Sundays', 'they behave riotously in the streets', the men exposing themselves to 'modest women passing by' and using 'language extremely indecent and offensive'. To put down and prevent such scenes, the clergyman had sworn in special constables and warned the innkeepers that their recognisances would be forfeited in the event of their having encouraged drunkenness. The constables were duly active in removing 'tippling part[ies]' from the alehouses, and, on the Sunday prior to the attack, one of the churchwardens confined a man in the stocks for having in a drunken state 'visited my Church and disturbed the congregation during the time of divine service'. Jenkins' campaign had 'given great displeasure', and, in fear for his life, he requested of the government 'the appearance of a few soldiers for a week or two' to 'infuse a little salutary Terror'.[14]

If by the turn of the eighteenth century, as E.P. Thompson put it, 'the "magical" command of the Church and of its rituals' on the people was 'still present' but 'very weak', by the 1820s the poor had defiantly gained a 'freedom from the psychic discipline and moral supervision' of the established church. Control over the feasts and festivals of rural workers had also been ceded, the marking of Saints' days was removed from the winter to the summer to coincide with the agrarian calendar, the secularisation of the festive calendar made complete by the money-making efforts of the hucksters, publicans and entertainers.[15] Parsons were reduced to the exercise of the law. Indeed, by 1830 they comprised 25 per cent of all magistrates – and a rather higher percentage in rural districts – and were often the most active of magistrates, affecting 'salutary terror', and using poor relief in an attempt to enforce church attendance and 'moral' behaviour.[16] In return, as Jenkins experienced, rural clergymen were increasingly the subject of protest. In the 1810s and 1820s, after farmers, clergy in the south were the most frequent targets of would-be assassins, victims of assault and incendiarism, and receivers of threatening letters.[17]

This is not to say that Jenkins' case was necessarily archetypal. Many rural clergy remained committed to the paternal idea(l) of tending to their flocks' needs: in the summer of 1830 clerical magistrate Price of

Lyminge, Kent, had attempted to prevent the farmers from mowing their wheat in fear that it was 'cruel to deprive the poor' of gleanings.[18] Moreover, the attendance of rural workers at the parish church did not completely fall off: it was higher in parishes with resident squires than those without, and lower in areas of forest, marsh and upland waste.[19] There is also evidence of popular cultural participation in church, with rural workers bell-ringing, playing in church orchestras and singing in choirs well into the middle of the 1840s.[20] Though, as Thomas Hardy's *Under the Greenwood Tree* portrayed, attempts to put down such popular participation was met by the protest of no longer attending church. And for those that did attend church – whether under a sense of piety or compulsion – there was the possibility that the sermon would rally against plebeian culture and the effects of poverty. For instance, during a Swing parley at St Mary Bourne, Hampshire, labourer John Simms took Reverend Easton to task for his sermon on the preceding Sunday that was 'against the poor'.[21]

Beyond issues of social control, James Obelkevich's study of religion and rural society in South Lindsey in Lincolnshire, Albion Urdank's parallel study of Nailsworth in Gloucestershire, and Keith Snell and Paul Ell's historical geography of the 1851 census of religious attendance, all attest to the persistence of the importance of religion in rural life.[22] This is perhaps evidenced most explicitly in three important forms of rural 'dissent': 'popular' opposition to Catholicism, especially as evidenced by rural manifestations of the Gordon riots of 1780; religious non-conformity as a form of resistance; and the influence of the Bible and religious teaching on discourses of popular protest.

Opposition to religious toleration, and in particular to Catholics in the form of the 1778 Catholic Relief Act, was at the heart of the Gordon riots, the spree of destruction that engulfed London in June 1780. Violent anti-Catholicism was not, contra historical orthodoxy, an exclusively metro-politan phenomenon. Rather, it was also manifest in provincial towns and in rural England. Before the outbreak of protests in London, some-thing precipitated by the march of at least 40,000 individuals in support of the delivery of a petition from Lord George Gordon's Protestant Association to the House of Commons, protests had occurred outside the capital. Affiliated Protestant Associations were formed in Carlisle, Canterbury, Newcastle upon Tyne and Rochester, while Gordon had supporters and correspondents in Cornwall, Hampshire, Norfolk and Yorkshire. Elsewhere petitions against the Relief Act were received from a variety of towns and more rural areas, including from Wooburn in Buckinghamshire, Maidstone and the surrounding villages in mid-Kent, and Helmsley Blackamore in Yorkshire.

The violence in London, though, did not transfer to the country-side in the form and ferocity expected, perhaps in part a reflection that in places such as Winchester and Cobridge (Staffordshire) attacks were expected and the authorities took precautions. However, as Colin Haydon has shown, anti-Catholic disturbances did occur, and were not just confined to major cities such as Birmingham and Norwich. At Bath, for instance, after being subdued by troops brought in from Devizes – where there had been disturbances, and Wells – where threats had been made against Catholics, the rioters went into the surround-ing countryside. There they continued their work at Hinton Blewett and Camerton, where the wealthy Catholic Coombs family had a chapel. An attack on Wardour Castle near Tisbury in Wiltshire, the home of the Catholic Arundell family was also only prevented by the interven-tion of the military. In the West Riding of Yorkshire and in Hampshire protests even occurred not at the instigation of mobile activists from nearby towns but were caused directly by rural residents.[23] As with the London riots, these protests were short-lived, being as much remarkable for marking the final violent protests against Catholicism – the protests against the 1829 Catholic Emancipation Act being just as vehement in tone but far less bodily assertive[24] – as for their actual force. As Jonathan Oates has asserted, though, 'popular' anti-Catholicism was a canonical part of loyalist expression, even being resorted to in and around York in response to the Jacobite Rebellion of 1745.[25] It is also important to note that the riots in no way targeted Catholic property reflexively. Rather, as George Rudé has shown, only the wealthier Catholics tended to be targeted, the protests, then, he claims, being as much about the poor settling 'accounts with the rich, if only for a day'.[26]

The second point is more simply made. By not attending the estab-lished church but instead visiting alternative places of worship, rural workers engaged in an act of defiance, hence the label 'religious dis-sent'. Methodism, the 'new dissent', in its various sects and guises, was arguably most clearly perceived to be a direct challenge to the author-ity of parish churches, especially so in the form of Primitive Methodism with its emphasis on a profoundly demotic democracy. The estab-lished church, as Navickas has pointed out in her study of Lancashire, might occasionally have needed to show greater tolerance to dissent, for instance, in the face of revolutionary threats in the 1790s, but was otherwise quick to attack and discredit every aspect of Methodism.[27] Critiques were not levelled just by the clergy. Henry Morton, Lord Durham's estate agent and colliery manager on his north-eastern estates, had 'an almost pathological obsession with the influence of Primitive Methodist preachers', while *The Times* in its coverage of the

Swing riots was quick to highlight the leadership role of 'Dissenting or Methodist teachers' in the protests.[28]

The reality of the impact of Methodism on workers, both rural and urban, has long been the subject of debate by historians. First Halévy, then Thompson, asserted that Methodism's evangelical message was an agent of capitalist domination of working life, the movement pacifying the potential for revolutionary fervour among working peoples. Conversely, Ward and Hempton have argued that Methodism perfectly complemented political radicalism through its message of optimism and democratic principles.[29] In a sense the argument tends to get in the way of the lived reality that dissent, both 'old' and 'new', was attractive because of its theological and socio-political difference from the establish church. As Gilbert notes, it offered emancipation from the social control of the paternalist world and a culture of religious engagement and mutuality more attuned to the needs of agri-industrial capitalism.[30] Thus whether protestors were disproportionately drawn from the dissenting sects, whether dissenting preachers took a key role in organising protests – as was undeniably the case in the later 'revolt of the field'[31] – is perhaps to ask a set of unhelpful questions. Instead, that religious nonconformity helped to foster a broader culture of dissent not just to the established church but more broadly to the established rural order is arguably more telling. In contrast to the illegal practices of riot, and (before 1824) combination, it offered the expression of a 'more or less legitimate opposition to a reactionary regime'.[32] Perhaps, then, the link to popular protest has been over-played. But Thompson's argument that 'Dissenting sects often carried the principles of self-government and of local autonomy to the borders of anarchy' reminds us that Methodism did teach workers how to organise. Moreover, this 'training' also afforded a route for many workers into less sectarian forms of politics, most notably Chartism (for which, see Chapter 7) that drew on both the Methodist camp meeting and the Methodist biblical rhetoric of social justice.[33]

What united Methodism and the established Church in influencing protest was the influence of the Bible and religious teaching on the framing of popular political claims and discourses. This was arguably strongest in relation to enclosure and food protests, where the Bible provided direct inspiration. As Wood notes, anti-enclosure protestors could take inspiration from Deuteronomy – 'Accursed be he who removeth his neighbour's doles and marks' – and Proverbs – 'Thou shalt not remove thy neighbour's mark, which they of old time have set in thine inheritance.' The later line was integral to Rogationtide rituals, whereby the bounds of the parish were paraded and new obstructions and barriers removed. If these obstructions were new enclosure fences and hedges, then the Bible and the ritual, if not the law, allowed for them to be levelled.[34]

Food rioters too could take direct inspiration from biblical texts, E.P. Thompson acknowledging the link by starting his pioneering 'Moral economy' paper with another line from Proverbs: 'He that withholdeth Corn, the People shall curse him: but Blessing shall be upon the Head of him that selleth it' (xi. 26). As Adrian Randall notes, 'voluminous popular pamphlets echoed these sentiments ... across the eighteenth century. It was such a commonplace that anyone seeking to argue in the first half of the century for an unfettered market and the removal of regulation would have found himself the recipient of scriptural refutation.'[35] Threatening letters offered arguably the best expression of the influence on working peoples, the exact reference being vague but the message all too clear for recipients. 'We have agreed in 5 parishes we mean to have provisions cheaper or Rescue our lives', started a threatening letter sent to a Rye (Sussex) farmer in early 1801:

> we are Led up by popery and oprestion the same as France was before the war begun ... you are agoing to have a fast to offer up prayer to God but it is an offer to the Devil[,] God will never hear the prayer of the unmerciful the time is short that we must give an account of our work.[36]

Or as the author of a threatening letter sent to a Lenham (Kent) farmer put it: 'God is of our sids you may se by the faverabel weather if God was as much a gainst the poor as the rich are we shall have been all starvd before now long agoe.'[37] That God was on the side of the poor – whatever claims to godly right the landed might also make – was the universal message, occasionally couched, as in the Rye letter, in terms of Millennial prophecies.

This played out in two notorious ways. First, through Joanna Southcott and her particular brand of Millenarianism, after her death in 1814 her followers combining religious 'radicalism' with political radicalism. Second, through the actions of the self-proclaimed Messiah and self-styled Sir William Courtenay, aka John Tom, in and around the wood-bound communities of the Forest of Blean in east Kent. There, in the days and weeks before 31 May 1838, Courtenay had 'recruited' a band of followers who, in a pseudo-military style, openly marched about the surrounding villages, Courtenay making occasional speeches on social, political and religious matters, exalting others to join them as they were going to 'put an end to the oppression of the poor by the rich'. Those who heeded Courtenay's call were a perfect cross-section of the male community: small farmers, labourers, woodsmen, beer-shop keepers, artisans. Several played in the Hernhill church choir, others attended Methodist meetings, several possessed religious books, others, like small farmer Edward Wraight, had refused to go to church 'to hear a man who robbed him every day of his life by taking tithe'.

On 29 May, Oak Apple Day, Courtenay began recruiting for the 'great jubilee' (the day, according to Leviticus, when every 49 years land was restored to those who had lost it, a common theme in English radicalism), when: '[A]ll the country would be up ... and we must be with 'em', i am going for a jubilee; any of you men that have nothing to do I shall fill your bellies with victuals, and nothing shall happen to you.' They would have, so Courtenay proclaimed, more to celebrate than just the restoration of Charles II. The authorities, becoming increasingly alarmed at his activities, determined to put down the marching band, their concerns being heightened by the fact that the locale had witnessed Swing mobilisations in 1830 and anti-New Poor Law protests in 1835. An attempt to arrest Courtenay on 30 May failed when one of the police was shot and stabbed, the murder precipitating military intervention. A detachment of the 45th Infantry was duly despatched and, on the afternoon of 31 May, Courtenay and his followers were confronted in Bossenden Wood. In what would be the last pitched battle on English soil, two soldiers and nine of the millenarian rebels, including Courtenay, were killed. Opinion as to whether Courtenay's men were engaged in insurrection is mixed. It is worth noting, though, that notwithstanding Courtenay having a stash of weapons and bullets, and many of his followers having poacher's guns, only two of his band were actually carrying firearms. If this was not open insurrection, it was almost certainly a drill for a future uprising.[38]

Custom and Protest

While religion was important in helping rural workers to frame their discontent into a clear protest discourse, custom and customary ceremony offered the justification to protest *and* gave form to acts of protest. Custom was the wellspring of common law,[39] underpinned pre-enclosure communal forms, and acted as the regulator, at least in pre-industrial society, of social relations. In this way, through repeated practice-use rights became accepted as common rights, forms of community sanction emerged and evolved, and rituals developed that marked important days in the agrarian calendar. Custom was not, therefore, some static body of praxis written down in the annals of the labouring poor. Rather, it varied from community to community, albeit often showing great similarities between different communities in the same district and region. It also changed over time. As Thompson asserted, 'custom itself *is* the interface [between law and practice], since it may be considered both as praxis and as law'.[40] This process of becoming was determined by two factors: common (i.e. pertaining to a *specific* community) usage and time out of mind. As common usage changed, for instance in relation to a technological project or land-use change, so custom was challenged, responded, adapted and evolved. As Adrian Randall and Leonard Schwarz have shown, industrial workers, whether in the city or the country, adapted customs from earlier guilds but were also quick to develop their own customs in relation to working practices, especially regarding hours of work, perquisites and wages.[41]

Outside of the work-bound customs of particular occupational groups, it was the broad similarity of need and community experience from parish to parish in any given region that created a culture that was more-or-less shared by rural workers. This, in turn, gave cohesion to the way in which protest found expression and form. As Peter Jones has noted in relation to Swing, these shared experiences and this shared culture gave a degree of cohesion to Swing's practices and claims as it spread across southern England in the autumn and winter of 1830.[42] This cohesion took two forms, first a shared experience, and thus sets of claims, that acceptable forms of behaviour towards rural workers had been broached, and second, the shared discourses and forms of customary ritual that were deployed in punishing transgressors and attempting to right the wrong.

As Julius Ruff has claimed for early modern Europe, many popular rituals were rooted in physically assertive performances of opposition. It was only the mutual understanding that the display was being acted out in the context of a long-practised community custom that allowed for physical aggression without recourse to legal sanctions.[43] This was particularly the case in 'rituals of justice', those practices that sought to punish, usually through a combination of bodily violence and mocking, those who had transgressed accepted forms of behaviour. The performing of 'rough music', a customary practice in which those who had supposedly abused or cuckolded their spouses were mock serenaded by the noisy banging of kettles and pots, was shared throughout Europe, being known in France as 'charivari'. 'Riding the stang', in which husband-beaters were placed backwards on a horse and paraded through the streets to rough music, was also a more-or-less universal practice. These rituals often combined bodily violence with forms of symbolic violence, for instance the carrying of weapons or the hanging of effigies. Symbolic forms assumed a dual role, first the avoidance of trial and retribution that assault might bring, and second, rather than targeting an individual, symbolic violence could be used to infuse terror in the wider community, the fear of what was possible, what might happen.[44]

While folklorists and early modernists have long since subjected the importance of such customary rituals in popular protest to systematic study,[45] scholars of modern England, while acknowledging the importance of ritual, have been slower to subject the link to such study. In part, this is perhaps because of the acknowledgement that by the turn of the nineteenth century many popular customs and rituals were being suppressed or sanitised by the rulers of rural England. However, as Alun Howkins and Linda Merricks note, even when suppressed, the influence of custom and ritual persisted.[46] Another possible reason is that 'early' studies of popular protest were invariably focused on attempting to uncover the making of 'modern' forms of protest, especially trades unionism and popular politics, at the expense of customary practice. Yet, again, this is somewhat unsatisfactory, for the simple reason that there was no neat, teleological shift from 'pre-modern' to 'modern' forms of protest. Instead, we see the influence of ritual and customary practice informing workers' responses to capitalist change and industrial change. For instance, on 7 July 1757 a riot occurred at Liverpool on the 'pretence' that potter Peter Higson was 'working under Wages', Higson being fixed on a pole and carried 'up and down the Town'. The ritual of 'riding the stang' thus being combined with techniques of industrial protest.[47]

It was E.P. Thompson who most provocatively forced historians of the Georgian and Victorian age to seriously consider the importance of custom. Long before the publication of his *Customs in Common* in 1991, in a series of essays Thompson suggested that custom underpinned all aspects of 'plebeian culture'. In the face of the dual, but contradictory, challenges of patrician rules and the commercialisation of agrarian capitalism, custom therefore provided the rulebook for when and how to oppose. In relation to the marketing of food, Thompson famously suggested that 'the expectations, traditions, and, indeed, superstitions of the working population most frequently involved in the [eighteenth-century food] market' represented a custom-bound value system he labelled the 'moral economy'.[48] This did not rest exclusively on expectations of fairness and transparency from farmers, dealers, millers and bakers in the selling of food – expectations in themselves in part rooted in the Tudor 'books of orders' – but also on magistrates that they would intervene to ensure that markets were not manipulated. Critically, in Thompson's formulation, custom was not some static entity but rather a system that adapted to change in the rural workers' habitus. Thus, when the authorities refused to intervene in the market, a function of the increased intellectual and commercial sway of political-economic values in the late eighteenth century, consumers innovated in the arts of resistance, breaking traditional compacts to assert their agency.[49]

This same dynamic was further addressed in Thompson's essay 'Patrician society, plebeian culture'. Analysing changing social relations in the eighteenth century, Thompson asserted that it was possible to read of a cultural struggle between the 'plebs' and the gentry, a challenge to deference and the regulation of social action. This occurred in three ways, 'the anonymous tradition, countertheater; and swift, evanescent direct action'.[50] If the latter could be read as public evidence of the muscular confidence of Thompson's plebs, and the former as evidence of the continued importance of the weapons of terror, counter-theatre was evidence of something truly distinctive. Until the 1760s, and in many cases long after, this opposition to the public performance of patrician cultural might was defiantly rooted in 'a language of ribbons, of bonfires, of oaths and of the refusal of oaths, of toasts, of seditious riddles and ancient prophecies, of oak leaves and of maypoles, of ballads with a political *double-entendre,* even of airs whistled in the street'. Combining customary ritual form and radical politics, this was a Jacobite language and symbolism designed to 'enrage and alarm' Hanoverian rulers. But if this is clearly far from what might be expected from a deferential culture, one could not conversely claim that it was evidence of a proto-revolutionary culture. Rather, so Thompson stated, it is suggestive of a plebeian culture that was both 'remarkably robust' and 'greatly distanced from the polite culture'. It sought a certain freedom from old forms of social servitude, yet also demanded respect and fairness, and stability in the form of the defence of the community and the household.[51]

How, in practice, did this play out? Charlesworth *et al.*'s analysis of the 'Jack-a-lent riots', a set of anti-turnpike protests that occurred in and around Bristol in 1749, provides a useful example. As noted in Chapter 3, protests against turnpike tolls were many from the late 1720s to the late 1740s, popular opposition predicated on the basis that the tolls were a *de facto* tax for what had previously been free at the point of use.[52] Protests in the Bristol area started on 24 July, five days after tolls were first levied on the Long Ashton Road, at Bedminster, on the southern fringe of Bristol. 'A great body of the country people of Somerset' armed with hatchets and axes destroyed the toll house and gates. So began a 'cycle of confrontation' between the protestors and the turnpike commissioners, gates and tollhouses being rebuilt and again attacked. Protests were not confined to south Bristol, the Somerset protestors calling on the support of the notoriously independently minded Kingswood colliers, and, eventually, miners from the Mendips. Beyond their shared grievances and history of, as the Bristol mayor put it, 'inveteracy', what bound these disparate communities together was a shared 'distinctive cultural fund of rituals and symbols'.[53] Indeed, as Binfield and Navickas have both demonstrated in relation to the Luddite disturbances of the 1810s, the very fact that individuals in different places with different experiences and grievances could organise and unite under a shared banner was testimony to the importance of both symbols and a shared customary culture.[54]

The Bristol area protests also drew upon two other customary forms that underpinned many eighteenth- and early nineteenth-century acts of rebellion. The first, 'processioning', usually took the form of either perambulating the parish or a procession to a place of local symbolic significance. The second took the form of the 'visit', wherein a group would visit a predetermined household and give a performance, for wassailing tides or mummers' plays, and demand refreshment or largesse. Collectively, such rituals are known as '*quête* customs'.[55] The anti-turnpike protestors' use of blackened faces, dressing up in women's clothes – disguise being pragmatic but also both an attempt to subsume individuals into the collective and to invoke carnival – the beating of drums and sounding of horns, and the use of handkerchiefs as flags were all drawn from this rich repertoire of customary ritual. When deployed, these motifs gave notice that normal life was suspended, that the carnival had commenced. Indeed, not only did these rituals give form and shared meaning to popular protest, but their deployment also served notice that normal social relations were on hold. Even the name the group styled themselves as, 'Jack-a-lents', contained a reference to the effigy of Winter or Judas Iscariot customarily burnt on Ash Wednesday. As Edward Muir has stated, rituals could be used to 'open up a labyrinth of dissonance' in opposition to 'neatly unified vision[s] of society'.[56] Or, as Bob Bushaway and Paul Custer have stated, many forms of customary ritual deliberately turned the social order topsy-turvy, 'crowds' performing 'turbulence' as an 'orderly parody of order'. The usually powerless were placed in a temporary position of power over those who normally determined the rules of rural social politics.[57] The following example from the parish of Owlsebury during the Swing rising of late 1830 is a case in point. As the group of labourers, artisans and small farmers processioned round the parish they were accompanied by a woman – a Mrs Deacle, wife of Swing sympathiser farmer Deacle – on horseback, the woman positioned, literally, over the men. The march round the parish was therefore not just a playing out of labouring strength but also a symbolic statement that all power was inverted, that conventional social relations, at least for that moment, did not apply.[58] For those wishing to invert the balance of power in rural society, customary rituals thereby provided the perfect script, rules and set of protest tools. But, as John Walter has asserted in the context of early modern England, '[c]rowd actions' were not just attempts to invert authority, rather they can be usefully 'understood as claims to exercise political agency in the context of a popular political culture'. Ritual was thus a way in which claims to 'political' legitimacy could be made.[59]

The customary calendar also provided inspiration as when to protest. Mass meetings were festivals as well as political events, especially as many, out of necessity and to gain the largest possible attendance, occurred on the public holidays of Good Friday, Whit Monday and New Year. While such meetings were invariably attended by large numbers of urban workers, they were often held on the edges of towns. For instance, as Navickas has shown for Lancashire, many meetings took place on the moors, mirroring the fact that on public holidays urban workers would normally go rambling or for picnics.[60] Bonfire Night – 5 November – was a favourite night for incendiarists, the traditional celebrations also being used as a front for pro-reform riots in Dorset and Somerset in 1831 and again in 1832. St Andring rituals of squirrel hunting and nut gathering were similarly used as a front for fence and hedge breaking,[61] while 'harvest home' celebrations were used to recruit potential machine-breakers in the first Swing mobilisations in the Elham Valley area of east Kent.[62] The timing of these examples was no coincidence. The customary calendar framed the resort to protest by virtue of the fact that custom legitimated opening the 'labyrinth of dissonance', and these were the dates when the world *could* be turned topsy-turvy.

The increasingly dim view of bodily violence *and* physically assertive forms of popular cultural expression taken by the rulers of rural England,[63] meant that protestors deploying such customary forms increasingly risked prosecution. The Special Commissions that tried Swing protestors in Berkshire, Buckinghamshire, Dorset, Hampshire and Wiltshire universally pronounced the door-to-door demanding of monies (a classic 'visiting' doling ritual) as felonious 'robbery' brutally attests that, in the eyes of the law, custom had no legitimising function.[64] This was no sudden change in the hearts of the rulers of rural England. In the national wave of food riots in the 1790s, evidence of the influence of ritual forms was just as explicit – processioning, bands of music, the parading and burning of effigies – and the reaction of the authorities just as severe.[65] And yet, notwithstanding the full might of the British state in putting down these customarily informed protests and the parallel attempts by the country gentry to suppress and sanitise popular cultural forms, the influence of custom and ritual in popular protest persisted.

Coda

The late seventeenth century witnessed a withdrawing of the wealthier villagers and the lesser gentry from a long-established role in leading rural revolt. The language of community ran deep, though. Calls to neighbours, the people of the village, and friends represented a continuity with earlier cultural forms that united communities in the face of external threats to the existing order. To uphold *legitimate* ways of being from, to quote Wood, 'alien innovation'.[66] But, against continuity, there was also a creeping sense that rural workers conceived of their interests as not being with their employers and the rulers of the parish but *against them*. Hence, the language of community was often decidedly partial: calls to the fellow poor; calls to the men; and, just as critically, against hard-hearted farmers and covetous parsons.

As David Eastwood has put it in relation to the early decades of the nineteenth century, rural England was 'a theatre for the making and remaking of class relations'.[67] So, we might paraphrase, the same was true of community. For even among rural workers there were differences, cliques even, the artisans having different social and cultural circles to the field workers, the horsemen having a profoundly different status among plebeian circles to the horselads, women a different status from men.[68] Community was not something that was necessarily spatially bounded, place-based even, for family diasporas could bind together individuals in different places in informing networks of shared (and the sharing of) experience.[69] Differences could also be as much driven by the influence of rural workers' social 'betters' – who to grant relief to; who to award an allotment to; who to employ; who to offer a house to, and so on – as they were the product of circumstance and character. The persistence of the idea that rural workers could be divided between the 'roughs' and 'respectables' in mid-nineteenth-century social discourse in part underpinned this making and remaking of difference.[70]

None of this is to say, though, that struggles in the village were not ultimately attempts to restore and reinvigorate the holistic community. Indeed, the importance of custom as a wellspring of protest is proof positive that many individuals and groups looked to the past to find their ideal(ised) model of how things should be. To call on what held for time out of mind was to escape the social dislocations and privations of the present and to perform the past. This was defiantly rooted in place, in the spaces of shared life in the parish, hence the persistence of calls and claims, so ably documented by Keith Snell, to the parish and being of the parish, and the attendant practices of opposition to outsiders, to foreigners.[71] The shifting sociology of opposition can therefore be read as

Realpolitik rather than any conscious attempt to build a *new* community. Or at least until the failure of Swing and the subsequent betrayal of the first reformed parliament heralded a quite different set of rural social relations and protests as much predicated on new ideals as old values. Differing community types and protest histories, though, *might* generate very different topographies of resistance. What follows in Chapter 5 critically examines this idea. Specifically, it considers this premise, advanced by David Underdown for the mid-seventeenth century and John Bohstedt for the late eighteenth and early nineteenth centuries, in relation to food rioting and cultures of incendiarism.[72]

Chapter 5: Protest Practice

The publication of Andrew Charlesworth's *Atlas of Rural Protest* marked a turning point in the way historians conceptualised the geography of protest. Through its 182 pages of detailed maps and supporting text, the *Atlas* suggested two things. One, that 'overt' protests tended to cluster in time and space; and two, that some areas appeared to be more protest prone than others. While both conclusions could in part be a function either of the unevenness of existing studies or the patchiness of archival coverage, it is hard to deny, for instance, that the mining areas of Cornwall were hotspots of food rioting or the Fenlands of Cambridgeshire and Lincolnshire were particularly prone to enclosure rioting.[1] Community context mattered when it came to protest: specifically, past successes and failures; work types and the economic base; local systems of control and support; and the juxtaposition between work and welfare. As noted in Chapter 4, and to paraphrase David Underdown and John Bohstedt, differing community types might generate very different protest histories, though, of course, the structure of a community could change dramatically over even short spaces of time.[2] Through a detailed analysis of the totemic protest practices of food rioting and incendiarism, what follows seeks to move beyond a reductionist model of how and where protest happened to instead offer a more fluid understanding of the resort to protest.

Food Rioting and the 'Moral Economy'

If the eighteenth century was the age of the riot, then the food riot – aka the bread riot, the corn riot, and the subsistence riot – was its archetypal form. As Adrian Randall, in his magisterial survey of riot in eighteenth-century England, notes, while foreign visitors were shocked at the prevalence of public disorder per se, it was the management and regulation of the food supply that prompted the most frequent and vehement of riots.[3] It has even been suggested that food riots accounted for two out of every three 'disturbances'.[4] Food riots took several different collective forms. Price fixing, otherwise known as *taxation populaire*, was by far the most common method, involving either forcing farmers, millers, dealers and bakers to sell at what the crowd thought was a fair price, or the taking of foodstuffs and leaving the fair price as payment. Other regularly assumed forms were attempts to prevent the export – simply meaning the moving out of the community – of foodstuffs; and forcing farmers and dealers to bring supplies to market. Those who transgressed expected market norms could also be the subject of symbolic mocking and being paraded in effigy, while calls were often made on magistrates to intervene in regulating the market. Following regional waves of rioting in 1709–10 and 1727–9 and national waves in 1740, 1756–7, 1766–7, 1772–3, 1783–4 and 1795–6, 1800–01 represented the last genuinely national 'wave' of extensive food rioting, though 1811–13, 1816 and 1847 also represented periods of geographically fragmented rioting. This is not to say that food riots were omnipresent.[5] They were not, either temporally or geographically. Rather, that a culture of food rioting assumed a greater popular potency and visibility than any other form of 'contentious gathering'. And, to quote Charlesworth, 'grew stronger and was enriched as a cumulative collective memory of previous struggles' as the eighteenth century unfurled.[6]

Notwithstanding an earlier paper by R.B. Rose which suggested that food rioting was 'a function of harvest [and trade] fluctuation' and favoured by 'such homogeneous working-class groups as the Cornish tin and copper miners, and ... the coal miners of the South-west and the West Midlands',[7] it was not until E.P. Thompson's famous study that the practice was subjected to critical scrutiny. Thompson's thesis posited that food riots did not occur simply because of scarcity or high prices, rather that the cause was invariably illicit market manipulation and sudden and suspicious price rises, though sudden price rises did not always lead to protests, such as in 1804–05 and 1808–09. This pricked the shared *mentalité* of consumers, the set of ideas and beliefs, values and expectations of what constituted proper behaviour in the food market that Thompson labelled the 'moral economy'. Consumers mobilised as 'the crowd' were the guarantors of the moral economy, exposing and attempting to right abuses, and punishing those who perpetrated them. It was not a rejection of capitalism, after all many price fixing rioters 'paid' what they thought was a fair price, with food rarely being taken without payment. Nor was it static and tradition-bound. Rather, it represented a shared value system that not only told consumers when to protest – the decision being considered rather than a reactive ebullience – but also how to protest.

Because claims as to what was customarily acceptable were being made, protestors needed to be measured in their actions, disciplined in making sure their actions never went beyond righting the perceived wrong. Violence was therefore contained and often symbolic rather than bodily, for instance, parading the effigy of a crooked miller through the streets as opposed to assaulting him. This modulation of anger was important in acting to legitimise their protests but also in calling on the magistrates to intervene *on their behalf*. Indeed, in this sense food riots can be understood as the playing out of a performance with very clear rules and directions, what Charlesworth has termed a 'stately gavotte' between protestors and the magistrates.[8]

Calls for the magistrates to act were necessarily predicated on the moral economy being a shared value system, or as Archer puts it, for the regulators of the market to subscribe to 'plebeian values'.[9] Before the turn of the nineteenth century, this was broadly true for three key reasons. First, as Thompson asserted, the rulers of England were in many ways 'prisoners of the people', the power of the protesting crowd – *force majeure* – impelling magistrates to act and legislators to regulate food markets more effectively.[10] Second, as Randall points out, in a state which 'claimed to derive its sovereign power from the observation of Christian principles', the authority of the Bible could not be ignored. The Old Testament was writ through with commands to the rich to protect the food supply of the poor, injunctions that Randall notes were 'elucidated at quarter sessions, preached from pulpits ... and from wayside chapels by itinerant evangelists in times of distress'.[11] Biblical and Christian teaching also underpinned 'a wider paternalist philosophy' that obliged the rich 'to protect the weaker members of the community from exploitation and extreme hunger'. But, as Thompson reminds us, this relationship was increasingly undermined in the eighteenth century by 'free labour', or rather greater freedom from discipline in and in choosing their daily work, and from coercive legislation that redefined property and notions of ownership.[12] Third, these social dynamics came together in specific legislation to regulate the marketing of food, most notably in the Tudor 'books of orders' for the prosecution and punishment of forestallers, regraters and engrossers, and to impose the Assize of Bread.[13]

The impact of the philosophy of political economy, systematised and popularised through the writings of Adam Smith, helped to challenge the idea that the rich and the state had a responsibility to the poor, as expressed through market regulation. Instead, markets, and therefore prices, were to find their own level. If supply was low in one locale, farmers and dealers from elsewhere would send their supplies to that market in the hope of securing a greater return. So, all else being equal, supply levels and prices would *tend* towards equilibrium between markets. Intervening, so the philosophy went, was therefore unnecessary and went against the 'natural law of the market'.[14] In practice, markets were riddled with imperfections: the cost and time delay in transporting goods from one locale to another to meet demand acted as a disincentive to send supplies to far-off markets, while farmers were obviously unable to meet demand instantly, unlike factories working on a twelve-month production cycle. The biggest potential problem, though, was that of market abuse, especially adulterating food – for instance, through adding alum to flour, using faulty weights and measures, and engrossing and hoarding supplies in times of dearth. Increasingly, the regulation and management of markets tended to make a practical distinction between these practices and those of forestalling and regrating. Indeed, in 1771, as part of a raft of legislation in the early 1770s on corn and bread, parliament repealed the original Elizabethan legislation against forestalling, regrating and engrossing.[15]

In some locales, though, magistrates continued not only to prosecute those who used faulty weights and sold foul or adulterated food, but also, in the face of central government wishes, actively censured forestallers. Parliament received frequent petitions, especially from the Common Council of London, requesting new protection, with bills even being brought before parliament in 1787 and 1797.[16] During the 1795–6 food crisis, magistrates in many country towns publicly resolved to put an end to the practice. At Shrewsbury and Worcester in May 1795 the magistrates were reported to have 'determined to put a stop to forestalling' of 'butter and other articles', while a meeting of a committee into the scarcity and high price of corn at York was advised that forestalling and regrating still remained punishable by common law.[17] During the 1799–1801 subsistence crisis, the corporations of numerous market towns entered into subscriptions to prosecute forestallers, regraters and engrossers, a committee at Winchester even offering a £50 reward for those who informed against forestallers.[18] Most notoriously, in early 1801, having been found guilty of the common law offence of forestalling by a City of Worcester jury and by a Middlesex jury in King's Bench, Lord Chief Justice Kenyon sentenced hop dealer Samuel Waddington to a £1,000 fine and four months' imprisonment.[19] By 1816, though, as Douglas Hay notes, 'the treatise writers declared that the law, so loudly proclaimed by the judges ... was dead'.[20]

All of this matters because food riots occurred in a complex, to quote Thompson, 'field of force', opposition being framed in the playing out of power, custom and social expectations between the poor, marketmen, farmers, and the gentry and nobility. Even given all the conditions that led to food rioting, it was never inevitable *if* the magistrates intervened. And intervene they did, at least for much of the eighteenth century. Steve Poole and Wendy Thwaites' studies of the civic management of markets, in eighteenth-century Bristol and Oxford, respectively, highlight that the mayors and magistrates in both cities readily market regulation in highly symbolic ways, both at the behest of poor consumers and as a way of waylaying riot.[21] Indeed, that market manipulation did not always lead to food riots is suggestive of the fact that riot was often not necessary as the authorities had acted quickly to right perceived wrongs. Or, conversely, riot was not possible because of the strength of repressive forces in the locality and/or the fear of repercussions. A recent riot, or one having occurred nearby, might also, in Archer's words, have 'concentrated the local authorities' minds wonderfully'. By the turn of the nineteenth century, though, magistrates tended no longer to view the tumultuous poor as a group to be negotiated with, but instead as a threat.[22]

To what extent, though, were food riots rural protests? The emphasis on food riots being market-bound has tended to mean that they have automatically been conflated with the urban sphere. Even John Bohstedt's innovative comparison of the differing food rioting practices in Devon and Manchester claimed that 'riot remained a tradition of the towns', albeit especially so in long-established market towns. Outside of London, Bohstedt suggests, of the three community types that turned to riot – industrial towns, small market towns and villages – three out of every four riots occurred in those settlements with populations greater than 1,500 people. 'Agrarian society', encompassing all other community types, 'was nearly untouched by riot'. '[C]ountry people', he concludes, 'very rarely rioted', being 'shielded from market fluctuations by receiving parish relief', especially so from the mid-1790s because of the introduction of Speenhamland scales, and subsidised grain. Moreover, not needing to mingle 'with market-town's society' and being unable to challenge their employers directly meant that rural workers neither understood the rituals of the urban moral economy in action nor were able to protest openly.[23] What few riots that did occur in the countryside were therefore 'undisciplined'. Bohstedt makes one exception to this neat model: Norfolk, a county where 'the farm workers were already involved in an agricultural system more orientated toward capitalist practices than most of rural England'. Freer from the social controls typical of most rural communities – especially the surveillance of the vestry, parson and employers – here the field workers, on low wages, had less to lose by rioting.[24] Bohstedt's later refinement of his model to include five community categories (small agrarian villages, medium-sized stable towns, rural industrial villages, big industrial boom towns, and London) left the core argument of the thesis unaltered. Another of Bohstedt's assertions is of import too. If, as he suggests, the people of the rapidly expanding northern industrial(ising) towns had no tradition of food rioting and consequently developed more confrontational forms than those deployed in the deeper-rooted communities of established market towns, then it is also possible that these recent immigrants from the countryside brought no culture of food rioting with them. They knew, so it follows, neither what form the protest should take nor what should be expected of the magistrates.[25]

In many ways, this is an attractive thesis, locating the wellspring of social action in different community forms. But, as explored in Chapter 1, many 'country' communities combined the agrarian and the industrial. Even 'classically' agrarian communities in the cornlands were composed of a diverse occupational mix of labourers, artisans and journeymen, their villages and hamlets linked to surrounding towns and cities through complex webs of kin and capital. Historians, though, as Randall has noted, 'properly regarding industrial workers and miners as the main instigators of food riots' have tended to assume that 'country people took no part in such protests'. 'Country people', so the position goes, neither had the 'community solidarity' to riot nor the actual need, being able to fall back on the exploitation of commons, pilfering and below-cost food from employers.[26] Yet while the rural food riot, and the role of country people in food riots, awaits systematic archival engagement, a close reading of research on popular responses to food crises suggests a more nuanced reality. In short, rural food riots appear to have been far more common than has been suggested, and evidence of countryside collective action against market manipulation can be found for all areas during all food crises, something detailed most graphically in Wells' study of the 1794–6 and 1799–1801 crises.[27] And this notwithstanding that rural riots are probably under-represented in the archive. As Charlesworth and Randall note of the 1766 wave of food riots, 'it was the larger actions ... of the earlier riots which caught the eye of the press and observers and dominated the courts', later actions of 'smaller mobs' who 'roamed' the countryside to the north of Stroudwater in Gloucestershire, and similar mobile 'mobs' in Wiltshire being 'generally under-recorded'.[28] We also need to be alert to the fact that just because a riot occurred in the countryside it does not necessarily mean that it was the work of country people. Sometimes we simply cannot know who was involved because of the diffuse wording of reports. In 1795 a riot broke out at Folkingham Fair, south Lincolnshire, when an individual was observed to be purchasing large quantities of butter. Given the location of the parish – being some 10 miles distant from Sleaford, the nearest market town – it might seem reasonable to assume that the regrater was attacked by rural workers. But given that it was a fair day, groups from the towns of Sleaford and Grantham might have been present.[29]

Evidence abounds that during food crises town dwellers often made journeys into the surrounding countryside to prevent exports of food-stuffs or to compel farmers, millers and dealers to bring their supplies to market. Conversely, there is also evidence that those who resided in the countryside, especially cloth-workers and colliers, invaded the towns to join or even instigate, food riots. In Bristol rare was the food riot that was neither instigated nor given force by the notorious Kingswood colliers, a group who frequently made the short journey into town to defend their rights and assert their collective might.[30] Journeymen, who lived in a per-petual state of mobility between city and country, were especially active participants in linking town and country together in riot, paper-makers being responsible for the diffusion of food rioting from west Sussex into Surrey in September 1800.[31]

Agricultural workers were also active food rioters. At Chichester on the evening of 13 April 1795, in consequence of an inflammatory hand-bill that had been circulated generally through the city and the neigh-bouring villages, 'a considerable body of the lower orders' of the city, assisted by some 'country people', assembled in the city to force a reduc-tion in the price of provisions. When joined later by a 'great number' of privates from the Herefordshire Militia, those assembled also marched out of the city to a farmer in a neighbouring village, who, it was alleged, had been withholding corn from the market. The farmer was compelled to promise that he would bring his corn to market and sell it at five shil-lings a bushel.[32] This was, by design, a coalition of poor consumers that combined rural and urban dwellers alike, and made permeable the divi-sion between the countryside and the city. As Charlesworth and Navickas have both suggested, contra Bohstedt's model, many residents of rapidly industrialising northern towns kept one foot in the country, maintaining close connections to rural cousins and often moving between town and 'semi-rural' neighbourhoods for work and leisure. The division between the urban and the rural has been over-played.[33]

There were, however, gaps in the compact. The Herefordshire Militia complained to the Chichester authorities that the 'country people' were relieved by their parishes and by subscriptions, and therefore had access to bread. The soldiers did not need bread money but needed bread itself. And yet, if this were the case without exception, rural workers would not have taken part in this complex set of disciplined protests. In short, some of the rural workers in the villages close to Chichester must not have had access to subsidised food and other forms of relief. Those deemed unworthy by rural vestries, those not employed by the farmers – including the artisans, industrial workers and the jobless – and those who did not want to be beholden to the vestry and charity were in no better position than their comrades in the towns.[34] Many pastoral and upland rural areas were, lest we forget, reliant on food supplies from elsewhere, Haslingden in Lancashire, for instance, being 'almost wholly dependent' upon meal, flour and potatoes from Cheshire and Yorkshire.[35] The rural–urban dynamic clearly worked both ways.

Identifying the 'faces in the crowd' has been an abiding obsession in protest studies since the publication of George Rudé's *The Crowd in the French Revolution*, first published in 1959.[36] This approach has its limits, though. Outside of individuals and groups self-identifying themselves, as in the above example, we are necessarily reliant on legal records of those taken into custody and/or arrested. What we do know is that, in addition to journeymen artisans, colliers and cloth-workers – especially in areas where the trade was in rapid decline such as Devon and Essex in the 1790s – farm workers also occasionally assumed prominent roles.[37] Agricultural labourers were also sometimes arrested; for instance, four labourers were prosecuted for stopping a cart going to Romsey in April 1800, while only five months later at the same place three labourers from agricultural Chilworth were among those arrested for a food riot.[38] Women, so critical in many urban food riots because of their household role in provisioning, were also occasionally involved in rural food riots.[39] The form that 'female' rural food riots took appears to be no different from that of (supposedly) all-male riots, though millers seem to have been their overwhelming target. During the crisis of late 1799 to early 1801, women were involved in at least three such 'riots' in Sussex alone. They were the sole instigators of an attack on millers at Northchapel; joined men and children in parading, hanging, burning and then drowning the effigy of a miller at Boreham; and, cut a millers' cloth used to dress the popularly-hated brown flour to shreds before threatening to destroy the rest of his equipment at St Leonard's Forest.[40]

The status of food – its price, availability and quality – as the foremost generator of popular protest was, by the turn of the nineteenth century, in question. According to Elizabeth Fox Genovese, from the late eighteenth century wage levels replaced the price of basic foodstuffs as the fundamental component in plebeian living standards.[41] If the economic and cultural importance of the wheaten loaf was on the wane among wage-earners, then, *ceteris paribus*, we would expect that, even during subsistence crises, protests would be concerned increasingly with wages and, where appropriate, poor relief entitlements. In certain industrial sectors, wages and attendant perquisites and customs had long been at least as important as food prices as the primary arbiter of living standards.[42] For most rural workers, however, it was not until the 1780s and 1790s that this altered significantly, several factors being important: the decreased regularity and increased seasonality of agricultural work; long-term decline in real wages; decreasingly generous, and more closely controlled, poor relief; yet, post c.1795, an increasing reliance on parish relief resulting from the introduction of Speenhamland-style wage subsidies.[43]

Combined, these factors tended to make wages and poor relief an increasing locus of conflict. Thus in times of crisis, so the logic follows, protests would be just as likely to target employers, overseers and vestries as those engaged in the marketing of foodstuffs. Wages and poor relief payments were not articulated as major factors during the 1740, 1756–7, 1766 and 1772 food riots, but in the 'minor' crisis year of 1790 and again during 1795 and 1800–01, complaints over wages and poor relief were frequently made in the countryside. Wells, who has done more than anyone else to improve our understanding of the subsistence crises of the Napoleonic period, has noted three parallel trends.

First, the emergent practice of large groups of men, sometimes accompanied by their wives and children, visiting either their parish overseers or magistrates' meetings. A 10-mile march in March 1795 by 37 'paupers' from Hurstpierpoint to attend the Lewes Bench to complain that their parish officers had refused them relief was typical in form, but the practice became central to the 1800 protests.[44] Of the eight recorded collective protests in Hampshire and Sussex during the spring and summer of 1800, five involved some juxtaposition of food prices with wages and/or poor relief. If evident in 1795, it was now universal and more precisely articulated than before.[45] Second, the sending of threatening letters protesting against low wages and poor relief, and the targeting of overseers and parish property in incendiary attacks. Perhaps atypically, a group of rural workers even tried to demolish the workhouse at Abbots Ann, Hampshire, in December 1800.[46] Third, an extension of trades unionists principles and methods in the countryside, most notably in East Anglia, the Home Counties and the south, perhaps inspired by the actions of building trades unions which had already penetrated the countryside. While in most places proto-union activity simply aped trades unions in throwing off work and stating their demands. At Heacham in Norfolk, farmworkers elected a clerk, proposed a 'general Meeting' and invited 'delegated messages of support' from the surrounding villages to come together and lobby parliament. Their petition was an extraordinary document, suggesting both a radical political understanding and a profound sense of collective solidarity:

> the mode of lessening his [the farmworker] distresses, as hath lately been the fashion, by selling him flour under the market price, and thereby rendering him an object of a parish rate, is not only an indecent insult on his lowly and humble situation (in itself sufficiently mortifying from his degrading dependence on the caprice of his employer) but a fallacious mode of relief, and every way inadequate to a radical redress of the manifold distresses of his calamitous state.

The labourers who went on strike in the Essex marshes in June 1800 went further than petitioning, by physically compelling other employees in the Steeple district also to throw off their work.[47]

Beyond 1801, food riots no longer assumed the same role in subsistence crises and became infrequent, the 1816 riots being the last 'wave' that assumed anything like a national prominence. Why, Wells asked, when there were moments of crisis in the nineteenth-century English grain trade that were broadly comparable to eighteenth-century crises, did the nineteenth century not witness anything like the resort to food rioting seen during the eighteenth century? Had the moral economy simply withered away in the minds of nineteenth-century consumers and market regulators? Or, as Charles Tilly's teleological model of protest change suggests, had 'traditional' forms of bargaining by riot given way to 'more sophisticated' protests in the form of organised labour and political lobbying?[48] The answer was no: the 'moral economy' was not dead, it just had to be articulated in different ways using different tools.[49] In a variety of contexts, from gleaning, the uses of machinery, and the wage-relief nexus, historians of rural England have asserted the continued importance of the moral economy in underpinning the regulation of social life.[50] In the towns, as Bohstedt has recently asserted, better organised systems of relief – both emergency subscriptions and publicly supported co-operative mills and bakeries – in times of crisis were critical in mollifying the populace and hence preventing riot. Such schemes had strong moral economic tones, often berating monopolisers of grain and promoting collectivity among both workers and the urban authorities alike.[51] If hunger was thus systematically dealt with in the towns, at least until the passing of the New Poor Law in 1834, in the countryside wages, poor relief and the use of machinery became the key drivers of protest. Here, beyond occasional strikes and collective claims to vestries and magistrates, the tools of covert terror, and especially incendiarism, became the key weapon of social protest.

The Culture of Incendiarism

During the night of 10 September 1756 the 'mills' at Okehampton, Devon, were set on fire. Only the sound of the walls cracking in the surrounding cottages alerted the sleeping residents to the fact of the fire, the residents close to perishing in the flames. This was, as the *Sherborne and Yeovil Mercury* confidently reported, a case of arson. Four months later, a very similar fire broke out in the mills at Botley in south Hampshire. 'In a few hours' during the early morning of Sunday 23 January, miller Arnold's property was completely destroyed, including all his stock of flour, meal and grain. Again, his family only narrowly escaped the 'sudden and fierce' flames. The cause was not related, the inference in the wording of the report clearly alluding to the suspicion that this was no accident.[52] In the context of the concurrent subsistence crisis, firing the very thing that was in such short supply might seem wilfully perverse. But if traditional moral economy sanctions, especially the food riot, had failed or would not work, then what difference did it make whether food was withheld, hoarded, or turned to ash? Besides, a carefully targeted fire could act to spread terror in the neighbourhood, forcing farmers, dealers and millers to bring their supplies to market. Arson could be an important tool in enforcing the moral economy. This role was expressed emphatically in a threatening letter addressed to the 'Clarge [clergy] and Gentery, and likewise to all Gentlemen Farmers' of the small east Sussex parish of Ninfield in February 1757:

> There hath bin, in a neighbouring Parish, a Barn of Corn destroied by Fire, if Wheat be not fell to the Price of 5s. per Bushell, the same Calamaty will happen in this Parish and sevaerl Parrishes ajoyning; for the Thing is decreed, and will soon be put in Execution, if not prevented by the Faul of Corn: Also several Dwelling Houses are conspired against, and I do asure you there will be but very few Barns standing in this Parrish, and many other ajoyning, in a Months Time.

The fear of being found out, so the writer alluded, was nothing to the indignity of starvation: 'Cruelty is the Cause and cruel will be the Reveng'. If the rulers of the parish were left in any doubt, the final sentence of the letter left no room for ambiguity: 'For as Mobs and Magistrates will not prevail we will run the hasard of our Lives before we will stareve. NINFIELD.'[53]

If riotous means of gaining redress were not possible and the magistrates were not alert to the sufferings, even the 'rights', of the poor, then more clandestine and 'cruel' methods would prevail. That the letter was signed 'NINFIELD', though, suggests the continued importance of stressing community and the importance of place-based solidarities. The letter-writer might be but an individual, but represented the community. Critically, this was no unusually lucid and forthright one-off. Earlier that month a similarly strident letter was received by a farmer at Brighton, then still a small settlement some 30 miles distant from Ninfield:

> You covetous and hard-hearted farmers, that heap your Stacks and Mows of Corn to starve the poor, if you will not take them in and sell them that we may some to eat, we will put them down for you by Night or Day, from [on a separate line] Jack Poor, Will Needy, Will Starve, Peter Fearnot, And others.[54]

So, 54 years later during the crisis of 1811–13, early on 4 November, a group of ten women and forty children 'in a very irritable state' applied to magistrate and local landowner William Milford at Petworth complaining that the previous evening Milford tenant and Tillington parish overseer John Colebrooke had not given them 'necessary relief'. Notwithstanding that the 'usual steps' to get all parties to attend the Bench were made, at 1am on 6 November the barley barn on Colebrooke's farm was set on fire and destroyed.[55]

For fire and the fear of fire to be so readily mobilised in times of dearth suggests that this was a well-understood protest tool. And yet in 2008 Steve Poole could still quite correctly comment that 'relatively few attempts have been made by historians to quantify or fully understand agricultural incendiarism. [With some exceptions] it has been an epidemic largely unexplored or else subsumed within broader arguments about rural proletarianisation.'[56] According to Hobsbawm and Rudé, the role incendiarism played both before and during Swing was ambiguous. It was a protest form, they claimed, that had 'been practiced' before, 'even in this part [of the South-East] of England'. It was not, however, the 'characteristic form of unrest' before or during 1830. Only after 1830 did incendiarism become 'the characteristic form of rural unrest'. All this is important because *Captain Swing*, published in 1969, was arguably the first study that took the role of incendiarism as a rural protest practice seriously.[57] Indeed, its influence was soon apparent in studies by David Jones and E.P. Thompson that positioned incendiarism not as some mysterious act but instead as a protest practice every bit as important as collective action in the rural workers' protest tool box. Jones' study of arson in the 1840s East Anglia not only showed historians how frequently resorted to it was – his study recording 671 committals for incendiarism in the assize courts of ten southern counties in the 1840s – but also that the government and social commentators were preoccupied with the challenge of incendiarism.[58] In this sense, Thompson's study of the actions of the Waltham Blacks in the 1720s showed a remarkable persistence: the repressive actions of the English state detailed in Chapter 2 also showed a fear of incendiarism. However, here the similarities end. The Blacks resorted only infrequently to incendiarism,[59] whereas by the 1840s incendiarism had reached, as Jones put it, 'epidemic proportions'.[60]

What happened between the 1720s and 1840s to increase the resort to fire-setting to such an extent that, as Poole has stated, incendiarism became 'a perennial factor in social relations in some areas of nineteenth-century rural England'?[61] Leaving aside – for now – both methodological complications and spatial variations, the Wells–Charlesworth debate on the relative importance of 'covert' forms of protest as opposed to 'overt' collective protests sought to answer this question. To reprise the argument as delineated in the Introduction: Wells suggested that, after the brutal suppression of the 1795 wave of food riots, 'traditional' moral economic forms of food rioting were no longer possible. Instead, and against a backdrop of increased social surveillance through extending the net of parish poor relief, deep grievances were expressed through a resort to incendiarism and the sending of incendiary letters. This was not just in response to food crises; rather, so claimed Wells, covert protest practices remained the standard form of protest until the 'faltering adoption of trade unionism' in the 1870s.[62] While Wells modified his thesis in acknowledgement of Charlesworth's reassertion of the importance of the Bread or Blood riots of 1816, the East Anglian protests of 1822, and Swing,[63] these were 'uncharacteristic explosions' set against a backdrop of a more frequent resort to the tools of rural terror.[64] This position was further honed in Wells' book *Wretched Faces*, his study of the response to famine in wartime England, and in an extended essay examining the evolution of south-eastern conflict between 1700 and 1880. Moderating his original assertion, Wells now claimed that the resort to arson became 'common' in the 1790s as a way in which '*public* as opposed to private vengeance' (original emphasis) was gained. Before the 1790s arson had a 'long history as a mode of exacting private vengeance' and had even on occasion been used to 'enforce [the] "moral economy"'. In response to Charlesworth's spatially-sensitive critique, Wells also claimed that the 'new and significant role' played by arson and threatening letters was most prominent in the south and east.[65] After a fine harvest in 1801, which eliminated supply problems and prompted a fall in prices, the incidence of incendiarism declined until markedly increasing again during the subsistence crisis of 1810–12.[66]

If it was Jones who first asserted the importance of incendiarism in the first half of the nineteenth century, and Wells who first stated the *relative* importance of incendiarism, it was John Archer who offered the first *systematic* analysis of the resort to arson over several decades. Focusing on the counties of Norfolk and Suffolk – thus replicating the central focus of Jones' study – and the period between 1815 and 1870, Archer's illuminating work revealed several important dynamics. First, incendiarism was resorted to far more frequently in the period than had hitherto been thought, peaking during Swing and 1844, the absolute nadir of the so-called 'hungry' 1840s, and maintaining higher levels *after* both crises. Second, there were few East Anglian parishes that had not been subjected to incendiarism at least once during the period. Arson was, so Archer concluded, a universal practice, a vital part of a shared rural culture of resistance. Third, incendiarism was a young man's game, the typical age of those indicted for fire-setting in Archer's East Anglia being the early twenties. This is important because it also tallies with the demographic of those indicted for animal and plant-maiming, those other widely practised 'covert' protest forms.[67] These young men were the most marginal members of rural society: the lads, those who lost out to married men in securing steady agricultural work, rural vestries invariably manipulating labour markets to support those who would otherwise be the biggest cost to relieve.[68] This is not to say that older men or women did not turn to incendiarism: they did, especially so in relation to younger women in service, who turned to arson against hard, exploitative and sexually-predatory masters.[69] Rather, that these were not the most frequent arsonists. Fourth, Archer's analysis shows that property was not, contra received opinion, frequently fired by revolutionaries or the 'mad'. The mentally ill and those with learning difficulties were, however, occasionally indicted.[70]

Fifth, while incendiarism only required one individual to strike the tinderbox, or, post-1830, the Lucifer match, it was often discussed and planned by small groups of men. Fires could also become foci for overt expressions of collective dissent, plebeian communities joyously gathering by the light of the flames and refusing to assist to extinguish them.[71] In such ways, incendiarism can be understood as a form of *popular* protest, as opposed to being simply a weapon of individual vengeance. This is perhaps best expressed by the apparent ineffectiveness of even very large rewards in securing evidence from working communities. As the radical *Brighton Patriot* put it in relation to a series of fires against those involved in the administration of the New Poor Law during the spring and summer of 1835, the 'poor seem to be happy about these fires'.[72] To sound a note of caution, though, as Poole notes, 'substantial progress has yet to be made' in understanding the 'mounting frustration' of the rulers of rural England 'over their inability to penetrate' the 'enormous solidarity' of rural workers towards incendiarists.[73]

Who were the victims of incendiarism? Both before, and especially after, 1815, farmers were the most frequent target of arsonists' wrath, their hay ricks and corn stacks being by far the most commonly fired combustible. When the archive details motivations, or usually perceived motivations, we can ascertain that farmers' property was normally targeted for two inter-related reasons: perceived exploitation of their employees, particularly as regards wages and working practices; and not treating their employees with respect. 'Mr. R. is not what is called a popular man amongst the labourers', reported the *Morning Post* after a devastating incendiary attack on farmer Robinson's farm at Chediston, Suffolk in October 1822, the second fire in the parish in a short period. Farmer Brown's premises and dwelling house at Uffcott in Wiltshire were destroyed in July 1825 after a 'woman by whom Mr. Brown had some means offended and who frequently declared she would be revenged' fired his ricks. Similarly, the outbuildings on Robert Greaves' farm at Hoo, Kent, were fired in August 1847 by a former farm servant in revenge for having been discharged earlier that day for leaving the horses in the field.[74]

When farmers assumed the role of parish overseer or poor law guardian, their personal property was even more likely to be targeted. During the early months of 1816, farmer and overseer Fisher at Terrington St. Clements, Norfolk, had been in the practice of employing those labourers out of work in 'dressing' flax in a barn on his farm 'rather than expend the Parish money on those who applied for relief in idleness'. On the night before the flax was to be sent to market, the barn was symbolically fired, 'strong suspicion' resting on 'the dissatisfied persons who had been so employed'.[75] Likewise, during the crisis year of 1822, the absolute low point of the post-Napoleonic depression, paranoid landowners in Sussex asserted that 'a system for the purpose of [firing stacks of overseers and clergy]' had 'been devised by incendiaries who are generally labourers out of employ'. Overseer Flurry at Burwash was one such victim. That he was perceived by Home Office correspondent and significant landowner E.J. Curteis to be 'a respectable man who has acted meritoriously in his public actions, never guilty of harsh or inappropriate conduct', was clearly not shared by the local labourers.[76] As Archer has suggested, incendiarism was far more prevalent when there was less work around, both seasonally – incendiarism peaking in the winter months – and during the most parlous economic times.[77]

Parish property and union workhouses were also obvious, symbolic targets. In areas dominated by the clothing trades, master manufacturers and their factories and warehouses were frequent targets during trade disputes. Clergy, because of their collecting of tithes and their assumed roles in regulating and controlling village life, were also symbolic and occasional targets, doubly so when they also officiated on the Bench. Shopkeepers, dealers and other employers of servants were relatively frequent targets of their employees' wrath. As noted above, during subsistence crises millers and others involved in the meal trade were likewise important targets. The one occupational and social group whose property was, after farmers, most likely to be subjected to incendiary attack, though, was the rural workers themselves. Indeed, in reading rural protest we all too often assume that it followed the classical Marxist form of proletarians attacking the property (or bodies) of the capitalists. Yet disagreements and feuds between rural workers were expressed by resort to arson and other forms of covert protest, informants being especially vulnerable to attack.[78]

In analysing incendiarism we must take special care, though, in reading the archive, as not all cases of arson involved an element of protest. Attempts to defraud insurance offices were especially common. Between 1790 and 1815 there were twelve cases of arson tried at south-eastern assizes, of which four were for arson with the intent to defraud, and one, probably a malicious prosecution, being a widely publicised case of the rector of Maresfield in Sussex for setting fire to his recently insured house.[79] Insurance companies thought the problem was even more widespread: according to S.J. Fletcher, the Sun Fire Office's Secretary, giving evidence to the 1867 Select Committee on Fire Protection, one-third of all fires in Great Britain were 'very unsatisfactory' in their origin. When a particular trade went into depression, Fletcher asserted, the number of fires in that trade rose.[80] Similarly, burglars occasionally resorted to arson to destroy evidence of their plundering: clearly pragmatic but imbued with a malicious edge.[81] The archive even relates that some fire-setters were not motivated by malice but instead by a desire to get transported. When in April 1850 the inappropriately named farmer Luck's barn was fired at Pembury near Maidstone, the culprit confessed to a Post Office messenger that he had set fire to the barn with a Lucifer because he wanted to get transported. 'Apparently', reported the *Maidstone Journal*, 'two boys in Maidstone Gaol from the [Poor Law] Union House intend to do the same when they come out' – being wrenched from one's community being deemed preferable to acute poverty and hunger.[82] We also need to take care in reading the archive, for the *precise* identification of incendiary fires before the establishment of bureaux of well-trained fire investigators was far from a scientific practice. As Jones notes, 'the problems of identification were considerable: it was not always possible to decide which fires were accidental, the result of drink and carelessness'.[83]

Ostensibly, the ways in which incendiarism was deployed stayed remarkably stable throughout the period, the targets of arsonists in 1850 being much the same as in 1700. Technological change, and technological projects, did, however, present new and novel targets. Threshing machines from their initial use in the early 1790s, and especially after their widespread adoption post-1815, became frequent subjects of the incendiarists' torch.[84] This practice followed a longer history of Luddism that, as Randall and Navickas have detailed, combined machine-breaking and incendiarism in both town and country. Indeed, during the 1812 Luddite disturbances, the local authorities in Yorkshire perceived the firing of threshing machines and the destruction of machinery in the clothing trades as being manifestations of precisely the same thing, resistance to the mechanisation of customary working practices.[85] Another significant technological change, as detailed in Chapter 3, that also increasingly drew the incendiarists' wrath was the mania for creating plantations post-1790.[86] The availability of the cheap, reliable Lucifer match from 1830 also made the would-be incendiarists' job easier than having to use a tinderbox. Arguably of even greater importance, though, is that the methods of reporting incendiarism in the period changed dramatically. Not only did the volume of correspondence from the provinces to central government rise exponentially – something systematised and encouraged by the creation of the Home Office in 1782 – but also the rise of the provincial newspaper, by far the most important source for the study of most protest forms in the period. By 1723 there were only 24 provincial newspapers, with many counties having no county newspaper; by 1795 there were 72 but these papers still notionally covered very large areas, while by the end of 1855 there were few towns and districts that did not have at least one dedicated *local* newspaper.[87]

All else being equal, we might reasonably expect that a fire in 1850 would more likely be reported than a fire in 1700. For instance, for the county of Dorset, Kevin Bawn has noted that the number of reported cases of incendiarism increased markedly from the mid-1820s, more or less coinciding with the first publication of the *Dorset County Chronicle* in 1822.[88] And yet this likely to be coincidental. Shakesheff's study of incendiarism in nineteenth-century Herefordshire also details that incendiarism became (relatively) more frequent from the mid-1820s; while studies of the south-eastern counties suggest that the level of incendiarism increased markedly with the start of the post-Napoleonic depression.[89] In drawing such conclusions, it is important to remember that we are usually dealing with very low numbers of cases, the shift from the occasional incendiary fire over several years to fires occurring with something like regularity. Yet even low numbers hide a complex social reality. A solitary incendiary fire could have major repercussions for both the target and other local residents alike. Incendiary fires were often dramatic and had devastating consequences. That in most communities they were infrequent occurrences also meant that they lived on in the community consciousness for decades.

It is for this reason that it is difficult to assess the impact of prosecutions for incendiarism. We know that the creation of county police constabularies from 1839 – not all counties establishing constabularies immediately on the passing of the County Police Act in 1839 – led to a greater arrest rate and conviction rate for reported incendiary fires. In Norfolk and East Suffolk, for instance, the creation of county constabularies in 1840 led to arrests being made in relation to one in every three fires and an almost doubling of the rate of successful convictions per committal.[90] Yet it remains unclear as to whether a successful prosecution – and a subsequent public hanging – deterred individuals from setting farmers' stacks on fire. If it is impossible to ever truly answer this question, it is still telling that the many hangings for incendiarism during and in the immediate aftermath of Swing appear to have had no impact, given that incendiarism in the early and mid-1830s assumed record levels. By way of example, within hours of labourer Richard Dixon being hanged at Penenden Heath, Kent, on 22 December 1831 for incendiarism, the barns of the overseer at nearby Ulcombe were set on fire.[91]

Either way, for those counties where systematic studies of the resort to incendiarism have occurred – admittedly focused more on the east and south than the west and north – 1815 and 1830 appear to have been pivotal moments. Before 1815, incendiarism was not a *constant* threat to farmers and other property owners in any county, being used only intensively in relation to either particular places or occasional, particular contexts. The small Purbeck market town of Wareham, for instance, had a history of arson going back to the Civil War, and between 1790 and 1838 was subject to seventeen incendiary fires.[92] While Wells has claimed that incendiarism was 'largely the tactic of the individual', a response to 'deprivation', a way in which the poor could set 'things right', before 1815 the most important, if occasional, context in which fire-setting occurred were food crises.[93]

If, notwithstanding Wells' pioneering labours, the role of arson in eighteenth-century food crises awaits systematic study, it is clear that, as the opening paragraphs of this section allude, the deployment of incendiarism was both a vital supplement to and an occasional substitute for food rioting. But the combining of arson with other protest forms was not confined to subsistence crises. Machine-breaking and incendiarism were deployed interchangeably depending on context in 1812 – something explored in detail in the following chapter – while the Waltham Blacks combined fire-setting with a wide range of other tools of rural terror. Rural workers, as Archer has suggested, were 'selective in their choice of tactics', combining 'open' and clandestine forms at will.[94] Arguably, the clearest articulations of this flexible and adaptable culture of protest came in the form of the Bread and Blood rising of 1816, the East Anglian rising of 1822, and, most explosively, the Swing rising of 1830. But the role of incendiarism in such dramatic episodes has, until recently, remained uncertain. While to many contemporary observers incendiary attacks on farmers' property were 'the most notable and memorable of "Swing" activities', to Hobsbawm and Rudé 'an element of mystery' surrounded incendiarism in Swing. 'Was it,' they asked, 'an integral part, or was it a largely intrusive or alien element?'. In attempting to answer these questions they concluded that arson played a different role from place to place, but ultimately that 'It lay at the fringe rather than at the core of the movement.'[95] Chapter 6 explores these three dramatic episodes, and the way in which the relationship between open, collective protests combined and the tools of rural terror gave form to these risings.

Chapter 6: Rural Rebellion

According to Charles Tilly, social movements were 'invented' in the Western world during the later decades of the eighteenth century, the organised agitation against colonial rule in Boston, America, and against John Wilkes, MP's arrest on the charge of seditious libel in London being critical turning points. To Tilly, the 'innovation' in techniques of protest, and emphases on financing and public displays 'pioneered' an entirely novel 'synthesis' of crowd action with formal appeals to supporters and the authorities. The English, and others, had made public claims and engaged in popular public politics before, but the events of 1768 marked something altogether new: the 'converting, expanding, standardizing, and combining' of earlier forms of popular expression into 'disciplined vehicles for the expression of the popular demands'. If this was not the *moment* at which the social movement was hatched, it was, against the background of 'war, parliamentariaztion, capitalization, and proletarianization', the point at which popular public politics moved 'toward social movement forms'.[1] By 1812, Tilly argued, all aspects of what we understand to be fundamental to social movements were in place, the increasing emphasis on institutionalised campaigning and a national basis for campaigns and co-ordination being especially distinctive compared to late eighteenth-century protests. Indeed, this point marked the shift from what political geographer Walter Nicholls has conceptualised as the 'first moment' of social movement formation – there being loose connections between many 'activists' who share common grievances, identify with a common discourse and employ similar tactics – to the 'second moment', when the network of 'loose' affiliates are 'activated' for more concerted and co-ordinated campaigns.[2] These 'early' social movements, again rooted in radical politics, made the shift from 'loose connection' to co-ordination. Moreover, as Sidney Tarrow has asserted, these early 'social movements' also marked a shift from 'more parochial attachments to local settings', as given expression in such protest practices as 'rough music' and effigy burning to 'modular weapons' such as boycotting. It was, in short, a product of rapid urbanisation, the rise of class consciousness and the politicisation of the poor.[3]

While historians might well shrink from such seemingly Whiggish readings of protest past,[4] the works of Tilly *et al.* are important in reminding us to think carefully about the ways in which forms of collective action changed in the eighteenth and early nineteenth centuries. For instance, the techniques and organisational forms adopted by the Chartists in the late 1830s and 1840s betray, as will be shown in the following chapter, a more striking resemblance to twenty-first-century mass lobby organisations than they do the actions of the Waltham Blacks. This notwithstanding, the series of early nineteenth-century rural rebellions that started with the so-called Bread or Blood rising of 1816 followed a long line of rural uprisings. Leaving aside the many regional revolts during the English Civil War, before the turn of the eighteenth century rural inhabitants were central to the Peasant's Revolt (1381), Jack Cade's Rebellion (1450), Buckingham's Rebellion (1483), the Cornish Rebellion (1497), the Pilgrimage of Grace (1536), Wyatt's Rebellion (1554), Kett's Rebellion (1549), and the Midland Revolt (1607), as well as the Diggers (1649). All had shared grievances and more-or-less shared objectives – the *sine qua non* of all forms of collective action, some degree of organisation and leadership, albeit often highly localised, and more-than-local ambitions.[5]

Early-nineteenth-century rebellions fitted into a long lineage of 'movements' that can usefully be understood as *protest movements*, something quite distinct from social movements but betraying many of the same characteristics. Indeed, the centrality of earlier protest movements in shaping the nature of the emergent British state, framing rural social relations and, as Andy Wood has so vividly demonstrated of Kett's Rebellion, their persistent potency in the public mind, attests to the importance of protests that were more than isolated events.[6] It attests to the *power* of protest movements. Using this definition, while compared to the proceeding centuries, eighteenth-century rural England was relatively free from protest movements, it was not without them. The Jacobite rebellions of 1715 and 1745 (for which, see Chapters 2 and 7), and the so-called Gordon riots of 1780 (Chapter 4) were arguably the most important of the eighteenth-century protest movements. But what marked out early nineteenth-century rural protest movements out from those of the eighteenth century and earlier was the emphasis on the social and economic dislocations caused by the mechanisation of agricultural and rural industrial tasks. What follows analyses these movements, starting with an analysis of Luddism (and pre-Luddite, anti-machine protests) in the countryside, before considering the 1816 Bread or Blood riots, the East Anglian protests of 1822, and the Swing rising of 1830. Chapter 7 continues the theme, considering the ways in which this period also evidenced the politicisation of rural workers manifest in rural trades unionism and that *bona fide* social movement, Chartism.

Luddism

If the Luddite protests of 1811–13, the Bread and Blood protests of 1816, the East Anglian riots of 1822, and Swing in 1830 were novel in intensity and scale – 1811–13 and 1830 being by far the largest ever episodes of machine-breaking in British history – they were not the first instances of machine-breaking. This had a far deeper history. The point could easily be over-played, for many new technologies were either happily adopted by promoters and users alike, or, after initial scepticism, became, as Glennie and Thrift have put it in relation to the acceptance of clock time, 'grooved into the body'.[7] Either way, as Humphrey Jennings' pioneering compendium of writings on the 'coming of the machine' shows, the introduction of new forms of technology that modified, revolutionised or even made redundant existing skills invariably provoked some form of opposition.[8]

The issue, as always, is whether such resistances were recorded in the archive. Popular, as opposed to merely individual, opposition was first manifested in the cloth industry. As Adrian Randall has demonstrated, the large amounts of capital invested in cloth production and the high labour costs involved drove technical innovation in the industry.[9] Before examining reactions to machinery, it is important to note that whatever the successes of anti-machine protests, technological inventiveness did not generate an automatic, reflexive, popular opposition. In many places and at many different times, machines met with no explicit opposition, though we can never rule out that their introduction did not provoke grumbling. Ultimately, the success of new technologies, and related new social technologies, was responsible for a huge rise in labour productivity and output in the late eighteenth and early nineteenth centuries. The machine was, as Joel Mokyr put it, the 'lever of riches'.[10]

None of this is to claim, though, that opposition was either minor or futile. It was not. Rather, the spatiality and temporality of resistance to machinery was complex and fractured. For instance, the introduction of scribbling, or carding, engines that mechanised the labour-intensive process of separating fleece into long fibres ready for spinning provoked different responses in the cloth industries of the west country than in the northern counties. After initial opposition in Lancashire in 1779 and in the mid-1780s in Yorkshire, the machines were broadly accepted as they fitted into the pre-existing 'domestic system' where scribbling was one of several processes undertaken by journeymen in clothier's workshops. In the west, though, scribbling was customarily a practice undertaken by specialist male workers employed directly by gentlemen clothiers. Because of this arrangement, resistance in the West country was more sustained. Initial attempts to introduce the scribbling engine by Bradford-upon-Avon manufacturer Joseph Phelps in the spring of 1791 met with fierce opposition, while subsequent attempts to introduce the machine elsewhere in Wiltshire and in neighbouring Somerset met with an equally vigorous response from local scribblers.[11] Resistance to the introduction of spinning jennies – machines that could spin multiple reels of wool compared to using a spinning wheel – was equally complex. The introduction of the first jennies in and around Blackburn and Bolton in late 1768 and early 1769 prompted muscular but short-lived resistance, the burning of machines and the demolition of weavers' houses containing the jennies soon giving way to a grudging acceptance as the rapid expansion of the cotton industry engaged otherwise displaced labour. New, powered, 'large' jennies introduced in the late 1770s provoked more bitter resistance, Arkwright's mill at Birkacre being destroyed by a determined group at the second attempt, after two of their number were fatally shot and another drowned during their first attempt. This and other riots delayed the uptake of the machines, though not by as long as in Somerset, where protests in 1776 and again in 1781 prevented the widespread use of spinning jennies in the region until the late 1780s.[12]

The most ferocious opposition to machinery in the west came in the form of the so-called 'Wiltshire Outrages' of 1802, a series of protests against new cloth-finishing technologies: the revised gig mill (used to bring up the 'nap' on cloth, displacing a skilled trade) and shearing frames (that sheared the nap on cloth, previously done by hand). Gig mills had long been a source of popular contention, both elsewhere and in Wiltshire, but despite a mill being destroyed at Horningsham near Frome in 1767 and an (unsuccessful) prosecution being brought against Samuel Cook for erecting an 'experimental' gig mill on the edge of Marlborough in 1795, other clothiers also introduced the new mills. Threatening letters and assaults followed, with rising tensions coming to a head when in April 1802 two Warminster clothiers introduced gig mills. A turn out of the workers on the introduction of the mills quickly spread to encompass shearmen in other local mills, and those refusing to strike being threatened. As the strike deepened, threatening letters were sent to the clothiers, one clothiers' trees were cut down, and incendiary attacks were made against the clothiers' agricultural property. Tellingly, even the 'agricultural' workers refused to assist in extinguishing the flames. This was not the end of it. When the strike spread to Staverton, the location of a new six-floor factory, proprietor John Jones responded by calling for military protection and, provocatively, by introducing shearing frames, the result being that the windows of his factory were broken. Only the intervention of the armed guards prevented further destruction. Further mills – and the property of clothiers – were duly set on fire, while Staverton was again attacked. Legal attempts to prove that gig and shearing mills were a 'nuisance' came to nothing, though, hardly surprising considering the terror generated among the property owners the Wiltshire grand jury represented. In some places wages were forced (temporarily) upwards, some offending mills put out of use, and outside of a small number of mills, gig mills and shearing frames were not adopted for several years, yet ultimately capital beat labour and customary regulation.[13]

In reading of the actions of the Wiltshire protestors one could easily come to the conclusion that compared to the later actions of the 'Luddites' their protests were squarely rooted in older, agrarian models of protest – incendiarism, plant-maiming, 'disorder' – rather than industrial forms of opposition. Yet this is to both deny the central role that trades unionism – theirs known as the 'brief institution' – and protestors' recourse to the law played. It is also to assume that machine-breaking was a fundamentally different form of protest. It was not. Like long-practised protest forms such as the food riot, it was a form of collective disorder, and like incendiarism it was a symbolic attack against an employer's capital. The similarities do not end there. The language and discourses of Luddite threatening letters was no different from those penned during eighteenth-century subsistence crises: religious imagery; the call to custom and community. And in the deployment of many customary and carnivalesque forms from 'rough music' to cross-dressing, Luddite actions appear to be little different from many earlier protest 'ceremonies'. The customary and paternalistic could be, and was, successfully mobilised in emergent and rapidly expanding industries such as cotton weaving.[14]

Nor did the later Luddite protests focus only on the urban and the industrial. Many mills were, as in the west country, located either on the urban fringe or in villages, while many mill owners in Cheshire, Lancashire and Yorkshire were also agriculturalists. As Katrina Navickas has shown, Luddite gangs used the moors as symbolic places to hold their 'drills' – industrial workers familiar with the moors as recreational spaces and as routeways – and even resorted to incendiarism against agricultural property and threatened the users of threshing machines.[15] In drawing together the rapidly emerging industrial, urban worlds with the rural and agrarian, the Luddites were able to draw on a rich protest tradition and mould it to their specific needs as well as continuing to hone 'new' forms of collective engagement. In Lancashire at least, as Navickas has suggested, the 'connections among all [protest] forms were ambiguous and fluctuating'.[16]

There is, however, a strong sense that the Luddites' resort to machine-breaking came in response to the failure of customary calls to, and for, paternal protection. The repeal of older legislation and the promotion of market competition rather than worker protection was already on the agenda, with many parliamentarians eagerly encouraged by the master clothiers wanting to gain whatever competitive advantage they could. Notwithstanding that a 3,000-strong Gloucestershire Cloth Weavers' Society had campaigned for a revision of the law to extend to 'loom-shops', in 1809 legislation prohibiting the hire of non-apprenticed workers in the woollen trades (2 and 3 Philip and Mary c.[11]) was repealed. This was a pivotal moment. Further mass petitioning, with one petition supposedly containing over 130,000 signatures, ensued, but this failed to find meaningful government support: the 1808 Select Committee into the weavers' grievances was a toothless sop. This failure provoked a bitter response. Mass meetings of weavers in St George's Fields, Manchester, were met by military force, with two weavers being shot dead and 30 arrested. A strike of rural and urban weavers that held for a fortnight was initially more successful, but the 20 per cent advance in wages secured did not last for long, as a stagnation in trade in late 1810 led to renewed wage reductions.[17] The reduction in wages also coincided with a severe dearth and a huge spike in the price of provisions. None of this, as Randall suggests, made Luddhism inevitable. Rather, it sowed the seeds for a crisis in which the question of machinery was to the fore.[18]

As is well established, what came to be known as the Luddite disturbances started in the Nottinghamshire hosiery trade in the early months of 1811, the early protests, again, linking town and country. The first act of machine-breaking occurred at Arnold, then a village on the northern fringe of Nottingham, where hosiery framework knitters removed the 'jack wires' from frames in a workshop. This was followed by a large gathering of knitters from the surrounding villages in Nottingham on 11 March to complain to the hosiers – their employers – about their conditions. Dispersed by the magistrates, some of the group reassembled later that day at Arnold, where they had resolved to destroy some of the stocking frames. Over the next fortnight, several other acts of stocking-frame-breaking occurred in the vicinity of Nottingham by small, orderly groups acting in disguise. A public meeting on 26 March, while condemning the attacks resolved to increase piece rates to previous levels, a measure that acted to pacify the stockingers for a while. However, worsening trade conditions and the increased use of new 'wide' frames which allowed for the deployment of cheaper female labour in place of male labour led to renewed tensions in late autumn. Frames were again smashed in the villages around Nottingham, something that followed the sending of threatening letters to several hosiers. The turning point came on the night of 10 November, when the house of hosier Hollingworth at Bulwell was attacked. Notwithstanding that one of the attackers was shot dead in the affray, the group still managed to gain entry to the house and destroyed all the wide frames and household furniture. Symbolically, the standard frames were not touched.

Thereafter attacks became more frequent and bolder, many occurring in daylight and by bigger groups. By late November frame-breaking had spread into neighbouring Derbyshire and Leicestershire, and even the stationing of the military in Nottingham did not prevent attacks in that neighbourhood, the protestors now reverting to smaller groups carrying out their attacks in outlying parishes in greater secrecy. Some standard frames being operated at reduced wages – or by women, a theme also raised in threatening letters sent to owners of Lancashire cotton mills[19] – were also now destroyed. Attempts to reconcile the stockingers and hosiers met several false dawns, agreements to increase rates and to listen to grievances not being followed through by all the employers and thus almost inevitably reinvigorating machine-breaking. The creation of a £2,000 fund by a 'secret committee' of Nottingham civil officers and leading hosiers to offer rewards for information leading to the conviction of the machine-breakers only tended to further strain social relations. Besides, popular support for the Luddites' cause tended to undermine the committee's efforts. Even the stationing of further troops and the passing of an emergency Frame Breakers Act, increasing the maximum punishment for frame-breaking from 14 years' transportation to death, proved ineffectual, machine-breaking continuing into March.[20]

By then attention had already passed to the cotton districts of Lancashire and Cheshire and the cloth-making areas of the West Riding of Yorkshire where power looms and shearing frames, respectively, were the primary targets. In Yorkshire, protests focused on the area around Huddersfield: a January meeting of hammer-wielding, face-blackened croppers stating their intention to destroy the frames being the first explicit manifestation of Luddism in the northern counties. The first acts of actual machine-breaking occurred on 22 February at Marsh near

Huddersfield and at nearby Crosland Moor, shearing frames in both cases being the target. After intensive machine-breaking in and around Huddersfield in late March, the protests spread to Leeds, where so intensive were the actions of the often-armed groups that within a fortnight most frames outside the largest mills had either been destroyed or were rendered inoperable by their owners. The shift was now to attack the larger mills, starting on 9 April when a group of 300 or so destroyed the frames, shears, cloths and windows in the mill owned by Joseph Foster at Horbury near Wakefield. This success begat other such attacks, though the attempt on William Cartwright's mill at Rawfolds on the night of 12 April was eventually repelled after a confrontation between the Luddites and the military force stationed at the mill, the fire fight claiming the lives of two Luddites. Enraged, the croppers resolved to murder the owners of the large mills: Cartwright survived an attack, but William Horsfall of Otiwells mill at Marsden was assassinated on his return from Huddersfield market. This 'success' encouraged the campaign to shift from attacking machinery to highly organised raiding for arms, a practice supported, so reports suggested, by the taking of secret oaths and military-style drilling. The impact of 20 years of war was clearly not lost on the wider populace. In adopting military forms and terms – the Luddites being led by the fictional 'General Ludd' – Navickas has persuasively asserted that workers were engaged in a 'cathartic reaction ... against the pressures of militarization'.[21]

Lancashire Luddism was based on a broader set of anti-machinery grievances compared to the East Midlands and Yorkshire and, arguably, in coalescing with food rioting and radical politicking, assumed a very different tone. As Binfield has suggested, in and around Manchester it was 'difficult to distinguish the various motivations' of the different groups, the artisan unions, weavers secret committees, Painette radicals and the 'ebullient Irish fringe' that Thompson listed as being active.[22] It was also more squarely, if not, as noted above, exclusively, focused on the mill towns, especially Manchester and Stockport, where the sending of threatening letters in February 1812 marked the start of the protests in the county. But assuming that those who were part of urban crowds and engaged in acts of urban Luddism were necessarily urban workers is to deny both the complex interplay between town and country in the lives of many industrial workers as well as the fact that many rural workers were involved in the spate of urban food riots. For instance, the food riot at Macclesfield on 13 April involved not only Stockport spinners but also carters and colliers from the surrounding villages. This same group on the following day turned their attention to a steam-powered factory at Edgley, destroying windows, and after having similarly damaged several mills and manufacturers' houses in Macclesfield returned to the Edgley mill, forced their way in and broke the looms.[23]

Luddism in Lancashire, as well as in the East Midlands and Yorkshire, was a community response as opposed to exclusively a trade response. Arguably, the influence of the 'secret' weavers' committees on the course of protest events was not as strong as the deeper regional connections that allowed for the participation of workers from outside the immediate neighbourhood and, critically, the immediate trade. The prominent involvement of colliers in and around Saddleworth and Stockport, for example, attests to the tight social bonds forged across employment in the south-west Lancashire coal belt and long community histories of inter-trade solidarity.[24] Even against an often underhand and brutal response from local magistrates, something especially profound in the area around Stockport and the border areas with north-east Cheshire, solidarities remained strong. Further evidence also comes from the firing of two threshing machines at Soothill and Birstall in the West Riding on the nights of 10 and 11 May, respectively. While no definite evidence attaches to the authorship of the fires, the belief that 'discontented' croppers were responsible suggests an understanding that the paths of industry and agriculture were not perceived as being mutually exclusive. Indeed, on 21 April, the deputy lieutenant of the West Riding had issued handbills advising farmers to keep watch over their threshing machines because of rumours that the Luddites were to turn their attention to agricultural machinery.[25]

Beyond local and regional connections, there is also tantalising evidence that suggests some contact between the different Luddite groups. One letter seized by a spy working for Huddersfield magistrate Joseph Radcliffe concerned the correspondence of 'Peter Plush, secretary to General Ludd senior at Nottingham' to a 'General Ludd, junior' at Huddersfield.[26] The ready use of 'Ludd' derived from a Leicestershire idiom for a machine-breaker, itself taken from a Ned Lud – the second 'd' was added later – who had destroyed stocking frames in Leicester in 1779. Thus the way in which the eponym Ludd was adopted in all of the machine-breaking areas attests to not only the way in which language and shared tropes gave cohesion to an otherwise only conceptually connected set of protests, but also to the ways in which knowledge could diffuse through pan-regional trade networks.

'Community' mattered on a number of levels. Luddism may have been more violent than many earlier trade-based disputes – the relatively little machine-breaking there was in Lancashire quickly gave way to arms raids, drilling and oath-taking as it had in Yorkshire – but it only took this form in desperation at the apparent abdication of community responsibility by the masters, magistrates and government ministers. It represented, as Thompson so perceptively noted, a 'crisis point in the abrogation of paternalist legislation, and in the imposition of the political economy of *laissez-faire* upon, and against the will and conscience of, the working people'.[27] These working people, we would do well to remember, were not just the industrial workers forging 'new' urban communities – and besides many had deep kinship networks that folded family links with trade societies – but also industrial and non-industrial workers in the countryside. What follows examines the working through of this 'crisis' by agrarian workers in the context of the events of 1816, 1822 and 1830.

Bread or Blood and 1822

The often-brutal repression of the Luddite protests and, especially in Lancashire and Yorkshire, the inability of direct action to undermine the heavily-mechanised factory system, effectively put an end to organised machine-breaking in the clothing trades. It did not, however, snuff out anti-machine sentiment or protests. Even in the Luddite heartlands, isolated acts of machine-breaking continued into the crisis year of 1816, while the spectre of open insurrection was kept alive through the sending of threatening letters signed by General Ludd.[28] But anti-machine protests in 1816 occurred in a profoundly different context from 1811–12. The end of hostilities in continental Europe occasioned the return of 300,000 demobbed soldiers in 1816, with another 32,000 in 1817, 'glutting' labour markets at exactly the same time as the price of agricultural commodities and manufactured goods collapsed. Mass unemployment and chronic under-employment followed.[29] The woollen and weaving districts of Essex and East Anglia were also in long-term decline, competition from more highly capitalised and machine-operating Yorkshire effectively putting the once huge cloth industry almost completely out of work.[30] These structural factors were further exacerbated when, from April 1816, rapid price movements in response to both localised supply problems, avaricious marketing practices and the anticipation of a poor harvest created a subsistence crisis.[31]

While the series of protests that occurred in the spring of 1816 were a response to this *rapid* deterioration in the fortunes of rural workers, they were not bolts from the blue. Most precipitately, anti-machine sentiment was evident in the spring and summer of 1815 in Suffolk, in what were the first ever (recorded) acts of threshing machine-breaking, though machines had long since been targeted by incendiarists.[32] While we can only speculate as to how this protest innovation came to be, the transmission of machine-breaking knowledge from workers in the cloth industries in this de-industrialising region to agricultural workers must be a strong possibility.

The initial collective protests in 1816 occurred simultaneously, and quite unconnectedly, on 17 April at Mile End Heath near Colchester, where threshing tackle was destroyed, and at Gedding in south Suffolk, where threshing machines and mole ploughs – which slashed labour costs for creating field drainage on the heavy local soils – were broken by a huge crowd. Beyond the firing of a malt kiln at Maunden later that month, for which 26-year-old ex-serviceman Joseph Bugg was hanged, no further protests were reported to have occurred in Essex. The Gedding protests, though, acted as the catalyst for a wave of protests in the area between Bury St Edmunds, Stowmarket and Lavenham over the following 10 days, including further acts of threshing machine and mole plough breaking as well as wages 'riots'.[33] This intensive wave of collective protests, combined with the 'dropping' of letters threatening 'vengeance for higher wages' in churchyards and farmyards alongside further fires created considerable alarm. According to one Home Office correspondent, the labourers were holding nightly meetings and 'taking oaths to stand by each other as in the <u>Meeting at the Nore</u>'. Landowner Major Marrie also reported on 25 April that one farmer had openly declared that he was 'ready to join the mob' to pressure the clergy into lowering their tithes. There 'did not appear', so Marrie warned, 'to be the least motion in the magistracy'.[34]

Stung into action, a general quarter sessions was hastily called to meet at Bury on 29 April. Those hoping for measures that would put down the protests were to be disappointed. Beyond 'signify[ing] their determination to take prompt and effectual measures to put a stop to all such assemblages, and to bring to justice all persons who are found offending against the peace', the gathered magistrates did nothing beyond agreeing that the civil force in each district would be strengthened. Lord Lieutenant of Suffolk, Lord Grafton, in a letter to all county magistrates after the meeting, acknowledged their 'discreet judicious and spirited conduct' but also 'strongly recommended' that if London police officers could 'be of help' then they should be 'immediately applied for'.[35] Either way, the measures taken were neither strong enough nor enacted quickly enough to prevent more widespread protests. A series of incendiary fires in south Suffolk and north Essex and threshing machine-breaking at Stoke-by-Clare in south Suffolk were followed by a shift to demonstrations in the market towns of East Anglia, though a seemingly isolated attempt by 50 labourers and artisans to force an increase in their wages also occurred at Swaffham Bulbeck in neighbouring Cambridgeshire.[36]

The first of these 'urban' protests was self-contained: a 100-strong 'mob' destroyed the windows of a flour mill at Needham Market on 7 May before being persuaded to disperse. What followed, though, was more persistent and determined. Bury was the scene of at least three days of riots starting on 14 May, the premises of a hosier containing spinning jennies only avoiding destruction through the intervention of the West Suffolk militia. On the 16 May protestors also took to the streets of both Norwich, where the populace attacked the military, and, famously, Brandon, where on the third day of rioting on Saturday 18 May the crowd carried a banner proclaiming 'Bread or Blood' and threatened to march on London.[37]

The example of Brandon was immediate, something Home Secretary Sidmouth felt was a result of the sympathy shown to the protestors by the local authorities. From Brandon, protests spread over the Norfolk border, and from there into the Fenlands of Cambridgeshire, in particular to the towns of Downham Market (20 May), Littleport (22 May) and Ely (23 May). This was, as Charlesworth has suggested, the tipping point.[38] The group active at Downham looted the contents of a flour mill and a butchers' shop, took bread and cheese from other food sellers and in fear were granted several concessions, including the release of several prisoners taken at protests at Southerey and Hilgay. News of this popular 'victory' quickly spread through the district. The effect was most obvious, and immediate, at Littleport, where protests started on 22 May and lasted for several days. The focus here was to win the same concessions as had been secured elsewhere; however, the interventions of the popularly detested clerical magistrate Vachell also led to his house being looted.[39] More seriously, the ever-expanding group also scoured Littleport for guns and other possible arms before proceeding to Ely where they joined with the 'refractory inhabitants' in the market place. The 500-or-so-strong crowd were met by the magistrates, who readily assented to their demands: flour at 2/6d, wages at 2s and beer at 2d.[40] Friday 24 May witnessed a very different response. Further protests in Ely were easily put down by the arrival of the Royston Volunteer Cavalry and a detachment of 1st Royal Dragoons, the military then heading to Littleport where they found many of the men drunk and up for a fight. In the ensuing battle, one labourer was shot dead, another had part of his jaw cut off by a sabre, and others received gunshot wounds while several soldiers were also hurt.

On Saturday 25 May, Home Secretary Sidmouth, alarmed at the inability of local law officers to prevent the spread of the protests, issued a royal proclamation. A £100 reward was to be given to anyone offering information leading to the conviction of any of the protestors, while a pardon was to be extended to any accomplice giving evidence leading to a conviction. Troops were also to be stationed throughout Norfolk and Suffolk. There is evidence that in some places a strong military force acted to prevent open protests. For instance, at Wisbech, 'inflammatory' speeches and placards threatening that the Downham men would be forcibly released from gaol on 25 May prompted the authorities to pack the town with 120 yeomanry and 300 special constables. No disturbance occurred. The prisoners were moved to Ely and regular troops stationed in Downham. Further collective protests over the bread–wage nexus did occur in the vicinity of Downham but these were isolated incidents. Arguably of greater concern was the renewal of threshing machine-breaking in Essex, a county outside the remit of the proclamation, machines being destroyed in several parishes north of Halstead in the old Essex cloth area.[41]

To reinforce the deterrent and wanting to make an example of the Ely and Littleport rioters, Sidmouth also ordered that a Special Commission of Assize be held to try the Cambridgeshire men. The trials opened on Monday 17 June and closed four days later when 24 men were sentenced to death. Nineteen of these men were reprieved, nine of whom were subsequently transported, the five not reprieved being hanged on 28 June. Two men, tried at the Norwich Assizes, were also executed, on 31 August, for their part in the Downham riots. In total, eight men – including Thomas Sindall, who was shot in the head by a Dragoon at Littleport – lost their lives, while 14 men were transported to Australia for their involvement at Downham, Littleport and Ely. Despite this heavy toll, it is important to note that while much property was destroyed and violence was often used in resisting the military, at no point did the protestors' calls ever exceed very modest demands: an end to the use of threshing machines; cheaper flour and bread; and a minimum wage or support from the parish of 2s a day. An analysis of those arrested for the Ely and Littleport riots also serves to remind us that those who were involved were not just agricultural labourers. Indeed, one in three of those arrested were small tradesmen and artisans, while one in seven had some land. As Andrew Charlesworth has asserted, in the complex 'peasant' economy of the pre-enclosed Fenland many others would have also earned money from cutting osiers, sedges, reeds and turfs.[42]

Beyond isolated episodes of collective protest,[43] the occasional fire and acts of animal and plant-maiming, rural East Anglia next exploded in widespread protest in the early months of 1822, the year that represented the absolute nadir of the post-Napoleonic War agrarian depression. While food prices were both significantly lower and far less volatile than in 1816, poor relief had become even more stingy, meaningful employment even harder to procure, and wages lower still.[44] Moreover, the penetration of threshing machines had significantly increased.[45] But as Paul Muskett has suggested, there was 'no anticipation of a second rising'. Even a flurry of (unrelated) incendiary fires in Suffolk and the sending of threatening letters generated little in the way of feverish comment.[46] When threshing machine-breaking erupted in mid-February to the north of Diss and in the vicinity of Eye, on either side of the Norfolk and Suffolk border, respectively, they both quickly assumed a localised intensity and caught the authorities unawares. The response though, in Diss at least, was swift: warrants were 'immediately' issued against several of those active in machine-breaking at Shimpling on 14 February, with six men arrested on Saturday, 16 February. The arrests did nothing to stop further acts of machine-breaking at nearby Winfarthing and at Tivertshall.[47]

Collective protests started again on 2 March, with at least 20 threshing machines being destroyed or dismantled over the next four days in at least 12 different parishes to the north of Shimpling, a 250-strong force mainly of mounted special constables eventually putting down the mobile groups even before the arrival of the Eye Yeomanry. Troops from Ipswich were also despatched to Diss as a precaution. A threshing machine was also destroyed at Southolt and at least a further six were also destroyed at Cratfield and Laxfield, some 11 miles east of Eye, on 4 March. There were other isolated protests too, both in the area in which protests had already occurred and, in the case of the resort to incendiarism, in areas otherwise unaffected by collective protests, the Reverend at Stonham Aspal twice being targeted.[48] The receipt of radically tinged threatening letters at Ipswich was also perceived to be evidence of 'an incendiary disposition', and Home Secretary Peel sent Bow Street police officers to assist as undercover detectives.[49]

Without a government-backed resort to a Special Assizes, the protestors were swiftly tried. Twenty-seven men were indicted at the Norfolk Quarter Sessions and a further six held over for the assizes. Of those tried at the sessions, two were acquitted, five bound over to keep the peace, the rest being sentenced to gaol terms of between one week and a year. At the Norfolk Assizes, Noah Peak and George Fortis, both Waterloo veterans but now reduced to being employed on the roads by the Bressingham parish surveyor, were found guilty of riot and of setting fire to poor law official John Kent's stacks by virtue of an accomplice turning King's Evidence. Both ended their lives on the Thetford scaffold. Three of the Laxfield protestors were also tried at the Bury Assizes for riot and sentenced to between one and two years' imprisonment.

Yet this was not the end of it in either county. Occasional acts of threshing machine-breaking continued throughout the spring, reviving again that summer in isolated cases in Suffolk and south Norfolk. One perambulating group in the parishes of the south-east Norfolk–north Suffolk border intent on destroying machines found only one threshing machine to destroy, so successful had the earlier machine-breaking been in inducing farmers to put their machines down. One final act of destruction occurred at Mendham, between Diss and Bungay, in mid-December.[50] What was striking about these 'post-trial' protests was the fact that not only had the earlier deterrents proved ineffectual but also that more individuals were brought to trial than for the earlier, more intensive wave of machine-breaking. As Muskett notes, 'nearly 120 men' were tried for their part in the protests during 1822, and all but five of these were farm workers. Of these five, two were farmers, one an innkeeper, one a carpenter and one a shoemaker. The protestors were, as Charlesworth suggested, far less socially heterogeneous than the 1816 protests. This most commercially orientated and highly capitalised part of rural England had become less socially diverse: the loss of small farmers and dual occupationalists supported in pre-enclosure parishes, the consolidation of ever larger farms with wealthier farmers, and chronically pauperised, under-employed field workers. Where smaller farmers held on they were commercially disadvantaged by the use of expensive threshing machinery by the large farmers, a dynamic best evidenced by farmer Goose inciting the men through bribes to break a threshing machine at Ditchingham.[51] This dynamic was, as the following section shows, also a key feature of Swing in areas where peasant producers and small farmers could still – just – eke out a living.

Swing

If the East Anglian protests of 1816 and 1822 had disabused Westminster of any notion that field workers were more inclined than industrial workers quiescently to accept their lot, there was still no sense in the early 1820s that a more-than-regional rural rebellion was possible. Claims in the London-published *Morning Chronicle* in April 1822 that 'outrages … among unemployed agricultural labourers' had also occurred in Kent and Sussex were denounced as 'evil' by the *Maidstone Journal*, the editor counter-claiming that the countryside was 'never in a more peaceful and tranquil state'. While this ignored evidence of incendiarism, the sending of threatening letters and even an assassination attempt on a farmer, the statement represented a fundamental belief that while occasional acts of rural terrorism were carried out, open revolt was improbable.[52]

An improvement in the rural economy between 1823 and 1827 offered some respite for rural workers – Archer recorded only two incendiary fires for Norfolk and Suffolk in 1826 compared with 64 for 1822[53] – but disastrous harvests in 1828 and 1829 checked this short-lived upturn in fortunes. As 'The poor labourers' of the Hundred of Cosford put it in an extraordinary letter to the *Suffolk Chronicle:* 'our class are starving weigh'd down with oppression and worn out with vexations'. 'We shall,' the letter continued, 'shortly fight for ourselves we count it an absolute right for us to rise for support for our wives and beloved children ... our side is strong and hang as it were by a thread ready ripened for a revolt.'[54] Now, and in stark contrast to 1816 and 1822, commentators readily predicted that the balance of rural society had tipped to the point that revolt was possible, even likely.[55]

A wretchedly cold winter and a wet spring in 1830 made matters worse still. In the Weald, crime was so bad that the Sussex press reckoned that rural workers were 'all now confederates, so that detection is scarcely possible'.[56] This was not something confined to agricultural workers: weavers in and around Norwich were locked in a long-running dispute, while a 'spirit of insubordination' among the cloth-workers of Painswick, Gloucestershire, was met in April by the stationing of a detachment of the 2nd Dragoons in the parish.[57] In an echo of 1816 and 1822, threshing machines were also destroyed between Finchingfield and Toppesfield, Essex, in early 1829,[58] and in mid-Suffolk during that autumn.[59] At Handsworth near Sheffield there was also reported to be an 'anti-thresh- ing machine spirit' among the 'flail workers' because of the arrival of a travelling threshing machine.[60]

A series of co-ordinated attacks on threshing machines in and around the Elham Valley area of east Kent proved rather more influential. The first recorded attack on a threshing machine occurred at Wingmore, a small hamlet between the villages of Barham and Elham, by a gang of 'three or four and twenty' men on 24 August. This was no 'bolt from the blue', as Hobsbawm and Rudé claimed, but rather was the result of long- running local disputes over the use of threshing machines. The group of labourers, artisans and small farmers had approached local farmers warning them that if they did not stop using their machines they would be destroyed. Some heeded the warnings. Those who did not were tar- geted. Over the following four weeks, the gang grew in size and destroyed machines over an ever-wider area. It was not until 22 September that the magistrates and 'gentlemen' finally met to discuss the unfurling protests, with arrests and the taking of recognisances starting five days later.[61]

Notwithstanding further machine-breaking episodes on the night of the arrests and again on 1 October, their protests duly turned to incendiarism and the issuing of threats, incendiary letters being sent by post to two individuals near Dover. Both letters were signed for the first time by 'the same significant word', 'Swing'.[62]

So started Swing. But what transformed a series of intensive but essentially localised protests into a more-than-local protest movement was the reaction of other workers elsewhere to the trial of the initial machine-breakers. Sentenced only to four days in gaol – the maximum sentence permitted being seven years' transportation – because one clerical magistrate and a further clergyman having compromised themselves, leading to the fear of reprisals if the maximum penalty was imposed, the actions of the Elham men were duly read as having been vindicated.[63] The sentence acted as a spur to protests beyond the gang's range, machine-breaking extending to the vicinity of Ash in east Kent and, more critically, wages protests to the area between Maidstone and Sittingbourne to the west.[64]

The sentence was even more extraordinary given the wider political context. In one sense, against the backdrop of the recent revolution in France, the death of George IV and the ensuing general election, Prime Minister the Duke of Wellington's fragile hold on power and the associated parliamentary reform crisis, the breaking of machines in Kent was small beer. Yet, given the relatively recent experience of Luddism and the 1816 and 1822 East Anglian riots, and the fear that the example of France would have an electric effect on English workers, was, many commentators argued, reason enough to make an example of the Elham men. This paranoia was indeed partly justified, for evidence of radical political discourse and sentiment was present in many Swing episodes. Even at Elham, where the agenda was purest, one machine-breaker was reported to have said, 'Next year we will have a turn with the Parsons, and the third, we will make war upon the Statesmen.'[65] But in some localities, like Maidstone, radical politics *underpinned* Swing: the symbolism of the tricolor combining with politically charged claims and speeches.

The protests in the vicinity of Maidstone were of note for reasons beyond the radical influence and the extension of Swing's canon to wages protests. Here, highly mobile groups led by two politically-active Maidstone shoemakers physically diffused protests throughout much of west Kent and into the Weald at the start of November.[66] Beyond the actions of the Maidstone groups, Swing was first manifested in the Weald through two indigenous sets of protests: at Battle over wages and poor relief starting on 1 November – here radical politics and in particular a recent lecture by William Cobbett were again implicated – and four days later at nearby Brede over poor relief. Thus in this area marked by chronic levels of unemployment and pauperisation, the agenda widened to embrace calls for more generous poor relief and, critically, better treatment of rural workers at the hands of poor law officials. In several locales, starting at the aforementioned Brede, salaried assistant overseers were even physically removed from the parish by protestors. A further impetus for protests here came from the large number of small and tenant farmers who expressed their willingness to support the labourers' cause if they, in turn, used their collective power to secure tithe reductions from the clergy.[67]

Between 8 and 14 November virtually every Wealden and south-west Kent parish rose, protests spreading in essentially predictable and linear forms. Thereafter, the protests lost their geographic coherence, having several concurrent foci, often at some remove from other centres of protest. On 13 November, labourers' assemblages occurred independently in the north-west Sussex parishes of Kirdford and Wisborough Green some 40 miles distant from Mayfield, the previous most westerly parish to 'rise'. Radical agitation over taxes and tithes at Horsham was central to several days of intense protests in the town and the surrounding countryside, as well as being responsible for the diffusion of wages and anti-tithe protests into the parishes around Dorking and Reigate in Surrey. A wave of threshing machine-breaking in the vicinity of Chichester – the most extensive beyond Elham – physically diffused into the south-east Hampshire parishes of Emsworth, Havant and Warblington on 18 November, the day after a series of wages assemblages had started in the vicinity of Whitchurch in north Hampshire.[68]

In both west Sussex and Hampshire incendiary fires and the receipt of threatening letters immediately pre-dated the start of collective protests. Yet there is no discernible link between these early fires and the first collective protests. The first incendiary fire in west Sussex after the spread of protests into neighbouring east Sussex occurred at Coldwaltham on the night of 12 November, some 20 miles distant from Kirdford parish, which 'rose' the next day.[69] In Hampshire, a flurry of incendiary letters, at least one of which was signed 'Swing', 'asked' the farmers to remove their threshing machines were received around Gosport on 11 November, the threat being made good against one farmer that night. But beyond the explicit link being made to the events in Kent and fears in the Hampshire press that the fire was not 'a prelude to the outrages which have for some time disgraced several neighbouring counties', there was no connection between these protests and the sustained start of collective action around Havant on 18 November.[70] In Berkshire, where Swing was first manifest in its overt form at Thatcham on 15 November, most of the fires that pre-dated collective action occurred in the forested eastern part of the county, an area that remained largely free from 'mobbings' in the winter of 1830.[71]

That no clear connection existed suggests that the incendiarists – notwithstanding that they might have been inspired by events to the east or were potentially attempting to provoke others into collective action – were part of any co-ordinated action to 'soften up' farmers. This is not to say, though, that the fires had no connection to the movement. Several factors are worth considering. First, the extent of incendiarism in 1830 was far greater than that for any previous year. For Hampshire, Kent, Surrey and Sussex, 40, 100, 37 and 58 fires, respectively, have been identified as occurring in 1830, of which 38, 88, 35 and 55 happened in the final five months of the year. This compares to 1, 2, 5 and 0 fires in 1828 and 7, 9, 0 and 7 fires, respectively, in 1829.[72] Incendiarism was also deployed as an overt tactic. This could take the form of open threats of incendiarism, as made against farmer Barnes at Shoddesden, a threat that was realised almost instantaneously when, after levying money and victuals from him, the supposedly 200-strong group set fire to his barn and destroyed his threshing machine.[73]

The foregoing analysis in many ways sums up the complexities of Swing in Berkshire, Hampshire and Wiltshire, the existence of multiple simultaneous poles of protest, the deployment of Swing's motifs as developed in Kent and Sussex, and, critically, the intensity. While it took over 12 weeks from the destruction of the first machine in the Elham Valley until Swing was first manifest in central southern England, so intensively did the protests take hold that by 24 November in Hampshire and 25 November in Berkshire collective protests had either run their course or had been repressed. This is even more extraordinary for Wiltshire, where despite the receipt of Swing letters and several fires from 15 November, collective action did not start until 19 November (through a combination of indigenous activism and physical spread) and was concluded effectively by 25 November.[74] The only area of these three counties where protests did not pass quickly was the Dever Valley in central Hampshire, where, much like at Battle and Maidstone, radical politicking and plotting through a Musical and Radical Society that met at Sutton Scotney gave the protests both greater temporal depth and a more resilient organisational form.[75]

Notwithstanding the sudden outbreak of protest in all three counties, the authorities coped far better than their Kent and Sussex counterparts, partly a function of the Home Office now readily agreeing to the deployment of troops. If initially the rapidity of Swing's diffusion caught magistrates on the hop, especially in and around Thatcham and Newbury,

the swearing-in of large numbers of special constables and ready deployment of troops quartered in various locations throughout the region
soon filled local gaols to capacity with arrested machine-breakers and
'rioters'. Still, the mobile nature of many of the groups, and the fact that
so many districts 'rose' at once, meant that it was hard to be proactive
in preventing protests. Groups at Kintbury, Yattendon and Lambourne
in Berkshire and in communities in Wiltshire close to the Berkshire and
Hampshire borders were thus able to destroy threshing machines with
an openness and rapidity more akin to the Havant protests than those
at Elham.[76] For north-west Wiltshire, though, Randall and Newman have
argued that pre-emptive wages and poor relief increases were particularly successful in helping to at least moderate protests in that locale.[77]

According to Hobsbawm and Rudé, some 97 machines were destroyed
in Wiltshire, with Berkshire and Hampshire being the next highest ranked
counties with 75 and 45 machines destroyed, respectively.[78] While their
figures have been critiqued as underestimating the scale of machine-
breaking, especially in Swing's initial centres,[79] their rankings highlight
the importance of machine-breaking as the key expression of discontent
in south-central England. Indeed, this was most profoundly given voice
in the destruction of machine works at Fordingbridge near the Wiltshire
border in south-west Hampshire and the aforementioned Tasker's at
Upper Clatford. However, if threshing machine-breaking was the primary motive in west Berkshire, south-east and north-west Hampshire,
and in south, east and mid-Wiltshire, it was not to the exclusion of other
claims. Machine-breaking groups on their perambulations were invariably to be found demanding higher wages and poor relief, doles – often in
payment for the 'work' done in breaking the machines – and a reduction
in tithes. In short, the many temporary alignments of individuals, 'mem-
berships' often overlapping parish boundaries and attachments that
were forged in the heat of Swing did not necessarily see the threshing
machine as the only evil. Rather, in many of these communities where
threshing machines had been in operation for many years, Swing gave
rural workers the *opportunity* to attack the symbols of their pauperisation,
of their oppression. In areas where threshing machines were not widely
used, most notably the heavily forested areas of east Hampshire and the
New Forest, Swing activists focused their attentions on other symbolic
targets, the destruction of workhouses at Headley and Selbourne on 22
and 23 November, respectively, being the most dramatic examples.[80]

Military interventions and the organisation of 'constabularies' of
special constables had a significant effect in south-central England
in dispersing Swing groups and making large numbers of arrests.
The mobilisation of still extant yeoman cavalries in Wiltshire and

neighbouring Dorset – yeomanries further east having long since been dissolved, many were now being revived but not in time to help with the repressive effort – were also important in dispersing many groups. This stiffening of governmental resolve and an increased preparedness as Swing diffused westwards ultimately changed the pattern and depth of subsequent protests.[81] Indeed, elsewhere in the south, Swing was only manifested in an intensive form in isolated pockets. In Dorset, for instance, Swing in its overt forms was limited to machine-breaking on Cranborne Chase (protests having spilled over from south Wiltshire and Hampshire), in the Blackmore Vale (the same group also destroying machines at Henstridge in neighbouring Somerset), between Blandford and Dorchester over wages and machines, and, finally, on the western fringes of the Isle of Purbeck. The individual who took it upon himself to lead the repressive response in the latter two areas was no less a figure than landlord and head of the local yeomanry James Frampton, Esq., conducting his men with a zeal and vitriolic force that would later be visited upon the nascent agricultural trades unionists at Tolpuddle.[82]

The extent to which Swing was truly meaningful as a coherent protest movement beyond Dorset is open to interpretation. Because, on the one hand, there were few, isolated, overt protests in the other western counties. Threshing machine-breaking at Hanley Williams and Wadberrow in Worcestershire was evidently inspired by the examples elsewhere, but food riots in Cornwall appeared to be little more than coincident expressions of grievance. Conversely, it is possible to read the spike in levels of incendiarism and the receipt of Swing letters as evidence of explicit linkages to the southern protests.[83] Arguably the strongest case can be made for south-east Gloucestershire and south Oxfordshire, where waves of threshing machine-breaking had diffused over the north Wiltshire border from 26 November and from Berkshire, respectively.[84] The destruction of the machinery of several paper mills in and around High Wycombe in Buckinghamshire and the concurrent receipt of Swing letters also attests to the power of the ideas that Swing, as a movement, embodied.[85]

The other major wave of protests occurred in East Anglia. Here, though, threshing machine-breaking on the north coast and south-west of Norfolk – Hobsbawm and Rudé recording 29 cases – and the less intensive wage and invariably farmer-supported tithe riots in south-east Norwich and east Suffolk were as much informed by the cultural memory of the events of 1816 and 1822 as they were by southern Swing. This is not to deny the importance of this third wave of collective action in 15 years, but instead to assert that the protests cannot be fitted neatly into the canon of Swing activity. Indeed, it is striking that while the claims made were similar to those issued elsewhere and the discourses were similar – the notions of asserting 'rights' and of work for fair wages – the use of the eponym 'Swing' was conspicuous only by its almost total absence.[86] Threshing machines were also destroyed in the neighbouring counties of Essex and Huntingdonshire, though protests in Cambridgeshire were manifested only in the form of several fires and unconnected wages demonstrations. In the former county, wage riots were Swing's more typical form, all occurring in early December in the separate poles of the far north-western corner, between Colchester and Harwich, and around Great Clacton, the parish where eight of the 15 threshing machines broken in the county were destroyed. In Huntingdonshire, owners of threshing machines had been threatened as early as 10 October at Bluntisham, a fire making good one threat in mid-November, while 15 machines were destroyed in the west of the county, Sawtry also acting as the pole from which on 26 November machine-breaking spread into Northamptonshire.[87] Fears that the Huntingdonshire men would also turn their attentions to Lincolnshire proved unfounded. There were protests – indeed Richardson's study of the county has shown that Hobsbawm and Rudé significantly underestimated the resort to machine-breaking and wages riots – but there was little geographical coherence outside of a cluster of protests in the Fenlands of the south. What was most striking was the resort to incendiarism that assumed an intensity otherwise not seen outside of the southeast, the western fringes of the Wolds in particular being affected.[88]

It is possible also to discern the influence of Swing – as shared grievance and discourse as well as threatening metonym – beyond the south and east, the areas where Swing constituted a protest movement through diffusion.[89] Using the resort to collective action and/or the receipt of a 'Swing' letter as the necessary qualification, Hobsbawm and Rudé claimed that Swing was seen in 37 counties, 16 being only marginally affected. Beyond Cornwall, Hertfordshire, London and Middlesex, these were all northern and Midlands counties. For instance, according to their tabulations, in 'marginal' Yorkshire only two threshing machines were destroyed and several Swing letters received. Herefordshire qualified on the basis of two Swing letters, and Lancashire because of one strike and five political demonstrations. One might argue that breaking threshing machines anywhere in late 1830 necessarily happened in the context of the intensive resort to machine-breaking in the south and east. Similarly, deploying the motif of 'Swing' was clearly to invoke the symbolic power of Swing as a movement. Yet, as Navickas has argued in her treatment of the 'riots' that occurred in Carlisle in November and early December, events that occurred outside of the areas where protests physically diffused from place to place were more likely to be expressions of long-standing local concerns rather than symptoms of 'contagion'. The cause of the riots in Carlisle, so Navickas asserts, had nothing to do with events elsewhere and everything to do with 'a running debate about policing and authority in the city', itself the 'culmination of growing social and political tensions among a divided population'. And yet, even here 'Swing', the word and the concept, was used to invoke terror and a more-than-local strength, while elsewhere in the county threatening letters were sent to the users of threshing machines, an atypical protest discourse in the northern counties in 1830.[90]

Peter Jones, in his study of Swing in Berkshire, has offered a similar reading. It was, he suggests, 'a series of discrete moments of impact, like pebbles in a pond, each specifically meaningful within its own locality, but creating overlapping ripples that had a marginal impact on other localities.' He continued, '[i]n this way, the disturbances formed a kind of "meta-movement", a series of events coherent and tangentially connected in terms of their concerns and the manner of their progress, but having no guiding principle or special end outside the localities where they occurred.'[91] For there was no 'guiding principle', no overall plan or organisation, however much the press were concerned about the possible existence of a 'Captain Swing'. Swing offered rural workers, to adopt a social movement theory perspective, a 'political opportunity' to rise, to voice grievances, to release tension, and to make claims. As labourer Richard Hodd, a member of a Swing group active on the northern fringe of Ashdown Forest, was quoted as exclaiming: 'he was never so happy in his life as he was on that day'. Swing offered a sense of release and of joy that the rural poor were being listened to.[92]

But to render Swing merely as a series of parochial risings connected only as ripples in a pond is to both deny Swing's unique power and to deny activists' agency. In many locations we find evidence of agents provocateurs and radical politicians trying to stir up protest – for further details of which see the following chapter – and field workers and artisans readily making common cause with distant others, often invoking politicised critiques of the national political-economic system. We would also do well to remember that many Swing groupings were highly mobile, their active diffusing of protests attesting a sensibility that was not just tied to the parish but rather thought about wider district and regional communities. The objectives of the vast majority of protestors in 1830 were simple and shared, their grievances made sense of by a shared value system – an agrarian moral economy, as Wells and Jones have put it – and given form through customary ritual and community protest histories. Their demands were modest, and their protests usually restrained, though the *possibility* of violence was often invoked, Swing itself in all probability being an allusion to swinging from the gallows. The destruction of property fits less neatly into this model but can be understood as an attempt to punish those who continued to transgress what the labourers considered to be acceptable conduct. Machines in particular were fair game as they represented an attempt by farmers and landlords to absolve themselves of age-old responsibilities to the poor.

As the foregoing analysis of the protests suggests, while in some localities magistrates, landlords, clergy and farmers were quick to respond to Swing's pleas by acting in a paternalistic way by increasing wages and poor relief allowances and stopping the use of machines, in others the response was not to listen to grievance but instead to repress all dissent. Wages increased through fear or, in an attempt to pacify protestors in the heat of movement, were all too quickly cut. For instance, a group of West Chiltington road workers marched on the Petworth Bench as early as 4 December 1830 to complain that their parish had reneged on a local agreement,[93] while the labourers of Twyford went on strike on 13 December after their wages had been cut to pre-Swing levels.[94] This is not to claim, though, that all farmers, vestries and landlords were as hard-hearted as to hide behind the state-sponsored repression in again cutting wages and poor relief allowances. As Jeremy Burchardt has shown, late 1830 marked the effective start of the allotment movement, Swing prompting many landowners in a quasi-paternalistic gesture to set aside blocks of land to let to rural workers.[95] Far harder was it either to repair broken machines or buy replacements, though many farmers tried and found themselves subject to incendiarism in the ensuing months and years. Arguably, this was Swing's greatest success, as threshing machines were not again in general use in many districts until the start of the 1840s. Indeed, elsewhere I have suggested that post-1830 there was a 'heightened hostility' to all forms of machinery in the countryside, paper mills and the property of early adopters of steam engines also being attacked.[96]

In the foregoing analysis, Swing protestors have been referred to as labourers, even artisans and small farmers, and always as men. With few documented exceptions, this was overwhelmingly true of the many collective acts that constituted the movement. However, it does not follow that women were not involved or that Swing had nothing to say about gender relations. First, mirroring Binfield's analysis of the earlier Luddites, Swing gangs and groupings were often rooted in a profound homosociality, building on pre-existing friendships and working relationships, bonds that were further forged through protesting – 'we are as one' – and drinking together.[97] Second, I have argued elsewhere that this sense of togetherness was, at least in part, a deliberate performance of a plebeian masculinity, something imperilled, neutered even, by being forced to be reliant on the parish vestry for support. In relation to threshing machines, this was a direct comment on the fact that, in robbing men of the wintertime occupation of flail threshing, male labour was often replaced by cheaper female and child labour in the feeding of threshing machines. As one member of the Elham gang was reported to exclaim during one of their machine-breaking ceremonies, 'Kill Her! – More Oil! – More Grease!', the machine being both gendered as female and the act of destruction graphically alluding to rape.[98] Third, the involvement of women was invariably in poor-relief-related protests; for instance, a large number of women and children were reported to have joined the procession that followed the Brede assistant overseer being wheeled out of the parish.[99] Fourth, there is also a sense that the groups of men that comprised most Swing mobilisations were attempting not only to restore their own masculinity and honour but also the honour of 'their women', their wives and daughters who had also been subject to brutalising forms of parish employment and demeaning investigations into their private lives at the hands of select vestries.[100] By way of example, at Ninfield in the Sussex Weald, a mobilisation on 9 November was motivated by the parish policy of shaving the heads of pauper women, the protest therefore allowing for the reassertion of laboring masculinity through the 'defence' of Ninfield women as well as the defence of femininity.[101]

While it is currently unknown how many individuals were *arrested* across the country for their involvement in the protests, in Berkshire, Buckinghamshire, Dorset, Hampshire and Wiltshire, where government-sponsored Special Commissions were held, 992 criminal cases were heard. Here, the sentence of death was passed on 227 individuals, of whom five were actually hanged, 359 were transported to New South Wales or Van Diemen's Land, 254 were gaoled, and two were fined. Across all of Hobsbawm and Rudé's Swing counties, it has been calculated that 1,976 cases were heard in 90 courts, with some 644 individuals sent to gaol, 19 executed out of 252 sentenced to death, and 505 men and women transported. This was the single biggest act of transportation. Yet these 'draconian punishments' did not totally, as Hobsbawm and Rudé suggested, demoralise rural workers.[102] Rather, in some locales the sentences generated bitter reprisals, in other areas there was unfinished business, and in others attempts to reinforce Swing's meagre gains required occasional protests. Incendiarism dominated, but wages strikes and the collective destruction of threshing machines were also important in many areas, including the original Swing centre of east Kent.

This pattern held until the imposition of the New Poor Law from 1834 fundamentally altered the social bonds of rural England for ever. This was the moment when Swing protestors' attempts to revivify paternalism gave way to a newfound bitterness, an altered social state in which frayed social relations were far more likely than ever before to find expression through a resort to the tools of rural terror. Incendiarism, animal and plant-maiming, and other attacks on property in the 1830s and 1840s reaching levels far in excess of the 1810s and 1820s.[103]

That Swing sought to restore old social bonds and yet was the justification for the passing of the Poor Law Amendment Act means that, whatever Swing's short-term gains, its most profound act was in hammering in the final nail of the old paternalist rural system. While the bloody repression of Swing and farmers and vestrymen's ready cutting of wages and poor relief acted as the decisive pivot on which the (further) politicisation of rural workers turned, that the influence of radical politics was so strongly writ through Swing suggests that even before 1830 popular political discourses has already infiltrated the countryside. Indeed, the 'failure' of Swing in most areas to significantly improve the labourers' lot was fundamental in establishing a new consciousness in which labourers no longer looked to their social 'betters' to ease their condition. This new consciousness created the ideal conditions for the 'new' forms of association and activism explored in the following chapter.

Chapter 7: Rural Popular Politics

Tucked away at the beginning of the second 'part' of E.P. Thompson's seminal *The Making of the English Working Class* is a short chapter devoted to 'the field labourers'. While historians of rural England have noted that 26 pages out of a total of 940 represents an imbalance between rural and urban workers – it being, in the words of John Rule and Roger Wells, 'essentially a book about London's artisans and the industrial workers of the north and midlands' – the chapter has proved influential for one critical assertion. The field worker was not the inarticulate, slow-witted, bestial 'Hodge' of popular Victorian imagination; rather, so claimed Thompson, by 1830, 'political ideas of further significance were abroad'. Moreover, this presence had temporal depth. The brief 'agitation' of the early to mid-1790s democratic movement 'diffused its ideas into ... many corners of Britain'. By the time the movement was put down there were individuals 'in every town and in many villages ... with a kist or shelf full of Radical books, biding their time, putting in a word at the tavern, the chapel, the smithy, the shoemaker's shop, waiting for the movement to revive'.[1] At first, this claim lay untested. Indeed, in his review of *Captain Swing*, Thompson took Hobsbawm and Rudé to task for ignoring, as he saw it, clear evidence of radical agitation – that is, politicking to extend the vote to a wider constituency – in the mobilisation. There was, he reasserted, a 'radical nucleus in every county, in the smallest market towns and even in the larger rural villages'. Hobsbawm and Rudé responded to this criticism in the revised 1973 edition of *Captain Swing*, detailing several cases of radical influence and expression, but this was little more than tokenism, the role of radical politics not being explored systematically. Nor did their revisions consider the roots of rural radicalism or the routes of radical transmission.[2]

For the period before 1830, there are no systematic stand-alone stud-ies of popular radicalism that focus solely on the countryside. However, through the work of several historians, notably Roger Wells, Ian Dyck, Malcolm Chase, and most recently Katrina Navickas, our understanding of rural radicalism has been greatly enriched.[3] Before thinking through these implications, it is worth remembering Linda Colley's assertion that only from the 1760s was a serious challenge made to the political domi-nance of the landed elites. Before this period of political crisis, pleas to popular challenges to elite politics were invariably made by dissidents from the very sphere they critiqued.[4] Colley's claim, however, does not stand up to scrutiny.

Beyond the dramatic, but not strictly speaking rural, risings of 1715 and 1745, opposition to the combined rule of the Whigs and House of Hanover found rural voice in the form of Jacobitism. As Paul Monod has revealed, many public celebrations and other forms of popular protest occasioned displays of Jacobitism, even before 1715. The coronation of George II in October 1714 was marked by significant anti-Hanoverian, anti-Whig and pro-Tory, Stuart unrest throughout the country. For instance, at Frome in Somerset, the rioters 'dressed up an Idiot, called *George*, in a Fool's Coat, saying, Here's our *George*, where's –'. Stuart birthdays – or opposition to the marking of Hanoverian birthdays – could provoke bonfires and the ringing of church bells, such as occurred at Hambledon in east Hampshire, on 10 June 1723, when 'poor, trick-ling, shuffling' churchwarden Collins 'suffered the bells to be rung both morning and evening' to mark the Pretender's birthday.[5] Elsewhere, in the Midlands and South-West, birthdays and other significant dates on the political calendar were often marked by, as Jonathan Oates puts it, 'Jacobite disturbances'. However, the wave of riots in northern towns in 1714 and 1715 that precipitated the passing of the Riot Act in 1715 might have deployed, to use Paul Monod's phrase, Jacobite rhetoric and symbolism, but the outbreak was only marked by one demonstration of popular Jacobitism, this being at Chester in opposition to celebrations marking the first anniversary of George I's coronation. Instead, popular opposition to dissenters rather than support for the Stuarts was the uni-versal driver of protest.[6]

Even after the rebellion of 1745 (the '45'), many families, even districts, because of the influence of powerful landlords, remained, as Daniel Szechi has suggested, 'obstinately Jacobite from generation to genera-tion'.[7] The geography of Jacobite disaffection shifted, though. By 1750, as Nicholas Rogers has recently stated, it was concentrated where Whig–Tory rivalry was 'still intense and sectarian animosity sharp', especially in parts of the Midlands and the north.[8] But popular expressions of Jacobitism faded, and relatively few such cases are recorded in the rural archive. At Nuneaton and Tamworth, for instance, in 1756 when food rioters refused to disperse 'til the Pretender came to stop them', or a year later in rural Kent where two men were arrested on a charge of 'drinking the health of the Pretender & his son Charles, cursing the King & the Royal Family' and 'wishing them back to Hanover'.[9] Before 1715, between 1715 and 1745, and after 1745, Jacobite plotting and organising and the public performances of Stuart support were not confined to Scotland and Ireland or the border counties of England. Rather, they were manifest everywhere, northern industrialising town and southern village alike. This then was, as Rogers has claimed, 'a protean phenomena', something that assumed different aspects and popular hues from place to place.[10]

The impact of the Wilkes movement in the late 1760s and the emergent reform movement from 1779 on the countryside remain largely obscure, but we do know the phenomenon was not exclusively a London affair. Indeed, the creation of reform 'associations' from 1779 actually had non-metropolitan roots, starting in Yorkshire before being imitated in London and then throughout the country.[11] This wave of popular radicalism did not suddenly materialise. Rather, it represented the flowering of a vigorous, persistent, but often hidden popular radicalism, both in the form of Jacobitism, a broader muscular resistance to Whig oligarchy, as well as the participatory radicalism that Wilkes espoused. Indeed, the early chapters of Rogers' *Crowds, Culture and Politics in Georgian Britain* are replete with examples that pertain to the depth of popular radicalism before the 1770s. Such 'radical' expressions found voice almost invariably, or at least as recorded in the archive, in the context of other protests: not least food riots and opposition to impressment and enlistment in the militia.[12] Notwithstanding Rogers' vital corrective, it is important to note that popular radicalism in the English *countryside* before the 1790s awaits its historian.

The Emergence of a Mass Platform: From Tom Paine to William Cobbett

It is the outbreak of war with revolutionary France in 1793 that marks the starting point of many studies of popular radicalism, the influence of events in France and the socio-economic pressures created by militarisation acting as a spur to English 'Jacobinism' as well as more 'moderate' political reformers. According to Wells, the 'insurrectionary' movement of the 1790s (and revival in the early 1800s), while primarily a product of the cities, found both voice and support in the countryside. This was not only the case in the semi-urban, semi-rural mill 'towns' – though notably in places like Lancashire and the West Riding of Yorkshire meetings of nascent democratic organisations were often held in woodland, on common land and on the moors[13] – but also in such ostensibly rural places as in Christchurch (Hampshire) and Witney (Oxfordshire). By way of example, at the former place John Cantelo publicly exclaimed his support for the mutineers at the Nore as 'Men of Spirit' whose 'Eyes were open ... that was the way to shake off the arbitrary Government', while watchmaker John Emblin, arrested for his involvement in the Despard Conspiracy to assassinate George III, was from the latter place.[14] Arguably more notorious were those in the provinces with links to the London Corresponding Society (hereafter LCS). At Chichester a 'three penny club which discusses different subjects' and by 1795 had 'struck into the path of the London Corresponding Society' was active in local politicking, despite attempts by the local magistrates to put their meetings down. In April 1795 the self-styled 'Friendly Society' were thought to be involved in circulating 'inflammatory hand bills' through the town and neighbouring villages calling on the people to assemble 'to lower the price of provisions'. Two years later a local soapmaker received, again presumed to be from the LCS, a 'large parcel of inflammatory handbills tending to excite Mutiny among the Soldiers'.[15]

Evidence for the operation of such groups as the LCS and the United Englishmen – inspired by the loosely affiliated anti-sectarian and pro-reform United Irishmen – is gathered via an archive that necessarily rests on evidence gathered by spies, informants and those who turned King's Evidence against their former comrades. It is, therefore, slight and partial. More emphatic evidence of the penetration of popular politics in the 1790s comes from the extraordinary sales of Tom Paine's *The Rights of Man*, the second and more controversial part being published in the spring of 1792. Taking both parts together, and including abridged versions, it sold some 200,000 copies, equivalent to one in every 25 adults purchasing a copy. While this in itself did not directly correspond to a politicisation of rural workers, the government proclamation against 'seditious writings' attested to the fears of the landed elites. Outlawed in December 1792, Paine left the country for the last time, but to loyalists he remained the 'great national enemy'. In this, to quote Frank O'Gorman, 'apocalyptic climate of fear', attempts to stir up anti-Paine feeling found expression in the burning of his books and effigies.[16] But such loyalist spectacles could backfire. At Shipley, Sussex, the parish clerk publicly defended Paine's ideas, while in a small village near Devizes a fiddler refused to play 'God Save the King' at one of the staged effigy burnings.[17] This was no passing phase, though. In 1794 labourer

John Thatcher of Sandhurst in Kent provocatively signed a threatening letter to the 'Gentleman and farmers' of the parish 'Thomas Paine'.[18] As Gwyn Williams put it, 'hundreds of statements' testify to *The Rights of Man*'s 'penetration into every hidden corner of society'.[19]

Critically, Paine's language of rights struck a ready chord with the many rural workers who had little truck with revolution and regicide, but through their grinding poverty and the often grinding attitude of farmers and parish officers found common cause with the sentiments, if not the direct political prescriptions, of radicals. Thus an anonymous letter posted on the market house at Odiham, Hampshire, in March 1800 threatening to fire the farmers' property also alluded to mysterious backers who wanted to see 'the poor righted'. As Wells notes, 'poachers, pseudonymists and incendiaries certainly did not envisage any major structural changes in society'; 'incendiarism', he continued '[was] not synonymous with political "radicalism"' but incendiaries did 'articulate ... sentiments pertinent to class war'.[20] This coming together of political language and popular protest played out most obviously in the food crises of the 1790s and early 1800s. 'Ordinary inhabitants', claims Navickas, had recourse to both the moral economy 'tradition' and 'the radical language [which] was utilized from an extensive lexicon'.[21] Beyond the fact that dearth provided fertile conditions for radical politicking – one notice posted up at Lewes in June 1795 calling on the populace to 'to save thy native land for see your Comrades murder'd, ye with Resentment Swell and join the Rage ... To down with George and Pitt, and England call to Arms'[22] – this moral economic–radical hybrid was typically expressed with less campaigning zeal. Indeed, it took many forms and expressions from the somewhat diffuse 'rights' rhetoric of the Odiham threatening letter, through attacks on forces of volunteers and yeomanry sent to put down food riots, through to invocations of secret societies and unions. As a threatening letter sent to a Rye farmer in February 1801 put it:

> we have agreed in 5 parishes we mean to have provisions cheaper or Rescue our lives Sir we have no ill against you only your being Captaing over these men that are kept under arms to keep people in Rougery and Slavery all the Days of our Lives we are Led up by popery and oprestion the same as France was before the war begun.[23]

The repression of radicalism forced the movement underground. There was some revival from 1807, the death of Pitt the Younger robbing Westminster politics of its recent stability, ensuing general elections of November 1806 and May 1807 therefore offering radicals 'new opportunities for action'. Moreover, in contrast to the relative secrecy of the

1790s, radicals now adopted a different strategy, using 'patriotism to gain the moral high ground', organising mass petitions for peace and then against corruption in what Peter Spence has labelled the revival of 'romantic patriotic radicalism.[24] This move was supported by open meetings: one organised by the long-established radical 'circle' at the Lancashire village of Royton held on Oldham Edge on Christmas Day 1807 drew a thousand people, the eventual petition containing 13,000 signatures – well over a quarter of the local population. Sir Francis Burdett's reform campaigning from 1810 appears, however, to have had little impact on the countryside, perhaps a reflection of the fact that it was stronger in and around London than in the northern heartlands of radicalism, where new local radical leaders emerged out of the particular regional context.[25]

After the peace, organised plebeian radicalism flourished through Hampden Clubs and Union Clubs, though, again, neither appears to have had much traction in the countryside outside of those small-scale industrial communities of Lancashire and Yorkshire with 'dense and stable social networks'.[26] Prone to schism, the battle between the ultra-radical followers of Thomas Spence, who believed in the abolition of private property, and the 'constitutional' approach of Burdett and Cobbett, acted to limit its influence. The Spencean message of land reform was obviously well geared to appeal to that majority of rural workers who had no access to land, but, again, there is little evidence that it was the major driver of the most dramatic radical episodes in the late 1810s.[27] Rather, the so-called 'March of the Blanketeers' in March 1817 and the huge gathering at St Peter's Field, Manchester on 16 August 1819 that ended in the death of 15 weavers on the charge of the yeomanry – better known as the Peterloo Massacre – were mobilised in response to the dire conditions in the cloth trade. The 'blanketeers', mainly spinners and weavers from the small communities in and around Lancashire, and those gathered at 'Peterloo', saw reform and parliamentary enfranchisement as the solution to their hunger and poverty rather than access to land. While the Spencean William Benbow had clearly inspired the March of the Blanketeers, the revolutionary fervour of Spenceanism, albeit without an explicit attachment to radical agrarianism, was most evident in the Pentrich Rising of stockingers from the eponymous Nottinghamshire village in June 1817. Ostensibly similar to the March of the Blanketeers in that the plan was to march on London, the aims of the Pentrich men were different in that they attempted to effect revolution rather than beg for reform. Whatever the influences, aims and strategies, rural workers were central to all three episodes – and all three episodes were brutally put down by military might. Arguably of even greater impact than the terror generated by unleashing the full force of the military was the judicial response: the passing of the so-called 'Six Acts' in late 1819 offering explicit sanction to put down 'seditious meetings', arrest those 'drilling', search for and seize arms, and sentence to transportation those guilty of seditious libel. 'The immediate consequence of the events of late 1819 and early 1820,' as Malcolm Chase has put it, 'was that radicalism somewhat withdrew in on itself.' Beyond a few poorly attended drills on the Yorkshire moors in the spring of 1820, and the open radical agitation in support of Queen Caroline against King George's attempt to divorce her, it is perhaps no coincidence that the passing of the Six Acts coincided with what Wright has labelled 'the decline of mass radicalism' in the 1820s.[28]

In some senses, though, the mass agitation of the late 1810s was only ever a feature of the Luddite districts. Elsewhere, political radicalism found a different voice. As the agrarian depression took hold, calls for parliamentary reform were increasingly made by a far wider rural constituency than before. High taxes to service government debts generated by the huge expense of the war effort were grievance enough among members of the middle classes, farmers and poor consumers – the notorious malt tax being a particular *bête noir* – but the huge cost of pensions and continued government sinecures also generated deep resentment. Between 1817 and 1830, hundreds of petitions praying for relief 'flooded to parliament and ministers', their rejection or their being ignored only, as Wells notes, 'galvanis[ing] fiercer representations'.[29] While not all speakers at the many county and borough meetings lamenting their shared distress called for political reform, this 'legitimate' platform did provide an opportunity to espouse radical views.[30] For instance, in March 1823, the Petersfield Farmers' Club met to propose that all agricultural societies should co-operate to campaign for reform as the government had made it clear that agriculture did not need relief. 'Nothing,' so the advert they placed in the *Hampshire Telegraph* proclaimed, 'but an effectual Reform in the Commons House of Parliament can be of any real utility either to the Agricultural Interests, or to those of any other class of society.'[31]

The voice for this rural constituency was William Cobbett, whose lecture tours, journalism and other acts of campaigning were fundamental in creating a link between the metropolitan and industrial radicalism and agrarian society, while at the same time as espousing a distinctive rural radical platform.[32] Cobbett's message was aimed not just at that symbol of 'earthy virtues', the decayed yeoman[33] – and as a farmer's son and a one-time farmer himself he purported to *know* farmers' interests – but also at rural workers, a constituency Cobbett called *his* 'Chopsticks'.

'There is no man', claimed Cobbett, 'who knows the English labourers so well as I do. I not only know all their wants, but their dispositions, their tempers.'[34] His *Weekly Political Register* was thus hawked about the countryside by pedlars finding a ready audience among smaller farmers, journeymen and artisans. Newspaper duties, though, meant the cover price of his *Register* by the start of 1830 was seven pence – out of reach of all but the best-off field workers. His response was to launch a shortened version called the *Two-Penny Trash*. Subtitled *Politics for Working People*, 'the main object' was 'to show the working people *what are the causes* of their being poor'.[35] While it is impossible to judge just how widespread his audience was – his publications being shared and read aloud in tap rooms and workshops – Cobbett believed his reach was absolute: 'There is not one single village, however recluse, in England, where my name is not known as the friend of the working people, and particularly of the farming labourers, and if ever man deserved any thing, I deserve this character.'[36]

Others agreed. Cobbett was tried for seditious libel in his *Political Register* of 11 December 1830, the motivation being the government belief that his newspapers had a 'prodigious effect' on the rural poor.[37] Many of the rulers of rural England also thought his effect profound. When in 1832 the Poor Law Commission undertook their survey of the state of rural England, in offering explanations as to the cause of Swing, respondents were often quick to invoke Cobbett's influence.[38] And so in Swing's archive we find – though perhaps in part a reflection of government paranoia about Cobbett – frequent references to activists being avid readers of his works or having attended his 1830 lecture tour. Certainly, as the previous chapter showed, evidence of radical agitation and actual influence on the protests is not hard to find.[39] In the critical Swing centres of Maidstone, Battle and the Dever Valley, all central to diffusing the protests into 'new' areas, radical beliefs underpinned mobilisations. Yet to call Swing a political movement would be unwise. It would be to ascribe a political agency to the vast majority of Swing protestors who may have been familiar with Cobbett's name, may have understood the arguments for parliamentary reform, may even have had feelings of solidarity with the poor French revolutionaries, but whose involvement in the protests was ultimately underpinned by a simple desire to be better treated. Similarly, to claim that Swing was pre-political, or even apolitical, is unhelpful. It is to deny what we might usefully call a shared 'instrumental' politics of everyday parish life, which informed Swing's claims and discourses and, critically, that rural workers readily made the link between this instrumental politics and arguments for their involvement in participatory politics.[40]

Political Unions and Trades Unionism

While Swing itself was the most emphatic evidence that by 1830 the cosmos of many rural workers was already political, it, as noted, acted to further politicise rural workers. The flurry of reform meetings and petitioning came not just from the cities and county towns but also from the smallest market towns and largest villages in support of the first Reform Bill in March 1831, and then again in late September and early October when the second Reform Bill was before the House of Lords. Indicative of the depth of support for reform among rural workers was the £20 subscription raised by the 'friends of radical reform' to support the expenses of getting Henry Hunt elected to the seat of Preston in the 1830 general election.[41] The first bill had been approved by the House of Lords but was held up in the final committee stages. Prime Minister Earl Grey duly dissolved his pro-reform administration, notwithstanding the reluctance of William IV to sanction the move, so that the people, or rather the enfranchised few, could decide the matter. The campaign was fought almost solely on the issue of reform and resulted in a substantial majority for Grey's Whigs and a second Reform Bill. The rejection of this second bill by the Lords on 8 October, with all but one of the Bishops voting against the measure, led to a series of urban riots, initially in Derby and Nottingham and elsewhere in the East Midlands before, explosively, in Bristol and the South-West.[42]

Most, including a series of riots in the small market towns in south Somerset and Dorset, were readily suppressed by military interventions. Notoriously, the circumstances at Bristol were very different. An attempt by a force of dragoons to put down a protest against the anti-reform Recorder of the city prompted a fierce attack by those assembled, the protests unfurling into a three-day riot. While it is unknown how many people were killed during the riots, as many people are believed to have perished in the numerous fires, it is clear that it eclipsed even the Peterloo Massacre for bloodiness, at least 100 people being killed or dangerously wounded in fighting on the second day alone.[43] Quite what the role of rural workers was in the Bristol riots awaits systematic study, though an analysis of those arrested for their role in the riots in Dorset shows that labourers *were* involved.[44] Auto-reflexively, one might claim that such involvement simply mirrored the established practice of election candidates hiring 'mobs' to physically and verbally harangue their opponents,[45] but it ignores the fact that these 'reform riots' were the autonomous acts of working people.

A third Reform Bill finally received royal assent on 7 June 1832, the perceived threat of revolution during the so-called 'Days of May' while the bill was in the House of Lords coming to nothing beyond feverish politicking. Infamously, the Birmingham Political Union was reckoned to be the greatest threat to political order, but, again, support for the bill also came from many villages. For instance, the pro-reform *Kent Herald* reported that in the Swing centres of Barham, Elham and Wingham, 'Reform Unions' had been founded and meetings held in support of the third bill, while at Ash-next-Sandwich the 'inhabitants' had even paraded the streets 'with a band of music'.[46] This wave of rural working support for reform transferred to euphoria at the bill's passing and assent, though almost invariably in the countryside celebrations were staged-managed affairs, local elites using the opportunity to inculcate loyalism by revivifying paternalist principles through spectacle. Thus at Wickham in south Hampshire, landlord W. Garnier, Esq. put on a 'substantial fare of roast beef, plum puddings, [and] other viands', the evening spent in 'dancing and in other rural diversions'. Even Cobbett adopted this model of 'old hospitality', his 'Chopsticks' Festival' being held symbolically at Sutton Scotney in July 1832 to 'celebrate the fall of the villainous boroughmongers'. Cobbett's festival, though, being part of a wider tour of market towns, was more than symbolic, the purpose being to remind those who politicked for reform that the bill would be 'a bundle of waste paper' unless the opportunity was taken to campaign for further change. His purpose was therefore to campaign for 'a *common understanding* amongst the people, with regard to *what measures ought to be adopted by the reformed Parliament*'.[47]

The message was certainly heeded. Locally, the political unions founded in the Dever Valley to the north of Winchester were active in campaigning during the 1832 general election – parliament having been dissolved so that the newly enfranchised could vote and that the disbanded rotten boroughs were no longer represented – to get Henry Hunt's son elected in place of popularly despised local grandee Bingham Baring.[48] By the time of the passing of the third Reform Bill political unions had been, as noted in the previous section, established in many rural locations. Indeed, as early as November 1831 the Worcester press could comment that political unions were 'forming in all parts of the Kingdom', though this was perhaps more evident in the West Midlands than elsewhere, unions then forming at Ludlow and Redditch.[49] In Hampshire, such was their penetration that, according to the rural informants of Lord Lieutenant the Duke of Wellington, half of all Hampshire field workers were believed to be involved 'in the clubs' and the farmers 'a good deal alarmed' by the latent possibilities of such large assemblages of labourers.[50]

Ultimately, rural political unions collapsed by the summer of 1833, in part because of the use of repressive tactics and pressure applied by employers. At Salisbury, for instance, a political union was thwarted when all 'Masters' resolved not to employ its members.[51] Perhaps more significant, though, were the declining fortunes of urban political unions, though these did live on into 1834, and the massive sense of disappointment that the first 'reformed' House of Commons had proved a poor friend to rural workers. Parliament had remained dominated by aristocrats and the landed elites that were setting about a series of reforms that seemed to those without the vote, as John Belchem has put it, that 'the state, having shed its old inefficiency and corruption, was taking on the form of an interventionist and exploitative dictatorship.[52] But before the most notorious of these reforms was passed, the Poor Law Amendment Act, or as it was popularly known the 'Poor Man's Robbery' Act, there is evidence that agricultural workers were engaged in trades union activism. Before considering the totemic example of Tolpuddle, it is necessary to analyse briefly the 'pre-history' of forms of trades unionism among rural workers.

As Hamish Fraser has suggested, there were very few later features of trades unionism that were not present in the eighteenth century, trades unions emerging not out of the factory system but among artisans, tailors, building workers and weavers operating in small workshops or their own homes. For much of the eighteenth century, though, attempts to improve pay and/or conditions of employment were focused on pre-existing organisations such as guilds or journeymen's associations rather than formal trades unions. Still, we do well to remember that C.R. Dobson delineated at least 383 organisations *forged* in specific disputes over pay and conditions between 1717 and 1800. From the final third of the century, government attempts to deregulate trades, a move partly predicated by lobbying from employers and partly as an ideological attachment to the principles of political economy, brought workers and their masters increasingly into conflict. Recurrent subsistence crises combined with tightening labour markets post- 1793 further heightened this tension, parliament legislating against labour combinations in specific trades until they passed the notorious General Combination Acts of 1799 and 1800.[53]

While industrial conflicts were a feature of urban life, acts of combination in the eighteenth century were not confined to the large towns and cities. The often rural location of workshops, mills and mines all in turn connected through mobile tramping journeymen, meant that any urban trades disputes were quickly manifested in the countryside too – and vice versa. Critically, rural acts of combination were not confined to the industrial and mining trades. C.R. Dobson records combinations of harvest workers at Ely (Cambridgeshire) and King's Langley (Hertfordshire) in 1761, and recurrent harvest-time strikes in Middlesex in the 1760s and 1770s. Similarly, the employment of Irish agricultural labourers led to strike action at Dartford in north Kent and over the Thames Estuary in Essex in 1736, and in Middlesex in 1774.[54] As noted in Chapter 5, during the 1790s and early 1800s subsistence crises, agricultural workers throughout the cornland counties of the south and east, from Lincolnshire in the north to Wiltshire in the west, used the tactic of the strike in attempts to force wages higher. Many of these temporary combinations were more akin to 'traditional' forms of collective bargaining by riot; for instance, at Wilcot in the Vale of Pewsey in the spring of 1790 the labourers gathered by the sound of a horn and threatened 'destruction' unless their demand for 9s a week was agreed to. Some instances, though, demonstrated a more-than-parochial ambition in organising. In 1793 Isaac Seer earned the reputation as the first known farmworkers' leader for his efforts in spreading a strike in rural Essex, something that was repeated again in 1800. Similarly in Norfolk, field workers united under the banner of 'the Labourer is worthy of his hire' in a county-wide organisation.[55]

While there were many strikes and industrial disputes in the towns and among weavers and miners during the post-Napoleonic depression, forms of proto-trades unionism among farmworkers were few. According to Wells, 'The scale of unemployment, and continued magisterial hostility to any form of rural combination ... ensured that farmworkers were prevented from adopting a unionist response.' By and large this was true, not even the repeal of the Combination Acts in 1824 acted as any great encouragement to field workers, quite in contrast to tradespeople such as brick layers, tailors, paper-makers, flax combers, lace makers, shipwrights, shoemakers, sawyers, and others, who all went on strike in the late 1820s.[56] As Chapter 6 detailed, though, collective protests over wages were an important factor in the East Anglian protests of 1816 and 1822, while a group of labourers were sentenced to between 12 and 18 months in gaol for their part in a 'confederacy to raise and set wages throughout [Romney] Marsh' in the summer of 1821.[57] Indeed, given the centrality of collectively meditated wage disputes to Swing, the knowledge of how to combine and throw off work in pursuit of higher wages was held within many agrarian communities.

Attempts to *maintain* wage increases won during the heat of Swing also frequently took the form of labourers' strikes – or planned strikes. Some, such as that focused on the east Sussex Swing centre of Battle, represented extensive plans to affect increases in wages. 'Many parishes in this part', grandee Sir Godfrey Webster informed the Home Office, 'communicate with each other by means of Delegates, and are determined upon a compulsory increase of wage[s]'. This attempt at organising continued into the summer of 1831, when it was reported that labouring societies had formed across the Kent–Sussex border, their meetings providing opportunities for labourers from different parishes to liaise.[58] Elsewhere in the southern cornlands there is evidence to suggest that there was some connection between political unions and trades unionism. An attempt by farmer Allec of Somborne in west Hampshire to cut his labourers' wages in November 1832 was resisted, the men stating that 'The Union' had directed them to accept no less than 10 shillings and would 'support' them. The 'Union' in question was a local political union rather than a bona fide trades union, but in many ways this is a false distinction for it was clearly assuming the role and functions of a trades union, members' weekly penny subscription supporting striking workers 'to keep up a certain rate of wages'.[59]

None of this is to claim that the countryside witnessed anything like the huge rise in trades unionism evident in the towns in the early 1830s. Nor is it to claim that in districts where the vast majority of employment was in agriculture and related trades did trades unionism penetrate popular consciousness in the way in which it did among, say, the miners of the Northumberland coalfield or the shoemakers in the villages around Northampton. Rather, it is important to assert that unionist principles and the language of trades unionism increasingly extended to farmworkers. The formation of the short-lived Grand National Consolidated Trades Union (GNCTU) in February 1834 marked a decisive turning point in that it not only brought together several pre-existing trades unions and attempted to expand the envelope of unionism – something also true of Robert Owen's October 1833 GNCTU precursor – but also actively attempted to 'get up a Union among the agricultural labourers'.[60] In this context, labourer and Methodist preacher George Loveless's formation of the Friendly Society of Agricultural Labourers at Tolpuddle in response to employers cutting wages from 7s a week to 6s a week in late 1833 can be better understood.[61] Indeed, the famous events at Tolpuddle were neither entirely exceptional nor unpredictable. It is, however, important to consider briefly the precise genesis of events in and around that part of south Dorset.

Topuddle had been central to local mobilisations during Swing; indeed to the first indigenous Swing mobilisation in the county. On 25 November labourers in the parish refused to work, and if by the end of the day all was supposedly quiet in the Bere Valley, there was the belief that further manifestations of protest in Tolpuddle 'should make others discontented'. There also appeared to be a radical element to Swing in the Bere Valley. A 'letter' addressed to 'the Labouring Inhabitants of Tolpuddle' and found by Squire Frampton in the village proclaimed:

> Whereas the Deputy for the National Civil Liberty have learnt that letters of an inflammatory and Destructive nature have been picked up in your streets in consequence of extortion, oppression and deprecating men's labour. Do here advise that no hasty attempts be made. First let one and all apply to their Masters or Employers to advance their wages and in consequence of a refusal Help shall be obtained from the loyal and obedient subjects of W.B.R. on this rock.[62]

A member of the Loveless family was also arrested – and subsequently escaped – for being involved in a Swing mobilisation. George Loveless, in his own words, became a spokesman for local labourers during wage negotiations in 1831–2 when 'there was a general movement of the working classes for an increase in wages'. His brother John was a flaxdresser in Bridport in west Dorset, the flax workers in that town having gone on strike in January 1826, while a flax-comber was found guilty of firing a flax shop in February 1833. Through John and a further brother called Robert who lived in London, George was in touch with several individuals soon to be involved in founding the GNCTU.[63] We also know that emissaries from London trades union organisations were active in the West country in the winter of 1833–4. In Devon, for instance, 'delegates' from London were administering oaths in symbolic ceremonies, meetings occurring at Tiverton and Horsebridge near Tavistock, while that at Exeter led to the arrest of 40 men. Clearly, authorities in the countryside were alert to trades union activity. Moreover, the issuing of oaths, as occurred for those who joined Loveless' Society at Tolpuddle, had a recent precedent.[64] The GNCTU were active elsewhere too: labourers reportedly 'flocked' into Brighton in the spring of 1834 to join the GNCTU.[65]

The formation of 'Societies' was not confined to Tolpuddle. Rather, as the Dorset Bench related to the Home Office in January 1834, 'Societies are forming ... in parts of the Dorchester and Wareham divisions, with known activities centred upon Tolpuddle in the former and Bere Regis in the latter.' So much appeared to be little different in scope and scale compared to other recent attempts to organise. Documents in the Earl of Ilchester's papers at the Dorset History Centre suggest, however, that attempts to spread the Society extended further than the bounds between the Dorchester and Wareham divisions, including attempts to encourage the agricultural workers of Mappowder and Hazelbury Bryan to join, these parishes being over 10 miles to the north of Tolpuddle and on the fringe of the Blackmore Vale.[66]

Two aspects were altogether novel. Through George Loveless's London contacts, two delegates of the emergent GNCTU travelled from London to Tolpuddle to address a meeting of some 40 labourers – at least one of whom was from Bere Regis – the delegates reading out a set of general union laws, regulations and rules. Then on 8 December 1833 the initial members were initiated into the new Society.[67] The other novel aspect was the tenacity and severity of the judicial response. The aforementioned James Frampton, landowner, head of the local yeomanry and active magistrate, having co-ordinated the response to Swing in central and southern Dorset, again took it upon himself to lead the judicial response to these nascent acts of agrarian trades unionism. Gaining Home Office support for his placing 'spies' in the Tolpuddle Society, Frampton's further suggestion that the unionists be prosecuted under the 1797 Mutiny Act, which allowed for the prosecution of administering illegal oaths, was initially met with the response that it was 'quite unnecessary'. Still, on 22 February, Frampton had handbills made up and posted round the countryside warning rural workers of the illegality of oath-taking on penalty of seven years' transportation. The societies having now been active for several months, the handbills had little chance of making any impact, for at dawn on Monday 24 February Frampton unilaterally decided to arrest the Tolpuddle leaders. Two of those arrested – Edward Legg and John Lock, both in attendance at the first initiation – cracked on questioning and gave sworn evidence detailing the act of oath-taking. Mindful that mass union activity in the countryside could prove a threat to the implementation of the Poor Law Amendment Act, Home Secretary Melbourne came round to Frampton's perspective. On seeing the written evidence, Melbourne eventually agreed to support the prosecution of six of the unionists, if not Frampton's request for an official proclamation offering rewards for evidence of union activity, in fear of encouraging others elsewhere to found societies.

What followed is so well-known as to have assumed an almost mantra-like status for trades unionists. At the Dorset Assizes held in Dorchester the six men were tried on 17 March and found guilty of administering illegal oaths, the maximum sentence as detailed on Frampton's handbill being passed by Judge Baron Williams two days later. The sentences were quickly seized upon by the GNCTU as evidence of a government-sponsored attempt to put down all trades unions, and was widely condemned by large sections of the press, even including the influential but anti-trades union *Times*. In this heady atmosphere, petitions complaining against the severity of the sentence were promptly got up, subscriptions for the support of their families raised, and several protest meetings held in London and Manchester. The first petitions were presented to parliament on 26 March, the day parliament went into the Easter recess. On its reassembling on 14 April, petitions, in the words of Joyce Marlow, 'started to pour in', Daniel O'Connell and the several other radical MPs 'stoutly' supporting the cause. Rebutted by the government, on 11 April prisoners James Loveless, John and Thomas Standfield, James Brine and James Hammett set sail on board the Surrey convict ship to Australia; George Loveless, being unwell, remained in England until the end of May. This did not stop further demonstrations, though, a reflection of trades unions wishing to publicly proclaim their continued defiance in the face of government hostility. On 21 April a 'mass demonstration' of the Metropolitan Trades Unions was planned to gather on Copenhagen Fields, a long-established meeting place of radicals, which would then march to the Home Office, over Westminster Bridge and then to an open space near Bethlem Hospital. A deputation of the Central Union Committee would also deliver a 'monster petition' containing 300,000 signatures to Melbourne at the Home Office. And so it passed off, *The Times* calculating that 35,000 individuals took part, the procession lasting two-and-a-half hours, while estimates of 200,000 others lined the streets to watch. The petition was received by Melbourne and the matter debated in both the Commons and the Lords on 28 April, petitions also being presented from Newcastle, Belfast and Scotland, but the ensuing debate failed to mention the petitions.[68]

Campaigning carried on rather more quietly and discreetly until Thomas Wakley, surgeon, founder of *The Lancet* and radical MP for Finsbury from April 1835, on 27 May 1835 detailed the plight of the martyrs' families and announced that he was to put forward a motion for a full debate on the matter on 25 June. By that date, Lord John Russell, the new Home Secretary, had already decided that the Tolpuddle men had been treated harshly and would grant a pardon on condition that all but the Loveless brothers would remain in Australia until they had been there two years, they having to remain in exile. Rather than back down, though, Wakley continued with his scheduled motion and pleaded that all six men be allowed home. Initially unsuccessful, ultimately further campaigning and petitioning won out. On 20 January 1837, George Loveless left Hobart for England, Brine, the Standfields and James Loveless following on 11 September; Hammett was left stranded in Windsor on a charge of assault. George arrived back to London on 13 June, and was welcomed by members of the campaigning London Dorchester Committee before returning as the victor to Tolpuddle where, funded by the Committee, he wrote an account of his travails.[69] Published that September, *The Victims of Whiggery* was to become a touchstone for

Chartists, its description of the labouring poor as 'England's white slaves' lighting up, to quote Marlow, 'Chartist meetings like fireworks'.[70] The others, Hammett excluded, docked at Plymouth on 16 March 1838 to a welcome from local trades unionists. Their official welcome was organised by the London Dorchester Committee and held on Kennington Common on 16 April, the triumphant procession that day symbolically reversing the route of the procession four years earlier.[71]

The arrest and trial of the Tolpuddle men was undoubtedly the pivotal moment in early nineteenth-century trades union history, but it did not mark the end of trades unionism among agricultural workers in the 1830s. Wage cutting in the autumn of 1834 led – as it had in 1831, 1832 and 1833 – to strikes in several counties. Wells has noted occurrences in Bedfordshire, Devon, Hertfordshire and Sussex, though this list is probably far from exhaustive, the lack of systematic studies of the Midland counties in all probability masking a more widespread resort to strikes among field workers. Either way, these were not single parish protests. Rather, as reports of the Sussex strikes detailed, 'it appeared as if the principles of the Trades' Unions was about being established'. Presumably with Frampton's example in mind, the authorities in Sussex were quick to react to a 'very large' meeting of labourers on 2 November on High Down Hill, Goring, a signal to those in other parishes to join them.[72]

Strikes among southern agricultural workers in late 1834 were carried out in the context not only of wage cuts but also attempts (as detailed in Chapter 1) to implement the *spirit* of the New Poor Law, in some places through issuing relief partly in kind, in others through withdrawing relief from those who refused to enter parish workhouses. And so it was that trades unionism and the tactic of the strike were used in protest against the lived reality of these new welfare regimes. The tactic also carried through into the wave of protests against the creation of the New Poor Law unions, most notably in a society known as the United Brothers of Industry that existed in south-east Sussex and the Romney Marsh of Kent in the spring and summer of 1835. Supported by major urban unions elsewhere – one meeting was organised 'to hear [the] opinion of the London, Manchester and Birmingham Unions on the "Poor Laws Amendment Act"' – and by the newly founded radical newspaper the *Brighton Patriot*, the United Brothers were initially founded in the area between Battle and Brede out of the experience of Swing and post-Swing proto-trades union activity. Rapidly expanding through founding branches in an area that spread as far west as Seaford – though a meeting was reported as having occurred at Pulborough, some 35 miles further west – and as far east as New Romney and Appledore, the United

Brothers reached the peak of their strength in early May before repressive measures diminished their effectiveness.[73]

The implementation of the New Poor Law also provoked strikes in Hampshire and Wiltshire in the autumn of 1835, with strikes also occurring in Norfolk the following year. It was in Essex in the summer of 1836, though, that the spirit of Tolpuddle and the United Brothers most obviously lived on, a self-styled 'Union Club' based at Thorp and operating in 23 parishes with a claimed 1,200 members in an attempt to secure £6 per month during the harvest and 4s a week for victuals, though rather than being the indigenous product of local labourers it was led by craftsmen, shopkeepers and beer-shop-keepers. Still, it appeared to gain some local traction but against the willingness of the farmers to engage labourers from neighbouring Suffolk, a lack of funds to support striking members and a judicial backlash – five labourers being tried at the Essex Summer Assizes – it was unlikely to fare better than its Dorset and Sussex counterparts. At the trial, the five members were acquitted on the charge of combination but found guilty of assault against Suffolk strike-breakers. This would be no Tolpuddle. Indeed, the trial did not deter further attempts at organising among the Essex field workers the following year.[74]

Chartism

The example of Tolpuddle usefully serves to remind us that protest was rarely reducible to actions alone. Rather, in the events leading to the arrest of the Dorset trades unionists we see the coming together of the written (and often printed) word, and a culture of speech-making and orality in helping to define and diffuse the concept of trades unionism. In many ways this was built upon a long-standing protest tradition that combined the spoken word as an organisational and motivational tool and the written word in the form of threatening letters, but in other ways the importance of oratory was something distinctive to political (or politically charged) protests. The absolute protest pinnacle of this coming together of the written and spoken word came in the form of Chartism, a social movement that was based on the potency of the written word in the form of the so-called 'People's Charter'. This document was conceived in the summer of 1837 by representatives of the London Working Men's Association (LWMA) and six radical members of parliament as a 'practicable step in favour of Radicalism'.[75] Containing six by now well-established radical demands – a vote for all men, secret ballots, no property qualification to stand for parliament, a wage for MPs, equal constituencies, and annual parliaments – the plan was to establish a more-than-London platform for reform behind the Charter. The campaign developed rapidly. On 21 May some 150,000 individuals gathered in Glasgow to hear speakers from the Birmingham Political Union (BPU), supported by two delegates from the LWMA, speak in favour of a single nation petition as opposed to many local ones. Several days later – the precise date is unclear – the Charter was published. These two landmark events combined with support from Feargus O'Connor, his *Northern Star* newspaper and his loose affiliation of pre-existing societies known as the Great Northern Union (GNU) quickly propagated support for the idea of one petition. By October, as Malcolm Chase has stated, the Charter was 'was beginning to be used as shorthand for a whole new political order', the terms 'Chartist' and 'Chartism' also rapidly gaining universal currency.[76]

As the Glasgow meeting suggests, even before the movement began to cohere in the autumn of 1838, the BPU, GNU and especially the LWMA were already actively supporting emissaries to spread the word. Not just to the towns and industrial districts often associated with Chartism, but also, as revisionist studies of Chartism have begun to demonstrate, to the market towns and villages of rural England.[77] Janette Martin's recent work on Chartist itinerancy has placed the 'oratory and the agency of the itinerant lecturer' at the very centre of the movement, the mobility of Chartist lectures combined with the theatre of the lecture allowing for the more immediate flow of information and ideas.[78] Crucially, itinerancy also connected town and country together in wider political networks. Henry Vincent of the LWMA, for instance, was stationed in Bath from May 1838, from where through his lectures he built support in the surrounding counties, and, with notable success, in South Wales. On the back of such 'missionary' work, during the summer and autumn of 1838 meetings were held throughout the country to discuss the Charter and also, at some meetings, to elect representatives to the proposed General Convention which would manage the national petition.[79] Many of these lectures and meetings, while targeted specifically at urban workers, occurred in the countryside, thus aping the time-honoured tactics of earlier Luddite and political agitation: the 'Manchester' meeting was held on Kersal Moor, that for the West Riding on Hartshead Moor, a small hamlet near Brighouse. Meetings were also held at places like the rural market town of Stratford-upon-Avon and at Trowle Common near Trowbridge, also potentially drawing on large surrounding rural populations.[80]

Beyond supposition, the archive explicitly relates that in Dorset agricultural workers were *directly* targeted by the national leadership. A renewed attempt at agrarian trades unionism in the villages between

Bridport, Shaftesbury and Wimborne in the summer of 1838 – George Loveless being one of the leaders – was supported by the LWMA with the intention of turning the 'very extensive' union into, in Wells' words, 'a populist, political organisation'. The extent to which the initial meetings of the labourers during August and a further meeting on 20 October were, as Colonel Wildman of the Dorset Yeomanry believed, 'excited by the mischievous people in London, Birmingham and other places for other purposes' is unclear beyond advice and encouragement given by the LWMA. What is certain, though, is that a further mass meeting held on 14 November at Charlton Down on the edge of Blandford Forum was attended by emissaries from several groups: the aforementioned Henry Vincent; Robert Hartwell, secretary to the Dorchester Labourers' Fund in London; and W.P. Roberts and Anthony Phillips of the Bath Working Man's Association. Prior to the meeting the area was flooded with handbills announcing the meeting and its purpose, to discuss '"The People's Charter", "Vote by Ballot", "Annual Parliaments"'. 'Several emissaries' from the LWMA had also been going 'round from village to village'. That only a quarter of the 5,000 or so attendees were agricultural workers is perhaps not too surprising given an orchestrated campaign by farmers threatening attendees with dismissal. Either way, the dominant theme debated was the low wages of farmworkers. Symbolically, Loveless was also elected to the putative General Convention.[81]

While by the end of 1838 Chartism had gained a foothold in all English counties barring Cornwall,[82] the Dorset mission's deliberate targeting of rural workers was in many ways exceptional. By way of contrast, Chartism in Essex and Suffolk was quickly established in major towns such as Ipswich and Colchester, but a 'hostile agricultural establishment in the market towns as well as dominant in the villages' meant Chartism failed to gain 'widespread and sustained support from farmworkers'.[83] In some senses, we should not be too surprised to find that where the movement was not nurtured by the national leadership or strong societies in provincial towns, it failed to truly flourish. In rural communities with established political cultures, it was more likely, however, that Chartism would take root. Among the knitting shops in rural Leicestershire and in the mill-working villages of the West Riding, for instance, a strong politically aware associational culture was already entrenched and better allowed for Chartism to establish than in more squarely agrarian districts. As Randall and Newman suggest of Wiltshire, it was among the weavers and tailors – an occupational group with a long history of activism – that Chartism took hold.[84] Even in areas without a well-developed popular political culture, the clarity of the Chartist message eased the work of national delegates. In west Cornwall, a county where the disciplining effects of Methodism had increasingly led to a political passivity, delegates Abram Duncan and Robert Lowery reported in 1839 that 'the People here have never heard Politics' but still they were successful in generating much interest in the Charter. Similarly at Sandbach in Cheshire and Leek in Staffordshire, the inhabitants, according to local activist and shoemaker John Richards, were 'fully Convinced that every thing was wrong and yet Ignorant of the means to cure the evil' but when explained that 'the privations of the Sons of Labour lay in want of the Franchise ... never have I witnessed more enthusiasm'. West Riding Chartist delegate and North Yorkshire native Peter Bussey was even able to stir up enthusiasm for the Charter in the chronically decaying hand-loom linen weaving communities of the Vale of York, a notoriously Tory domain.[85]

None of this is to say that the field workers were not interested in or receptive to Chartism. On the contrary, where evidence permits the archive does relate examples of field workers attending Chartist meetings and embracing the anti-New Poor Law analysis of Chartist speakers. In January 1839 the audience for Robert Hartwell of the LWMA, and publisher of the *Poor Man's Guardian* Henry Hetherington at Tonbridge (Kent) was made up of a 'large proportion of ... agricultural labourers'.[86] Chartists at Brighton and Lewes also found success in their mission to extend Chartism into the surrounding countryside, so much so that after successful public meetings in Southwick and Patcham in December 1838 farmers in the vicinity threatened to dismiss those who attended the meetings. This forced the Brighton and Lewes emissaries to change tack, holding their rural meetings furtively in the early months of 1839 as they ventured further into rural Sussex. Tellingly, when Bronterre O'Brien, the official Chartist 'missionary to the Southern Counties' gave a lecture tour in March and April he included the village of Cuckfield on his itinerary.[87]

The combination of lock-outs, special constables and spies, as well as other tools of coercion effected by grandees, magistrates and farmers, perhaps made the possibility of mass labouring support improbable. Still, O'Brien and Marsden were exceptional as 'national' speakers in that they deliberately *attempted* to inculcate the support of agricultural workers. By contrast, Henry Vincent, on returning to the west in the early spring of 1839, confined his attentions to established Chartist centres and to textile and rural industrial communities, places such as the Wiltshire villages of Bromham and Holt.[88] Perhaps even more decisive was the turn to physical violence, first manifested through a series of Tory-orchestrated attacks on Chartist meetings at rural Devizes in March 1839, then through disturbances at the Welsh town of Llanidloes, and the arrest of Lancashire Chartists for armed drilling. Most notoriously, though, after the 'failures' of the first petition, notwithstanding its 1,280,959 signatures, and the damp squib of the 'sacred month' of co-ordinated strike action, the National Convention considered plotting a general rising.[89] Little is known about this, or how advanced such national plans were, but in South Wales, Tyneside and Yorkshire a plot *was* afoot. The latter places were to rise in tandem, with three separate marches from different parts of South Wales that were to take control of Abergavenny, Brecon and Newport. This plan was abandoned, but the Newport march went ahead on the evening of 3 November. The men who gathered – estimated at between 1,000 and 5,000, and mainly miners – were confronted by a force of infantrymen in the town and in the ensuing battle at least 22 Chartists were killed and 50 severely wounded. This was, then, the greatest number of fatalities in a civil disturbance in modern Britain. Over 200 Chartists were subsequently arrested and 21 were tried for High Treason, the three leaders – John Frost, Zephaniah Williams, and William Jones – being found guilty and sentenced to be hanged, drawn and quartered.

The massacre, and the judicial response, was the pivot on which Chartism inevitably turned. For while a mass petitioning campaign succeeded in convincing the government to commute Frost's, Williams' and Jones' sentences to life transportation, Chartism now had to confront new realities.[90] The reconvened General Convention agreed that a National Charter Association of Great Britain (NCA) should be formed and organised through urban branches.[91] In practice, then, notwithstanding O'Connor arguing that manhood suffrage needed to be mirrored by the Spencean ideal of restoring urban workers to the land through the provision of smallholdings,[92] Chartism now perceived itself to be an essentially urban movement. But while the 1842 national petition contained a much-reduced number of signatures from rural areas than the first petition, its rejection by the House of Commons on 3 May similarly provoked a response that *was* of the countryside. The general strike of the summer of 1842, aka the 'Plug Plot' riots, started in June 1842 among the colliers of north Staffordshire, before spreading to other mining and industrial communities, especially in West Yorkshire, Lancashire and Cheshire, lasting in many places until late August.[93]

Before Chartism's last grand hurrah in 1848, the movement went into something of an abeyance, falling back on its urban and largely industrial strongholds. The exception to this lack of vigour was the adoption of what was labelled as 'the Chartist Land Plan' by the thinly attended 1843 Convention. Through membership of the NCA individuals would be able to opt into the Land Plan, their subscription paying for the purchase of land and erection of buildings. While the scheme was targeted, as per O'Connor's earlier plan, at urban and industrial workers, for labourers and rural artisans, who were faced with the day-to-day reality that the land they worked on belonged to someone else, the ideal appealed too. Only about a quarter of the Land Plan register survives, but analysis of what remains shows rural workers did subscribe. For instance, within a 10-mile radius of Blandford, the initial Chartist centre and branch in Dorset, of the 132 subscribers over half were labourers. The numbers may be small but they still speak an essential truth.[94]

Indeed, initially the Plan was a huge success. It acted to reinvigorate Chartism, with new members joining and in some places even new branches forming. Some new branches were based in growing industrial centres; for instance, Swindon, then rapidly developing around the railway works, but some were defiantly agrarian. A 'land branch' was founded at small rural Exning in west Suffolk in late 1847, and this followed a wave of new branches established in small agrarian market towns such as Witham and the former textile centre of Halstead.[95] In March 1846 the first estate was purchased by the scheme: 103 acres at Heronsgate near Rickmansworth in Hertfordshire. The second estate quickly followed, Lowbands in Worcestershire opening in August 1847, while preparations at two further estates, Minster Lovell in Oxfordshire and Snigs End in Gloucestershire, were also under way.[96]

Growing strength led to growing confidence, represented both in an increasing internationalism in Chartist mentalities and a renewed effort to recruit in the countryside.[97] The vibrant Swindon NCA, for instance, held meetings in seven neighbouring villages during March 1847, while on 12 March 5,000 individuals attended a rally at Peep Green near Hartshead Moor organised by West Yorkshire Chartists. Growing confidence also led to the drafting of a third national petition.[98] The credibility of the claimed 5,700,000 signatures on the petition was quickly undermined, though, by a House of Common's Committee suggesting the total was at most 1,975,496 signatures. While these figures were probably equally spurious, the petition now, as Chase put it, 'hung round the neck of Chartism like the proverbial albatross'.[99] Initially, the movement maintained its momentum, some rural places, like Cirencester in south Gloucestershire, even being drawn back into Chartism for the first time since 1839, and others like Beverely and Driffield in East Yorkshire becoming new Chartist branches. The call for simultaneous meetings throughout the country on 12 June was determined to show this vitality. While this was not an attempt at a national rising, in London there was something approaching revolutionary intent in defiance of the government hurriedly banning mass meetings in the capital.[100] In this atmosphere of confusion and disappointment, Chartism fell away quickly. While at least in theory the NCA continued until 1860, this was effectively its end. A parliamentary investigation into the Land Plan in 1848 concluded that the scheme was illegal and besides would take at least 150 years to settle all the subscribers on Chartist estates. It was duly wound up by act of parliament in 1850, having ultimately only settled 234 families on its estates. Given Chartism's weak and fluctuating relationship with the countryside, it is therefore a deep irony that arguably its last 'success' was the election of Chartist candidate Samuel Carter to the rural Devon seat of Tavistock at the July 1852 general election.[101]

Conclusion

While the landscapes of large parts of rural England had changed
markedly since 1700, the protest landscape in many ways remained little
changed by 1851. The major forms of protest deployed by rural workers
in the early years of Victoria's reign would have been familiar to those
who tilled the land and worked in rural industries in the final years of
William III: the making of threats; riotous assembly; incendiarism; maiming; and the destruction of property. Indeed, the three major agrarian
rebellions of the early nineteenth century were arguably the most widespread resort to riot the countryside had witnessed since the Civil War.
It can even be asserted, albeit with less conviction, that the 'new' forms
of protest that rural workers were deploying with increasing confidence
from the 1830s – specifically radical politics and trades unionism – were
already present in the protest canon of 1700. Persistences, underpinned
by the defence of custom, the potency and transmission through time of
popular cultural forms, and the fundamentally unchanging nature of
grievances, were profound.

Yet such an account is to fail to appreciate the very real changes in
scale, spatiality and tone of rural protest in the period. Simply put, the
drastic deterioration in the fortunes of rural workers, and especially of
farm workers, from the middle of the eighteenth century, and reaching
crisis points between 1815 and 1837, and again from 1842, was mirrored
by an increasing resort to both overt and covert forms of protest. Nor
does it consider the ways in which the tools of rural terror so systematically deployed by the Waltham Blacks and outlined in the Black Act went
from being rarely practised in the late eighteenth century to being almost
endemic by the early 1830s. It also fails to appreciate that by the early
1830s at the latest, and arguably as early as the 1790s, much in the way of
collective rural protest was underwritten by radical political discourse,

'collective bargaining by riot' giving way, in part, to the demonstration and the meeting. We do well to remember, though, as Chapter 7 showed, that 'even' 'modern' Chartism was occasionally prone to a reliance on both physical force and symbolic violence. Either way, rural workers had to adapt their protests, and even innovate in the arts of protest, to meet changing social and cultural realities.

As Chapters 3, 4 and 5 detailed, some dynamics became less important as generators of protest through time: the dislocations of enclosure in many parts of England by the late 1830s, for instance, were consigned to community memory, while the targeting of religious non-conformists had almost totally ceased to be a major concern by the 1820s. Similarly, collective acts of levelling houses and business premises that were so important as customary tools for exacting popular justice against the transgressors of accepted community codes of being – from adulterers to the adulterators of flour – were undoubtedly far less readily (and widely) practised by the turn of the nineteenth century. Arguably, though, as John Bohstedt has suggested, in socially and demographically stable small market towns many forms of collective protest were longer-lived. Indeed, in the cloth towns of East Anglia and the west of England, food riots continued into the 1810s – even the 1820s in Wiltshire – whereas in many locales they effectively died out in 1800. Yet one could argue that this localised persistence was a function not of stability but instead of community collapse, the 'traditional' resort to food rioting as a muscular defence of plebeian interest giving way to desperation.[1]

Arguably, the biggest area of debate regarding persistences and continuities was the changing role of 'riot'. As identified in Chapters 3 to 7, collective acts of protest were no less important in the early decades of the nineteenth century than they were in the eighteenth century. Smuggling, poaching and criminal gangs, acts of trades unionism, political unions and the massive scale of Swing all attest to the continued power of rural workers combining to change their lot. Riot was different, though. The Riot Act of 1714/15 was enacted not in response to the power of combination in the countryside but rather, as Adrian Randall notes, perceived Jacobite threats in light of the 1710 'Sachaverell Riots' and the frequent recurrence of food rioting that often plunged towns into apparent chaos and disrupted marketing networks.[2] The extent to which riot, that is to say, a gathering of twelve or more people as defined by the conditions of the Riot Act, was ever truly a 'rural' problem to the authorities is perhaps best attested by the fact that Randall's survey of eighteenth-century riot includes only one chapter devoted exclusively to the countryside. Similarly, the passing of the unparalleled Black Act a mere eight years after the passing of the Riot Act suggests it was a tool inadequate to the needs of rural magistrates. In truth, riot was not *one* practice, whatever the niceties and specificities of law. Rather, the act of multiple individuals gathering took many forms: meetings to discuss grievances and politics; to poach; to demand higher wages; to break machinery; to stop the shipment of grain; to demolish a transgressor's house. What tied together these disparate practices was community memory, experience and the guiding hand of custom, which gave form and discipline to the act.

It is similarly unsatisfactory to claim that the focus of protest shifted increasingly to politics, for such a statement is to deny the political in acts which were not necessarily driven by the deepening reform and democratic movements: it is to privilege participatory politics over instrumental, everyday politics. Besides, forms of popular, radical, politics were made possible by the politicising effects of enclosure and proletarianisation, un- and under-employment, pauperisation, and degrading treatment at the hands of employers, poor law officials and magistrates. As Gareth Stedman-Jones has stated, before people can mobilise they require a political language to provide a 'diagnosis of the sources of their problem'.[3] But it is equally unsatisfactory to make the teleological claim that Chartism and trades unionism represented a progression of protest practices, for this is to claim that earlier protests – from popular Jacobitism, the Blacks, food rioters, Swing protestors – were engaged in something reactionary and simplistic.

What it is impossible to truly assess is whether by 1850 English rural workers were more likely to resort to protest than their forebears in 1700. In part, this is because it is necessarily unknowable. For beyond the fact that the archive does not record every act of obvious, visible protest – a deliberate fire, a tithe demonstration,[4] rural workers protested in many ways – grumbling, foot-dragging – that were by virtue of their deliberately hidden nature beyond the archive. Moreover, claims that after the bitter repression of the food riots of the 1790s the resort to collective action in the countryside fell away as rural workers turned to the tools of terror is open to question. To what extent were the 'exceptional' mo(ve) ments of protest in 1816, 1822 and 1830 really exceptional? That collective action could – especially in the cornlands – flare up in times of crisis, is suggestive that a culture of collective action persisted in the countryside, but only occasionally found voice. We can also say with some degree of certainty that the early decades of the nineteenth century saw a significant increase in crime – both social and more straightforwardly acquisitive – and in the resort to incendiarism, plant maiming and animal maiming. Of course, we cannot truly discount the possibility that the simple dynamics of steep population growth from the 1810s and the widening net of provincial newspapers' reporting was in part responsible for these increases. However, the studies of incendiarism by Roger Wells, Steve Poole and David Jones, as well as by this author, all attest to the apparent fact that, post-1795, incendiarism became almost the default rural protest practice. It became part of rural working culture, an ever-present possibility as opposed to something unusual.[5]

Another complication in attempting to answer this question is that the issue of how much we know of past protests is simply a reflection of how the law framed and prosecuted protest (and therefore also recorded acts of protest). As Chapter 2 showed, many acts of resistance were reactions to, or even created by, the criminalisation of practices and/or the passing of new statutes. Many protests and acts of resistance, then, are only recorded in the archive by virtue of their having been legislated against, the acts of wood-taking and plant maiming being notable examples. There is also a sense, as per Thompson's moral economy thesis, that the actions of protestors were often framed in relation both to law – the practices of food rioting being a selective invocation of earlier Books of Orders – and in relation to expectations as to how magistrates should and would act. Hence, Charlesworth has stated that the playing out of food riots resembled a 'stately gavotte', the protestors, the authorities and the marketers all knowing their moves in relation to everybody else's.[6] In this sense, protest was not only framed and defined by law but also undertaken as a negotiation with the *application* of law, through the magistrates, police officers, and even the army. The extent to which law acted as a deterrent is far harder to assess. The presence of a strong repressive force, especially in the form of military detachments, did much to deter collective acts of protest, while, as related in Chapter 5, the creation of county police constabularies from 1839 led to a significant increase in both arrest and conviction rates for incendiarism. Similarly, Wells' thesis on the shift from overt to covert protest forms from 1800 rests on the idea that the military and judicial repression of food rioters in 1795 forced protestors to adopt the tools of terror, as open protest was no longer feasible.[7] But if law and expressions of power might have forced those who sought redress to adopt different protest tactics, there is no sense that, against stronger policing, the evolution of law and the strengthening of central state bureaucracy at the Home Office and War Office, that it became ever harder to protest. It did not – as the record levels of incendiarism and the vigour of Chartism in the 1840s demonstrates. Rural workers found a way to protest, to resist their lot, whatever the context.

Were shifting protest practices underwritten by changing causes of protest? Put simply, absolute poverty remained arguably the key reason why people resorted to protest. Indeed, that many of the peaks of protest in the countryside mirrored the spikes in Rostow's 'social tension' chart – 1795, 1800, 1812, 1819, 1830–01, 1839, 1842, 1848 – gives credence to Cobbett's maxim, 'I defy you to agitate a fellow with a full stomach'.[8] Yet, this does not explain why in times of crisis many people and many communities did not protest. Nor does it allow for the fact that absolute privation alone is not the only reason rural workers rebelled. We cannot explain the Jacobite rebellions, the acts of the Blacks, the anti-Militia Act riots, let alone the rise of popular radicalism, by resort to crude models that essentially reduce protestors to machines, reflexive and acting hysterically against a given hardship. Nor, contra theories of 'mob psychology', did other 'grievances' automatically lead to the firing of ricks and the maiming of cattle. The reasons for protesting – and not protesting – are many and complex. As E.P. Thompson famously suggested, the protests of the eighteenth-century marketplace were underpinned by a set of *values* shared across social groups in the community. The breaking of a compact or contract, the pricking of a principle, the abandoning of social responsibilities, were all more likely to lead to conflict than just being poor and hungry.[9] As Stevenson has suggested, much in the way of eighteenth- and early-nineteenth-century protest was defensive,[10] an attempt to protect 'accepted practice', to defend custom, to remind their employers, the clergy, the magistracy and the gentry of their obligations through public performances that were suggestive of the muscular power of the poor.[11]

What evidence do the foregoing chapters provide, then, of changing social relations? In some sense, it is possible to argue that as the position of labour deteriorated relative to that of capital, so the relations between rural workers and their employers and the rulers of rural England became more fraught. Certainly, post-Swing, the huge upsurge in the resort to the tools of rural terror and the anecdotal evidence of frosty employee–employer relations is highly suggestive of a new state of being in the countryside. One could also argue that post-1750, with the declining generosity of poor relief, not least in the northern counties, it is also possible to discern a deepening division between rural workers and other members of rural society. Beyond such historical pivots, the evident shift from food to wages and/or poor relief being the key nexus on which social relations turned marked an important shift in the everyday functioning of parish politics, the vestry increasingly becoming the key space in which the tone and tenor of relations were determined.

It is also possible to argue that the increasing mechanisation of many agricultural practices (especially threshing), the turn to hop and orchard planting, the decline of living-in service, and the casualisation of much agricultural labour fundamentally altered the balance between male and female labour. This was necessarily spatially uneven. For in every place where changing agrarian practice and the growth of rural craft offered new opportunities for female labour – and displaced male labour – there were far more places where, as Nicola Verdon put it, '[i]deological and economic forces coalesced to circumscribe women's involvement in the rural labour force'.[12] Indeed, if protest was not universally a masculine thing, engaging in those totemic acts of rural protest such as incendiarism and wage-bargaining were almost exclusively the preserve of young men, but many acts of resistance spoke of a more complex set of relations. Women and children, for instance, were *the* key activists in that great act of rural resistance, wood-taking, while many 'male' acts of protest were attempts to defend the dignity of their female relatives. The following case is instructive. At Ninfield near Hastings as part of an attempt to remove the assistant overseer during Swing, a pair of giant mocked-up scissors were paraded through the village. This seemingly obscure act was in reality a devastating critique of abuses committed against young girls in the parish poorhouse. First detailed in an expose in the *Brighton Herald* before being picked up by the London press, it transpired that on the transportation of a smuggler called Ford, his four daughters were placed into service by the parish, but the 'stigma' attached to their father meant they were soon forced to leave their places. On their attempt to enter the Ninfield poorhouse, they were refused by the parish, though the decision was overturned on an appeal to the local magistrates. In spite of this, on entering the house, the vestry hired a man to cut the girls' hair, but on their resisting the barber gave up. Several farmers then forcibly held the girls, while another farmer cut off their hair with such violence that their clothes were 'literally torn from their backs'. Some friends of the girls commenced a prosecution, and the farmers offered £100 to settle the 'disgraceful affair'. The parading of the scissors was therefore an attempt by the men of the community to defend the girls' honour and their right to assert their femininity.[13]

Yet, we need to be careful not to fall into making any totalising claims, for social relations are always in a state of flux, social change happening in the challenging of existing orders and ways of being. The actions of the Blacks, of anti-enclosure rioters, and those who attacked the creation of new unionised workhouses in mid-eighteenth-century East Anglia were evidence that at many moments and places in the eighteenth- and early nineteenth-centuries, countryside social relations could, and did, break down catastrophically. That those great moments where the existing social order was challenged – the actions of the Blacks, Luddism, Swing – were used to justify more stringent laws and social reform is proof positive that against the claims of protestors existing elites always try to bolster their own positions. Claims to custom, to authority, to respect were one thing, but the moral economy of the English countryside had its absolute limits against commercialising imperatives.

All this begs two final questions: to what extent by 1850 was it still meaningful to talk of the rural as a distinctive spatial-cultural realm – and as something in which a distinctive resort to protest was made? If by 1850 a slender majority of the population of England lived in the towns and cities – remembering the caveat stated in the introduction – the largest single occupational group were the agricultural labourers, while the majority of urban residents had either been born in the countryside or were one generation removed from their rural roots. If, economically, England was an urban, industrial nation, culturally its people self-identified as being rural, agrarian even, something perfectly elucidated by the back-to-the-land politics (and nostalgia) of the Chartist Land Plan. At the other end of the political spectrum, land remained the source of power and much wealth, successful urban industrialists and bankers buying country estates to consolidate their influence, and to assert their power and prestige.[14] The idea of the countryside, then, transcended the bounds of fields and gardens. But this representation of the countryside as exclusively agrarian, a bucolic idyll, was only just beginning by 1850, the rural still being recognisably a space of industrial production, of mining, of craft and artisanal production, as much as it was agricultural.[15]

The rural was not *a* place, something clearly bounded and defined, but rather a set of overlapping spaces, something that assumed different appearances and meanings from one district to another and from one person to another. As such, there was no rural protest canon per se. Indeed, many protest practices transcended the rural and the urban, while, as Chapters 5 and 6 have shown, the actions of mobile groups and gangs rendered any border between town and country more flexible than rigid. From the beginning of the period covered by this book to 1850, no single protest movement was entirely of the countryside, but instead drew in urban residents, entered urban spaces, and made claims to urban polities. Even those forms of resistance and opposition that by virtue of being practised solely in the fields, woods, commons and parks of the countryside – enclosure protests, wood-taking, poaching – could be described as 'exclusively' rural were practised by urban workers whose lives were partly lived in the country. The rural, then, was not hermetically sealed but something fluid. Still, as suggested in the Introduction, through the playing out of place-bound customs and rituals, through the ways in which the laws of settlement and poor laws bound individuals to the parish and generated attachments,[16] the rural was experienced and lived in as something truly distinctive. The rural was a patchwork of parishes and communities, each having different ways of being and customs, different links to the urban, different blends of agricultural and industrial, but still ultimately wrought together by the shared experience of being on and of the land. It was a set of spaces made by the constant interplay between, on the one hand, the commercialising imperatives of agrarian capitalism and the re-making of the British state as a defender of property, and on the other the persistent attempts by rural workers to defend their way of life, their families and communities, their rights, and their dignity.

Notes

Preface

1. J. Eddows, *The agricultural labourer as he really is; or village morals in 1854* (Driffield, 1854), 13.
2. M. Freeman (ed.), *The English rural poor 1850–1915: Volume 1: the moral and material condition of the mid-Victorian rural poor* (London, 2005), 2.
3. For two excellent studies of East Yorkshire hiring fairs, see: G. Moses, 'Reshaping rural culture? The Church of England and hiring fairs in the East Riding of Yorkshire c. 1850–80', *RH*, 13, 1 (2002), 61–84; Moses, 'Rustic and rude': hiring fairs and their critics in East Yorkshire c. 1850–75', *RH*, 7, 2 (1996), 151–75.
4 J. Marsh, *Back to the land. The pastoral impulse in Britain from 1880 to 1914* (London, 1982), 60.
5. M. Freeman, 'The agricultural labourer and the 'Hodge' stereotype, c.1850–1914', *AgHR*, 49, 2 (2001), 172–86. See also: A. Howkins, 'From Hodge to Lob. Reconstructing the English farm labourer, 1870–1914', in M. Chase and I. Dyck (eds), *Living and learning: essays in honour of J.F.C. Harrison* (Aldershot, 1996), 218–35; K.D.M. Snell, *Annals of the labouring poor: social change and agrarian England, 1660–1900* (Cambridge, 1985), 5–14, 381–91.
6. J. Dent, 'The present condition of the English agricultural labourer', *Journal of the Royal Agricultural Society*, 2nd series, 7 (1871), 343–4, cited in Freeman, 'The agricultural labourer', 173–4.
7. J. Stevenson, *Popular disturbances in England 1700–1832* (London, 1992); J. Archer, *Social unrest and popular protest in England, 1780–1840* (Cambridge, 2001); A. Charlesworth (ed.), *An atlas of rural protest 1548–1900* (London, 1983). Also see: C. Tilly, *Popular contention in Great Britain 1758–1834* (Cambridge, MA, 1995); F. Darvall, *Popular disturbances and public order in Regency England* (Oxford, 1969, first published 1936).
8. B. Latour, *We have never been modern* (Cambridge, MA, 1993).

9. For the outstanding study of Jacobitism see: P. Monod, *Jacobitism and the English people, 1688–1788* (Cambridge, 1993). For a rare study of the efforts of the Anti-Corn Law League in the countryside see: E. Billinge, 'Rural crime and protest in Wiltshire 1830–1875', (Ph.D. thesis, University of Kent at Canterbury, 1984). See also: E. Newman, 'The Anti-Corn Law League and the Wiltshire labourer' in B.A. Holderness and M. Turner (eds), *Land, labour and agriculture 1700–1920* (London, 1991).

Introduction

1. H. More (aka 'Will Chip'), *Village politics: addressed to all the mechanics, journeymen, and day labourers in Great Britain* (York, 1793).
2. 'Francis Swing' (pseud.), *The history of Swing, the noted Kent rick burner, written by himself* (London, 1830); 'Francis Swing', *The genuine life of Mr. Francis Swing* (London, 1831); R. Taylor, *Swing: or, who are the incendiaries? A tragedy [in five acts, in prose and in verse]* (London, 1831); G.W. (Gibbon Wakefield: pseud), *A short account of the life and death of Swing, the Rick-Burner; written by one well acquainted with him* (London, 1831); J. Parker, *Machine-breaking and the changes occasioned by it in the village of Turvey Down. A tale of the times* (Oxford, 1831).
3. See especially A. Brundage, *The people's historian: John Richard Green and the writing of History in Victorian England* (Westport, CT, 1994), ch.6.
4. E. Hobsbawm and G. Rudé, *Captain Swing* (London, 1969), 11.
5. *Westminster Review*, 31, 4 (London, 1836), 451.
6. For example, see E. Gonner, *Commonland and enclosure* (London, 1912).
7. J.L. Hammond and B. Hammond, *The village labourer* (London, 1978, first published 1911), 4th edition, chs 10–11.
8. See S. Webb and B. Webb, *History of trade unionism* (London, 1894) and *English poor law policy* (London, 1913); J.L. Hammond and B. Hammond, *The skilled labourer 1760–1832* (London, 1919).
9. The best of these studies are several interwar analyses of Swing: A. Colson, 'The revolt of the Hampshire agricultural labourers and its causes, 1812–1831' (MA dissertation, London University, 1937); N. Gash, 'The rural unrest in England in 1830 with particular reference to Berkshire' (B.Litt dissertation, Oxford University, 1934); W.H. Parry Okedon, 'The agricultural riots in Dorset in 1830', *Proceedings of the Dorset Natural History and Archaeological Society*, 52 (1930), 75–95.
10. As Eric Hobsbawm damningly put it, accounts by 'Fabians and Liberals' were necessarily flawed because of their default ideological position of believing 'that strong-arm methods in labour action are less effective than peaceful negotiation': 'The machine-breakers', *P&P*, 1 (1952), 57. For excellent analyses of the limitations of, and a survey of subsequent critiques, of *The village labourer*, see: A. Charlesworth, 'An agenda for historical studies of rural protest in Britain, 1750–1850', *RH*, 2, 2 (1991), 231–40; S. Poole,

'Forty years of rural history from below: Captain Swing and the historians', *Southern History*, 32 (2010), 1–20.

11. Hobsbawm and Rudé, *Captain Swing*, 13–14, 15 and 18.

12. E. Hobsbawm, The machine-breakers', *P&P*, 1, 1 (1952), 57–70; Hobsbawm, *Primitive rebels: studies in archaic forms of social movement in the 19th and 20th centuries* (Manchester, 1959); Hobsbawm, *Labouring men: studies in the history of labour* (London, 1964).

13. G. Rudé, *The crowd in the French Revolution* (Oxford, 1959); Rudé, *The crowd in history: a study of popular disturbances in France and England, 1730–1848* (London, 1964); Rudé, 'Rural and urban disturbances on the eve of the first Reform Bill, 1830–1831', *P&P*, 37 (1967), 87–102.

14. E.P. Thompson, *The making of the English working class* (London, 1980, first published 1963), 10.

15. Hobsbawm and Rudé, *Captain Swing*, 17–19.

16. For which, see the 2010 special issue of *Southern History* and C. Griffin, *The rural war: Captain Swing and the politics of protest* (Manchester, 2012).

17. E.P. Thompson, 'Rural riots', *New Society*, 13 February 1969, 251–2. For analysis of other reviews see: Griffin, *The rural war*, 5, 17–18.

18. I. Robertson, '"Two steps forward, three steps back": the dissipated legacy of Captain Swing', *Southern History*, 32 (2010), 85–100.

19. A. Charlesworth, *Social protest in a rural society: the spatial diffusion of the Captain Swing disturbances of 1830–1831* (Norwich, 1979); E. Richards, '"Captain Swing" in the West Midlands', *IRSH*, 19, 1 (1974), 86–99.

20. D. Jones, 'Thomas Campbell Foster and the rural labourer: incendiarism in East Anglia in the 1840s', *SH*, 1, 1 (1976), 5–37.

21. E. Hobsbawm, 'Distinctions between socio-political and other forms of crime', *Bulletin of the Society for the Study of Labour History*, 25 (1972), 5–6; E.P. Thompson, 'The moral economy of the English crowd in the eighteenth-century', *P&P*, 50 (1971), 76–136.

22. D. Hay, P. Linebaugh, J. Rule, E.P. Thompson, and C. Winslow, *Albion's fatal tree: crime and society in eighteenth-century England* (London, 1975; 2nd edition London, 2011).

23. D. Hay, 'Property, authority and the criminal law', in Hay et al., *Albion's fatal tree*, 21, 26; H. Fielding, *Tom Jones: a foundling* (London, 1749).

24. E.P. Thompson, *Whigs and hunters: the origin of the Black Act* (London, 1975).

25. Cited in R. Follett, *Evangelicism, penal theory and the politics of criminal law reform in England, 1808–30* (Basingstoke, 2001), 1.

26. P. King, *Crime, justice and discretion in England 1740–1820* (Oxford, 2000), 232–7.

27. E.P. Thompson, 'Patrician society, plebeian culture', *Journal of Social History*, 7, 4 (1974), 382–405; Thompson, 'Eighteenth-century English society: class struggle without class?', *SH*, 3, 2 (1978), 133–65.

28. Thompson, 'Patrician society', 382, 385.

29. A. Gramsci, *Prison notebooks, 1929–1935, Vols 1 to 3* (London, 1971); Thompson, 'Patrician society', 388.

30. Thompson, 'Class struggle', 164, 165.

31. R. Wells, 'The development of the English rural proletariat and social protest, 1700–1850', *JPS*, 6, 2 (1979), 115–39. For Williams, see his classic: *Artisans and sans-culottes: popular movements in France and Britain during the French Revolution* (London, 1968).

32. A. Charlesworth, 'The development of the English rural proletariat and social protest, 1700–1850: a comment', *JPS*, 8, 1 (1980), 101–11.

33. R. Wells, 'Social conflict and protest in the English countryside in the early nineteenth century: a rejoinder', *JPS*, 8, 4 (1981), 514–30. This study was followed up by a further, exhaustive study of Burwash: Wells, 'Crime and protest in a country parish: Burwash, 1790–1850', in J. Rule and R. Wells, *Crime, protest and popular politics in southern England 1740–1850* (London, 1997), 169–235.

34. J. Archer, 'The Wells-Charlesworth debate: a personal comment on arson in Norfolk and Suffolk', *JPS*, 9,4 (1982), 277–84; D. Mills and B. Short, 'Social change and social conflict in nineteenth-century England: the use of the open–closed village model', *JPS*, 10, 4 (1983), 253–62; M. Reed, 'Social change and social conflict in nineteenth-century England: a comment', *JPS*, 12, 1 (1984), 109–23; and, D. Mills, 'Peasants and conflict in nineteenth-century England: a comment on two recent articles', *JPS*, 15, 3 (1988), 395–400. These essays were collected together in an edited volume with some further reflections by the editors: M. Reed, 'Class and conflict in rural England: some reflections on a debate', and R. Wells, 'Social protest, class, conflict and consciousness, in the English countryside, 1700–1880', in M. Reed and R. Wells (eds), *Class, conflict and protest in the English countryside, 1700–1880* (London, 1990), 1–28 and 121–98. Subsequent references are to the essays reprinted in the edited book.

35. R. Wells, *Wretched faces: famine in wartime England 1763–1803* (Gloucester, 1988); A. Randall and A. Charlesworth (eds), *Markets, market culture and popular protest in eighteenth-century Britain and Ireland* (Liverpool, 1996); A. Randall and A. Charlesworth (eds), *Moral economy and popular protest: crowds, conflict and authority* (London, 2000). Also see: J. Bohstedt, *Riots and community politics in England and Wales, 1790–1810* (Cambridge, MA, 1985); Bohstedt, *The politics of provisions: food riots, moral economy, and market transition in England, c. 1550–1850* (Farnham, 2010).

36. M. Chase, *The people's farm: English radical agrarianism, 1775–1840* (Oxford, 1988); I. Dyck, *William Cobbett and Rural Popular Culture* (Cambridge, 1993); R. Wells, 'Mr. William Cobbett, Captain Swing and King William IV', *AgHR*, 45, 1 (1997), 34–48; Wells, 'Southern Chartism', *RH*, 2, 1 (1991), 37–59.

37. A. Randall, *Before the Luddites: custom, community and machinery in the English woollen industry, 1776–1809* (Cambridge, 1991).

38. See notes 35–41. In addition: J. Archer, *By a flash and a scare: arson, animal maiming, and poaching in East Anglia 1815–1870* (Oxford, 1990); B. Reay, *The last rising of the agricultural labourers: rural life and protest in nineteenth-century England* (Oxford, 1990); Reay, *Microhistories: demography, society, and culture in rural England, 1800–1930* (Cambridge, 1996); J. Neeson, *Commoners, common*

right, enclosure and social change in England 1700–1820 (Cambridge, 1993);
J. Rule and R. Wells, *Crime, protest and popular politics in southern England,
1740–1850* (London, 1997); R. Wells, 'The moral economy of the English
countryside', in Randall and Charlesworth, *Moral economy and popular protest*, 209–72.

39. R. Cobb, 'A very English rising', *Times Literary Supplement*, 3, 524 (11
September 1969), 992.
40. B. Reay, *Microhistories: demography, society, and culture in rural England,
1800–1930* (Cambridge, 1996); E. Muir, 'Introduction: observing trifles',
in E. Muir and G. Ruggiero (eds), *Microhistory and the lost peoples of Europe*
(Baltimore, MD, 1991), viii.
41. J. Neeson, 'The opponents of enclosure in eighteenth-century
Northamptonshire', *P&P*, 105 (1984), 114–39; D. Eastwood, 'Communities,
protest and police in early nineteenth-century Oxfordshire: the enclosure
of Otmoor reconsidered', *AgHR*, 44, 1 (1996), 35–46.
42. A. Howkins, 'Labour history and the rural poor 1850–1980', *RH*, 1 (1990)
119–20; D. Underdown, 'The chalk and the cheese: contrasts among the
English clubmen', *P&P*, 85 (1979), 25–48; D. Levine and K. Wrightson,
The making of an industrial society: Whickham 1560–1765 (Oxford, 1991). For
a post-1850 study, see: E.T. Hurren, 'Agricultural trade unionism and a
crusade against outdoor relief: poor law politics in the Brixworth union,
Northamptonshire, 1870–75', *AgHR*, 48, 2 (2000), 200–22.
43. Griffin, *The rural war*, 20.
44. A. Ludtke, *The history of everyday life: reconstructing historical experiences and
ways of life* (Princetown, NJ, 1995).
45. Rule and Wells, *Crime, protest and popular politics*; Randall and Charlesworth,
Moral economy and popular protest.
46. Charlesworth, 'An agenda', 231–40.
47. Randall and Charlesworth, *Markets, market culture*.
48. See especially: B. Bushaway, *By rite: custom, ceremony and community in England
1700–1880* (London, 1982).
49. J. Scott, *Weapons of the weak: everyday forms of peasant resistance* (New Haven,
CT, 1985); Scott, *Domination and the arts of resistance: hidden transcripts* (New
Haven, CT, 1990).
50. Thompson, 'The moral economy'; Thompson, *Customs in common* (London,
1991).
51. A. Randall, *Riotous assemblies: popular protest in Hanoverian England* (Oxford,
2006).
52. http://www.historyworkshop.org.uk/new-approaches-to-popular-protest-
and-resistance-in-britain-and-ireland-1500–1900. Accessed 26 August 2012.
53. K. Binfield (ed.), *The writings of the Luddites* (Baltimore, MD, 2004);
S. Hindle, 'Custom, festival and protest in early modern England: the Little
Budworth wakes, St Peter's Day, 1596', *RH*, 6, 2 (1995), 155–78; S. Hindle,
'Persuasion and protest in the Caddington common enclosure dispute
1635–1639', *P&P*, 158 (1998), 37–78; A. Wood, *The politics of social conflict: the*

Peak Country, 1520–1770 (Cambridge, 1999); Wood, *Riot, rebellion and popular politics in early modern England* (Basingstoke, 2002).

54. K. Navickas, 'The search for General Ludd: the mythology of Luddism', *SH*, 30, 3 (2005), 281–95; Navickas, *Loyalism and radicalism in Lancashire, 1798–1815* (Oxford, 2009); Navickas, 'Moors, fields, and popular protest in south Lancashire and the West Riding of Yorkshire, 1800–1848', *Northern History*, 46, 1 (2009), 93–111; Navickas, 'Captain Swing in the north: the Carlisle riots of 1830', *History Workshop Journal*, 71 (2011), 5–28; B. McDonagh, 'Subverting the ground: private property and public protest in the sixteenth-century Yorkshire Wolds', *AgHR*, 57, 2 (2009), 491–506; P. Jones, 'Swing, Speenhamland and rural social relations: the 'moral economy' of the English crowd in the nineteenth century', *SH*, 32, 3 (2007), 272–91; Jones, 'Finding Captain Swing: protest, parish relations, and the state of the public mind in 1830', *IRSH*, 54, 3 (2009), 429–58; I. Robertson, 'The role of women in protests in the Scottish Highlands', *Journal of Historical Geography*, 23, 2 (1997), 187–200; Robertson, 'Governing the Highlands: the place of popular protest in the Highlands of Scotland', *RH* 8, 1 (1997), 109–24. Some aspects of this new 'agenda' were with impressive foresight set out in the essay by Andrew Charlesworth: 'An agenda'.

55. R. Poole, 'The march to Peterloo: politics and festivity in late Georgian England', *P&P*, 192 (2006), 109–53; K. Navickas, '"That sash will hang you": political clothing and adornment in England, 1780–1840', *Journal of British Studies*, 49, 3 (2010), 540–65.

56. F. O'Gorman, 'The Paine burnings of 1792–1793', *P&P*, 193 (2006), 111–55; Jones, 'Finding Captain Swing'; Jones, 'The true life and history of Captain Swing: rhetorical construction and metonymy in a time of reform', *Southern History*, 32 (2010), 101–17; C. Griffin, 'The violent Captain Swing?', *P&P*, 209 (2010), 149–80.

57. Arguably the best such study relates not to rural England but to rural Scotland: see Robertson, 'The role of women in protests'. For other, older, more reductionist studies, see: M. Thomis and J. Grimmett, *Women in protest 1800–1850* (London, 1982).

58. S. D'Cruze, *Everyday violence in Britain, 1850–1950: gender and class* (London, 2000); Binfield, *Writings of the Luddites*; Griffin, *The rural war*, ch. 8; Griffin, 'Animal maiming, intimacy and the politics of shared life: the bestial and the beastly in eighteenth- and early nineteenth-century England', *Transactions of the Institute of British Geographers*, 37, 2 (2012), 301–16.

59. D. Featherstone, 'Skills for heterogeneous associations: the Whiteboys, collective experimentation and subaltern political ecologies', *Environment and Planning D: Society and Space*, 25, 2 (2007), 284–306; Featherstone, *Resistance, space and political identities: the making of counter-global networks* (Oxford, 2008); Navickas, *Loyalism and radicalism in Lancashire*; and, 'Swing in the north'.

60. Navickas, '"That sash will hang you"'; C. Griffin, '"Cut down by some cowardly miscreants": plant-maiming, or the malicious cutting of flora, as an act of protest in eighteenth- and nineteenth-century rural England', *RH*, 19: 1 (2008), 29–54.

61. Binfield, *The writings of the Luddites*; J. Martin, 'Popular political oratory and itinerant lecturing in Yorkshire and the North-East in the age of Chartism, 1837–60' (unpublished Ph.D. thesis, University of York, 2010), chs 4 and 5; R. Ganev, *Songs of protest, songs of love: popular ballads in eighteenth-century Britain* (Manchester, 2009), esp. chs 2 and 3; K.D.M. Snell, 'Deferential bitterness: the social outlook of the rural proletariat in eighteenth- and nineteenth-century England and Wales', in M. Bush (ed.), *Social orders and social classes in Europe since 1500: studies in stratification* (London, 1992), 158–84. Here the influence of Thompson's essay on threatening letters, Howkins and Dyck's work on the languages of rural radicalism, and Gareth Stedman-Jones's work on the languages of class have proved hugely influential: E.P. Thompson, 'The crime of anonymity', in Hay *et al.*, *Albion's fatal tree*, 255–344; A. Howkins and I. Dyck, '"The time's alteration": popular ballads, rural radicalism and William Cobbett', *History Workshop Journal*, 23 (1987), 20–38; G. Stedman-Jones, *Languages of class: studies in working class history 1832–1982* (Cambridge, 1983).

62. Navickas, '"That sash will hang you"'; Griffin, 'The violent Captain Swing?'; Poole, 'The march to Peterloo'.

63. Charlesworth, 'An agenda', 238.

64. T. Shakesheff, *Rural conflict, crime and protest: Herefordshire, 1800–1860* (Woodbridge, 2003); Robertson, '"Two steps forward"'; R. Soderlund, 'Resistance from the margins: the Yorkshire worsted spinners, policing, and the transformation of work in the early industrial revolution', *IRSH*, 51 (2006), 217–42; Navickas, 'Moors, fields and popular protest'; Navickas, 'Captain Swing in the north'. For an older but still important study, see: T. Richardson, 'The agricultural labourers' standard of living in Lincolnshire, 1790–1840: social protest and public order', *AgHR*, 41, 1 (1993), 1–19.

65. Jones, 'Swing, Speenhamland and rural social relations'; Jones, 'Finding Captain Swing'; Griffin, *The rural war*; R. Wallis, '"We do not come here … to inquire into grievances we come here to decide law": prosecuting Swing in Norfolk and Suffolk', *Southern History*, 32 (2010), 159–75.

66. A. Charlesworth, 'The spatial diffusion of rural protest: an historical and comparative perspective of rural riots in nineteenth-century Britain', *Environment and Planning D: Society and Space*, 1, 3 (1983), 251–63; Bohstedt, *Riots and community politics*.

67. BPP, *Census of Great Britain, 1851, Tables of the population and houses in the divisions, registration counties, and districts of England and Wales; in the counties, cities, and burghs of Scotland; and in the islands in the British seas* (1851) vol. xliii, 73.

68. http://www.historyofparliamentonline.org/volume/1820–1832/constituencies/steyning, accessed 20 August 2012.

69. See C. Cordle, *Out of the hay and into the hops: hop cultivation in Wealden Kent and hop marketing in Southwark, 1744–2000* (Hatfield, 2011).

70. For example, see: Randall, *Before the Luddites*, 17–26, 45, 127–9.

71. B. Reay, *Rural Englands: labouring lives in the nineteenth century* (Basingstoke, 2004).

Chapter 1

1. For such a view see: D. Chambers and G. Mingay, *The agricultural revolution, 1750–1880* (London, 1965); A. Armstrong, *Farmworkers in England and Wales: a social and economic history, 1770–1980* (London, 1988).

2. L. Patriquin, *Agrarian capitalism and poor relief in England, 1500–1860* (Basingstoke, 2007), 60; J.R. Wordie, 'The chronology of English enclosure, 1500–1914', *EcHR*, 36, 4 (1983), 489.

3. D. Hay and N. Rogers, *Eighteenth-century English society: shuttles and swords* (Oxford, 1997), 99. The outstanding study remains Michael Turner's *English parliamentary enclosure: its historical geography and economic history* (Folkestone, 1980).

4. L. Shaw-Taylor, 'Parliamentary enclosure and the emergence of an English agricultural proletariat', *Journal of Economic History*, 61, 3 (2001), 640.

5. Ibid., 659.

6. H. French, 'Urban common rights, enclosure and the market: Clitheroe town moors, 1764–1802', *AgHR*, 51, 1 (2003), 67.

7. For the classic assertion of the tendency towards larger, market-orientated holdings, see: Chambers and Mingay, *The agricultural revolution.*

8. L. Shaw-Taylor, 'Family farms and capitalist farms in mid-nineteenth-century England', *AgHR*, 53, 2 (2005), 189; B. Reay, *Rural Englands: labouring lives in the nineteenth century* (Basingstoke, 2004), 24.

9. J. Neeson, *Commoners, common right, enclosure and social change in England 1700–1820* (Cambridge, 1993); B. Short, 'Environmental politics, custom and personal testimony: memory and life space on the late Victorian Ashdown Forest, Sussex', *Journal of Historical Geography*, 30, 3 (2004), 470–95.

10. M. Reed, '"Gnawing it out": a new look at economic relations in nineteenth-century rural England', *RH*, 1, 1 (1990), 83–94; M. Winstanley, 'Industrialization and the small farm: family and household economy in nineteenth-century Lancashire', *P&P*, 152 (1996), 157–95.

11. *Taunton Courier*, 22 February 1816.

12. C. Searle, 'Custom, class conflict and agrarian capitalism: the Cumbrian customary economy in the eighteenth century', *P&P*, 110 (1986), 106–33.

13. J. Rule, The *experience of labour in eighteenth-century industry* (London, 1981), 13.

14. B. Reay, *Microhistories: demography, society, and culture in rural England, 1800–1930* (Cambridge, 1996), 3–5.

15. Rule, *The experience of labour*, 11–12; Hay and Rogers, *Eighteenth-century English Society*, 27; Reay, *Rural Englands*, 20. According to Keith Wrightson, the rural 'non-agricultural' population rose from 28% of the total population in 1700 to 33% in 1750: *Earthly necessities: economic lives in early modern Britain, 1470–1750* (New Haven, CT, 2000), 235.

16. Ibid., 244; D. Defoe, *A plan of the English commerce* (London, 1728), 192, cited in Rule, *The experience of labour*, 11.

17. Wrightson, *Earthly necessities*, 241–2.

18. P. Hudson, *The genesis of industrial capital: a study of West Riding wool textile industry, c.1750–1850* (Cambridge, 2002, first published 1986).

19. G. Timmins, *The last shift: the decline of handloom weaving in nineteenth-century Lancashire* (Manchester, 1993).

20. M. Berg, *The age of manufactures, 1700–1820: industry, innovation and work* (Routledge, 1994), 94–6.

21. Reay, *Rural Englands*, 28–30.

22. H. Cunningham, 'The employment and unemployment of children in England c.1680–1851', *P&P*, 126 (1990), 120–1; J. Humphries, *Childhood and child labour in the British industrial revolution* (Cambridge, 2010).

23. D. Defoe, *A tour through the whole of island of Great Britain* (London, 1986, first published 1724–6), 85–6.

24. See N. Verdon, *Rural women workers in nineteenth-century England: gender, work and wages* (Woodbridge, 2002), 47.

25. Wrightson, *Earthly necessities*, 243; Reay, *Rural Englands*, 28.

26. E.A. Wrigley, 'Men on the land and men in the countryside: employment in agriculture in early-nineteenth-century England', in L. Bonfield, R.M. Smith and K. Wrightson (eds), *The world we have gained. Histories of population and social structure* (Oxford, 1986), 295–336; R. Wells, 'Social protest, class, conflict and consciousness, in the English countryside, 1700–1880', in M. Reed and R. Wells (eds), *Class, conflict and protest in the English countryside, 1700–1880* (London, 1990), 130–1.

27. E.A.Wrigley, 'Urban growth and agricultural change: England and the continent in the early modern period', *Journal of Interdisciplinary History*, 15, 4 (1985), 683–728.; Wrightson, *Earthly necessities*, 235.

28. Verdon, *Rural women workers*; Verdon, 'The employment of women and children in agriculture: a reassessment of agricultural gangs in nineteenth-century Norfolk', *AgHR*, 49, 1 (2001), 41–55; P. Sharpe, *Women's work: the English experience 1650–1914* (London, 1998); Humphries, *Childhood and child labour*; C. Steedman, *Labours lost: domestic service and the making of modern England* (Cambridge, 2009).

29. G. Clark, 'Too much revolution: agriculture and the industrial revolution, 1700–1860', in J. Mokyr (ed.), *The British industrial revolution: an economic assessment* (Boulder, CO, 1999), 211.

30. J. Humphries, 'Enclosures, common rights and women: the proletarianization of families in late eighteenth- and early nineteenth-century Britain', *Journal of Economic History*, 50, 1 (1990), 19.

31. S. Hindle, 'Power, poor relief, and social relations in Holland Fen, c. 1600–1800', *Historical Journal*, 41, 1 (1998), 85.

32. D. Stead, 'Delegated risk in English agriculture, 1750–1850: the labour market', *Labour History Review*, 71, 2 (2006), 123–44; K.D.M. Snell, *Annals of the labouring poor: social change and agrarian England, 1660–1900* (Cambridge, 1985), 20–1 and 74–5.

33. P. Bowden, 'Statistics', in J. Thirsk (ed.), *The agrarian history of England and Wales, volume V, 1640–1750, Part 2, Agrarian change* (Cambridge, 1985), 877–9; Rule, *The experience of labour*, 69.

34. P. Bowden, 'Agricultural prices, wages, farm profits, and rents', in Thirsk, *The agrarian history... agrarian change*, 3.

35. H. Fraser, *A history of British trade unionism, 1700–1998* (Basingstoke, 1999), 4.
36. J. Hatcher, 'Labour, leisure and economic thought before the nineteenth century', *P&P*, 160 (1998), 66.
37. *Sherborne Mercury*, 15 July 1740.
38. *Salisbury Journal*, 20 January 1739; J. De L. Mann, *The cloth industry in the west of England from 1640–1880* (Stroud, 1987), 109–10; A. Randall, *Riotous assemblies: popular protest in Hanoverian England* (Oxford, 2006), 141–3.
39. For two classic papers see: P. Lindhert and J. Williamson, 'English workers' living standards during the industrial revolution: a new look', *EcHR*, 36, 1 (1983), 1–25; S. Horrell and J. Humphries, 'Old questions, new data, and alternative perspectives: families living standards in the industrial revolution', *Journal of Economic History*, 52, 4 (1992), 849–80.
40. A. Armstrong, *Farmworkers in England and Wales: a social and economic history, 1770–1980* (London, 1988). 23–5.
41. Cited in Verdon, *Rural women workers*, 43.
42. S. King, *Poverty and welfare in England, 1700–1850* (Manchester, 2000); Snell, *Annals of the labouring poor*, 37–8 and 91.
43. P. Parthasarathi, 'Rethinking wages and competitiveness in the eighteenth century: Britain and south India', *P&P*, 158 (1998), 79–109. Also see Armstrong, *Farmworkers*; D. Hay, 'War, dearth and theft in the eighteenth century: the record of the English courts', *P&P*, 95 (1982), 128.
44. P. Linebaugh, *The London hanged: crime and civil society in the eighteenth century* (London, 2003, first published 1991), 271.
45. Snell, *Annals of the labouring poor*, 59.
46. B. Kerr, *Bound to the soil. A social history of Dorset, 1750–1919* (London, 1968), 93.
47. After considerable delay, tenders were finally issued fourteen months later: Berkshire Record Office, D/P 110/8/1, Shinfield Vestry minutes, 28 December 1768 and 12 February 1770.
48. S.A. Shave, 'Poor law reform and policy innovation in rural southern England, c.1780–1850' (unpublished Ph.D. thesis, University of Southampton, 2010), ch.4.
49. See A. Digby, *Pauper palaces: the economy and poor law of nineteenth-century Norfolk* (London, 1978), 44–7.
50. P. Muskett, 'A picturesque little rebellion? The Suffolk workhouses in 1765', *Bulletin for the Society for the Study of Labour History*, 41 (1980), 28.
51. Digby, *Pauper palaces*, 216–17.
52. A. Crossley (ed.) 'Parishes: North Aston', *A history of the county of Oxford: Vol. 11: Wootton Hundred (northern part)* (1983), 6–21; Crossley, 'Parishes: Cropredy', *A history of the county of Oxford: Vol. 10: Banbury Hundred* (1972), 157–75. Though note Havering-atte-Bower in Essex. In 1736 it resolved that a poor child should be lodged on the 'roundsman' system, and in 1745 it passed a general resolution to the same effect: W. Powell (ed.), 'Havering-atte-Bower: Economic history and local government', *A history of the county of Essex: Vol. 7* (1978), 17–22.
53. Berkshire County Record Office, D/P 110/8/1, Shinfield Vestry minutes, 17 April 1780.

54. M. Neuman, *The Speenhamland county: poverty and the poor law in Berkshire, 1782–1834* (New York, 1982), 186.

55. Cited in Wells, 'Social protest', 135.

56. R. Wells, 'The moral economy of the English countryside', in A. Randall and A. Charlesworth (eds), *Moral economy and popular protest: crowds, conflict and authority* (London, 2000), 229–31; Snell, *Annals of the labouring poor*, 87–98.

57. Wells, 'Social protest', 136; N. Goose, 'How saucy did it make the poor? The straw plait and hat trades, illegitimate fertility and the family in nineteenth-century Hertfordshire', *History*, 91 (304), 530–56.

58. S. Williams, 'Malthus, marriage and poor law allowances revisited: a Bedfordshire case study, 1770–1834', *AgHR*, 52, 1 (2004), 58, 78.

59. For example, see Hampshire County Record Office (herein HCRO), 78M72 PV1, Long Sutton Vestry minutes, 28 February 1800; Dorset History Centre, PE/MOT/OV/1/3, Motcombe Vestry minutes, 5 December 1809.

60. E. Fox Genovese, 'The many faces of the moral economy: a contribution to a debate', *P&P*, 58 (1973), 161–8.

61. TNA, HO 42/61, fos 156–8.

62. *Reading Mercury*, 6 and 11 May 1795; M. Neuman, 'A suggestion regarding the origins of the Speenhamland plan', *English Historical Review*, 84 (1969), 317; Wells, *Wretched faces*, ch. 17; and 'Social protest', 135–8.

63. Neuman, *Speenhamland county*, 165; R. Wells, 'Historical trajectories: English social welfare systems, rural riots, popular politics, agrarian trade unions, and allotment provision, 1793–1896', *Southern History*, 25 (2003), 89.

64. Snell, *Annals of the labouring poor*, 27.

65. Hobsbawm and Rudé, *Captain Swing*, 74. Snell's work has done much to increase our understanding of overall trends, though: Snell, *Annals of the labouring poor*, especially chs 1, 4 and 5.

66. HCRO, 4M69, PV1, Eling Vestry minutes, 11 July 1816; Aggregated annual average based upon: BPP, 'Abstract of the answers and returns, pursuant to Act 51 Geo. 3, for taking an account of the population of Great Britain in 1811' and 'Abstract of the answers and returns, made in pursuance to Act 1 Geo. 4, for taking an account of the population of Great Britain, 1821', (1812) Vol. xi, 299, and (1822) Vol. xv, 298.

67. BPP, 'Report from the Select Committee on the poor laws', (1817), Vol. vi, 51, 86–7.

68. BPP, 'Report from the Select Committee on the poor laws', 116.

69. Armstrong, *Farmworkers*, p.66; BPP Commons, 'Report from the select committee relating to the employment or relief of able-bodied persons from the poor rates', (1828), Vol. iv, 50.

70. J.P. Kay, 'Earnings of agricultural labourers in Norfolk and Suffolk', *Journal of the Royal Statistical Society*, 1 (1838), cited in Reay, *Rural Englands*, 73.

71. J. Burnette, *Gender, work and wages in industrial revolution Britain* (Cambridge, 2008), 211–15.

72. Wiltshire and Swindon History Centre, 1902/47, Fisherton Anger Vestry minutes, 7 June 1817; HCRO, 43M67/PV1 and 90M71/PV2, Amport Vestry

minutes, 30 April 1817 and 21 April 1820, and Minstead Vestry minutes, 11 December 1829; Centre for Kentish Studies, P164/8/2, High Halden Vestry minutes, 14 April 1823.

73. For an excellent example of opposition, see the case of Reverend Wake of Over Wallop (Hampshire) against his vestry's policy of 'the stemming of men': H. Wake, *Abuse of the poor-rate!! A statement of facts* (Andover, 1818); BPP. Commons, 'Employment or relief of able-bodied persons', evidence of Henry Boyce, overseer, Walderslade, 10 June 1828.

74. BPP, 'Report from the Select Committee on labourers wages' (1824), Vol. vi evidence of Reverend Anthony Collett, Haevingham, 12 May 1824.

75. Such schemes await systematic analysis. For a summary see: C. Griffin, *The rural war: Captain Swing and the politics of protest* (Manchester, 2012), 40–3, 69–70.

76. C. Griffin, 'Parish farms: a poor law policy response to unemployment in rural southern England, *c*.1815–35', *AgHR*, 59, 2 (2011), 176–98.

77. HCRO, 25M60 PV1, Fawley Vestry minutes, 31 March 1831.

78. K.D.M. Snell, 'The culture of local xenophobia', *SH*, 28, 1 (2003), 21–3.

79. J. Archer, *By a flash and a scare: arson, animal maiming, and poaching in East Anglia 1815–1870* (Oxford, 1990), 14; T. Richardson, 'The agricultural labourers' standard of living in Lincolnshire, 1790–1840: social protest and public order', *AgHR*, 41, 1 (1993), 1–19.

80. Quoted in S. Williams, *Poverty, gender and the life-cycle under the English poor law* (Woodbridge, 2011), 8.

81. For instance, in 1800 four parish cottages of Appledore Vestry (Kent) were set on fire, while in 1807 the House of Industry at Cranley (Surrey) was also fired, leading to the life transportation of labourer Edward Longhurst for the crime: *Kentish Gazette*, 21 February 1800; TNA, Assi 94/1616, Surrey Lent Assizes 1808.

82. Griffin, *The rural war*, 53–5.

83. *Maidstone Journal*, 23 February, 2 March and 20 April 1830; *Reading Mercury*, 27 September 1830.

84. BPP, 'Report from His Majesty's commissioners for inquiring into the administration and practical operation of the poor laws' (1834), Vol. xliv, 1495.

85. BPP, 'Return to an address to His Majesty ... of any documents which may be in the possession of the Poor Law Commissioners, with regard to the Labour Rate Bill' (1833), Vol. xxii, 2.

86. BPP, 'Report from His Majesty's commissioners for inquiring into the administration and practical operation of the Poor Laws' (1834), Vol. xliv, (various responses, 1791, 1867, 1981, 1987, 196, 2099, 2147, 2244, 2255 and 2305.

87. A. Brundage, *The making of the New Poor Law: the politics of inquiry, enactment and implementation, 1832–39* (London, 1978); P. Harling, 'The power of persuasion: central authority, local bureaucracy and the New Poor Law', *English Historical Review*, 107 (1992), 30–53.

88. J. Knott, *Popular opposition to the 1834 poor law* (London, 1986), 89.

89. K. Navickas, *Loyalism and radicalism in Lancashire, 1798–1815* (Oxford, 2009).

90. Knott, *Popular opposition*; M. Rose, 'The anti-poor law movement in the north of England', *Northern History*, 1 (1966), 70–91; K. Navickas, 'Moors, fields, and popular protest in south Lancashire and the West Riding of Yorkshire, 1800–1848', *Northern History*, 66, 1 (2009), 93–111.

91. *Northern Star*, 14 September 1838.

92. TNA, MH 12/5019, Sir Francis Head, Ashford, to Poor Law Commission, 4 March 1835.

93. A. Randall and E. Newman, 'Protest, proletarians and paternalists: social conflict in rural Wiltshire, 1830–1850', *RH*, 6, 2 (1995), 216.

94. C. Griffin, '"As lated tongues bespoke": popular protest in south-east England, 1790–1840' (unpublished Ph.D. thesis, University of Bristol, 2002), 220–23.

95. Knott, *Popular opposition*, 67–8, 79–80.

96. Griffin, 'As lated tongues', 236; Knott, *Popular opposition*, 81, 82–3.

97. Ibid., 74–5; I. Anstruther, *The scandal of the Andover workhouse* (London, 1973); R. Wells, 'Andover antecedents: Hampshire New Poor-Law scandals, 1834–1842', *Southern History*, 24 (2002), 91–227.

98. G. Boyer, *An economic history of the English poor law, 1750–1850* (Cambridge, 1990), 233–64.

99. R.F. Haines, *Emigration and the labouring poor: Australian recruitment in Britain and Ireland, 1831–1860* (Basingstoke, 1997), 10.

100. R.N. Thompson, 'The working of the Poor Law Amendment Act in Cumbria, 1836–1871', *Northern History*, 15 (1979), 117–37.

101. A. Gritt, 'The census and the servant: a reassessment of the decline and distribution of farm service in early nineteenth-century England', *EcHR*, 53, 1 (2000), 84–106; A. Howkins and N. Verdon, 'Adaptable and sustainable? Male farm service and the agricultural labour force in midland and southern England, c.1850- 1925', *EcHR*, 61, 2 (2008), 467–95.

102. J. Huzel, 'The labourer and the poor law, 1750–1850', in G. Mingay (ed.), *The agrarian history of England and. Wales, VI, 1750–1850* (Cambridge, 1989), 806. On the persistence of outdoor relief under the New Poor Law, see: K.D.M. Snell, *Parish and belonging: community, identity and welfare in England and Wales, 1700–1950* (Cambridge, 2006), ch. 5.

103. *Brighton Herald*, 3 December 1842.

104. *Kentish Gazette*, 21 November 1843.

105. *Sussex Agricultural Express*, 12 and 26 November and 24 December 1842; *Maidstone Journal*, 3 January 1843.

106. J. Burchard, *The allotment movement in England, 1793–1873* (Woodbridge, 2002).

107. *Brighton Herald*, 29 December 1849.

108. For the classic statement of labouring despair in the 1840s, see: D. Jones, 'Thomas Campbell Foster and the rural labourer: incendiarism in East Anglia in the 1840s', *SH*, 1, 1 (1976), 5–37.

Chapter 2

1. A. Wood, 'Custom, identity and resistance: English free miners and their law, c.1550–1800', in P. Griffiths, A. Fox and S. Hindle (eds), *The experience of authority in early modern England* (Basingstoke, 1996), 249–85.

2. E.P. Thompson, *Whigs and hunters: the origin of the Black Act* (London, 1975), 21.

3. J. Langton, 'Forests in early-modern England and Wales: history and historiography', in J. Langton and G. Jones (eds), *Forests and chases of England and Wales c.1500–c.1850: towards a survey and analysis* (Oxford, 2005), 1–9.

4. G. Jones, 'Swanimotes, woodmotes and courts of "free miners"', in Langton and Jones, *Forests and chases of England and Wales*, 42–3.

5. For a useful summary of these dynamics, see: Langton, 'Forests in early-modern England and Wales'.

6. Thompson, *Whigs and hunters*, 197.

7. Ibid., *passim*.

8. *London Gazette*, 22 March 1720.

9. *London Gazette*, 2 February 1723.

10. L. Radzinowicz, *A history of English criminal law and its administration from 1750: Volume I* (London, 1948), 77.

11. Thompson, *Whigs and hunters*, 21.

12. F. McLynn, *Crime and punishment in eighteenth-century England* (London, 1988), xiii–xiv.

13. P. King, *Crime and law in England, 1750–1840: remaking justice from the margins* (Cambridge, 2006), 63.

14. A. Randall, *Riotous assemblies: popular protest in Hanoverian England* (Oxford, 2006), 49.

15. TNA, SP 36/14, fols 96–7 and 36/15, fols 8–9; *London Gazette*, 23 July 1733.

16. McLynn, *Crime and punishment*, 209.

17. C. Griffin, '"Cut down by some cowardly miscreants": plant-maiming, or the malicious cutting of flora, as an act of protest in eighteenth- and nineteenth-century rural England', *RH*, 19, 1 (2008), 29–54.

18. McLynn, *Crime and punishment*, 84, 141.

19. For instance see: *Hampshire Chronicle*, 15 June 1818 (arson and plant-maiming) and 3 April 1820 (arson in a forest); *Hampshire Telegraph*, 28 June 1819 (head of a fish pond destroyed).

20. C. Emsley, *Crime and society in England 1750–1900* (London, 1996), 252.

21. For the classic invocation of poacher as rustic, see H.E. Bates' semi-fictionalised novel *The poacher* (London, 1935). For an excellent analysis of poacher as folk hero, see: G. Seal, *Encyclopaedia of folk heroes* (Santa Barbara, CA, 2001), 246.

22. J. Thirsk, *Food in early modern England: phases, fads, fashions, 1500–1760* (London, 2007), esp. 243.

23. E. Hobsbawm, 'Distinctions between socio-political and other forms of crime', *Bulletin of the Society for the Study of Labour History* 25 (1972), 5–6.

24. J. Rule, 'Social crime in the rural south in the eighteenth and nineteenth centuries', *Southern History*, 1 (1979), 135–53.

25. R. Wells, 'Sheep-rustling in Yorkshire in the age of the industrial and agrarian revolutions', *Northern History*, 20 (1984), 127–45; B. Bushaway, 'From custom to crime: wood-gathering in eighteenth and early nineteenth-century England: a focus for conflict in Hampshire, Wiltshire and the South', in J. Rule (ed.), *Outside the law: studies in crime and order 1650–1850* (Exeter, 1982), 65–101; M. Freeman, 'Plebs or predators? Deer-stealing in Whichwood Forest, Oxfordshire in the eighteenth and nineteenth centuries', *Southern History*, 21, 1 (1996), 1–21; T. Shakesheff, 'Wood and crop theft in rural Herefordshire, 1800–60', *RH*, 13, 1 (2002), 1–18.

26. Wells, 'Sheep-rustling'.

27. C. Cheeseman, 'Geography and modernity: changing land, law, and life on Cranborne Chase in the nineteenth century' (unpublished D.Phil thesis, University of Oxford, 2008), Ch. 6.

28. W. Hudson, *A shepherd's life: impressions of the south Wiltshire downs* (London, 1910), 96.

29. Cited in J. Rule, 'Social crime in the rural south in the eighteenth and early nineteenth centuries', in J. Rule and R. Wells, *Crime, protest and popular politics in southern England, 1740–1850* (London, 1997), 158.

30. W. Chapman, *A letter to the noblemen, and gentlemen, proprietors of lands in Cranborne Chace ... for the disenfranchisement of the said Chace* (Tarrant Gunville, 1791), 102–03.

31. R. Manning, *Village revolts: social protest and popular disturbances in England, 1509–1640* (Oxford, 1989), 98, 101–02, 262–3.

32. Bushaway, *From custom to crime*, 77–8.

33. J. Fisher, 'Property rights in pheasants: landlords, farmers and the Game Laws, 1860–80', *RH*, 11, 2 (2000), 165–80.

34. A. Everitt, 'Farm labourers', in J. Thirsk (ed.), *The agrarian history of England and Wales, Vol. IV: 1500–1640* (Cambridge, 1967), 459.

35. C. Griffin, 'Becoming private property: custom, law, and the geographies of 'ownership' in 18th- and 19th-century England', *Environment and Planning A*, 42, 3 (2010), 747–62.

36. P. King, 'Prosecution associations and their impact in eighteenth-century Essex'; and D. Phillips, 'Good men to prosecute, bad men to conspire: associations for the prosecution of felons in England 1770–1860', in D. Hay and F. Snyder (eds), *Policing and prosecution in Britain, 1750–1850* (Oxford, 1989), 171–207 and 113–70; *Salisbury and Winchester Journal*, 3 May 1791.

37. J. Cooke, 'Timber-stealing riots in Whittlebury and Salcey forests in 1727–8', *Northamptonshire Notes and Queries*, 1 (1886), 123–7.

38. J. Archer, 'Poaching gangs and violence: the urban–rural divide in nineteenth-century Lancashire', *British Journal of Criminology*, 39, 1 (1999), 25–38; R. Wells, 'Popular protest and social crime: the evidence of criminal gangs in rural southern England 1790–1860', *Southern History*, 13 (1991), 32–81.

39. H. Osborne, 'The seasonality of nineteenth-century poaching', *AgHR*, 48, 1 (2000), 27–41.
40. See note 38.
41. D. Hay, 'Poaching and the game laws on Cannock Chase', in D. Hay, P. Linebaugh, J. Rule, E.P. Thompson and C. Winslow, *Albion's fatal tree: crime and society in eighteenth-century England* (London, 1975); Hay, 'War, dearth and theft in the eighteenth century: the record of the English courts', *P&P*, 95 (1982), 117–60.
42. Archer, 'Poaching gangs'.
43. H. Hopkins, *The long affray: the poaching wars in Britain* (London, 1985), 73.
44. J. Archer, *By a flash and a scare: arson, animal maiming, and poaching in East Anglia 1815–1870* (Oxford, 1990), 239–40.
45. E. Hobsbawm and G. Rudé, *Captain Swing* (London, 1969/1973), 77–8.
46. McLynn, *Crime and punishment*, 206–7; Hopkins, *The long affray*.
47. D. Landry, *The invention of the countryside: hunting, walking and ecology in English literature, 1671–1831* (Basingstoke, 2001), ch. 3.
48. Manning, *Village revolts*, 165.
49. G. White, *The natural history and antiquities of Selborne* (London, 1837; first published 1789), 29; Landry, *The invention of the countryside*, 73.
50. For a useful introduction see: R. Platt, *Smuggling in the British Isles: a history* (London, 2007). On smuggling and consumption see: J. Black, *Trade, empire and British foreign policy, 1689–1815: politics of a commercial state* (London, 2007), 34.
51. W. Harvey, *The Seasalter Company: a smuggling fraternity 1740–1854* (Whitstable, 1983).
52. G. Daly, 'Napoleon and the city of smugglers', *Historical Journal*, 50, 2 (2007), 344–5. This was not a new phenomenon: for a study of merchant involvement in sixteenth-century smuggling, see O. Jones, *Inside the illicit economy: reconstructing the smugglers' trade of sixteenth-century Bristol* (Farnham, 2012).
53. J. Woodforde, *The diary of a country parson 1758–1802*, edited by J. Beresford (Oxford, 1978), esp. entries for 15 September and 12, 23 and 24 October 1792, 421–4.
54. G. Morley, *Smuggling in Hampshire and Dorset, 1700–1850* (Newbury, 1983); M. Waugh, *Smuggling in Kent and Sussex, 1700–1840* (Newbury, 1998); Waugh, *Smuggling in Devon and Cornwall, 1700–1850* (Newbury, 1991).
55. C. Winslow, 'Sussex smugglers', D. Hay et al., *Albion's fatal tree*, 121.
56. Daly, 'City of smugglers', 334.
57. W. Cole, 'Trends in eighteenth-century smuggling', *EcHR*, 10, 3 (1958), 395–410; H.-C Mui and L.M. Mui, 'Smuggling and the British tea trade before 1784', *American Historical Review*, 84 (1968), 44–73; Winslow, 'Sussex smugglers'; Daly, 'City of smugglers'; P. Monod, 'Dangerous merchandise: smuggling, Jacobotism, and commercial culture', *Journal of British Studies*, 30, 2 (1991), 150–82.
58. Waugh, *Smuggling in Kent and Sussex*; R. Philp, *The coastal blockade: the Royal Navy's war on smuggling in Kent and Sussex, 1817–1831* (Horsham, 1999).

59. Cited in Winslow, 'Sussex smugglers', 123.

60. Information for this and the previous paragraph is taken from Winslow, 'Sussex smugglers'; and Anon., *Smuggling & smugglers in Sussex: the genuine history of the inhuman and unparalleled murders of Mr. William Galley* (Brighton, 1749).

61. Waugh, *Smuggling in Kent and Sussex*, 76.

62. Ibid., 147; Morley, *Smuggling in Hampshire and Dorset*.

63. For instance, see Mui and Mui, 'Smuggling and the British tea trade'.

64. Quoted in Daly, 'City of smugglers', 344.

65. TNA, ADM 51/4093 Coastal Blockade reports: a log of the proceedings of the Coastal Blockade under Capt Wm. McCulloch Esq.

66. See C. Griffin, 'The violent Captain Swing?', *P&P*, 209 (2010), 167.

67. Old Bailey Proceedings Online, T18210411–64, www.oldbaileyonline.org, accessed 12 October 2011, trial of Richard Wraight and Cephas Quested, April 1821.

68. Waugh, *Smuggling in Kent and Sussex*, 82–3; *Kentish Gazette*, 24 May 1822; *Sussex Advertiser*, 20 February; *The Times*, 30 October and 21 November 1826.

69. TNA, HO 77/28, Calendar of prisoners for trial in Newgate Gaol, 11 April 1821; *Sussex Advertiser*, 20 February 1826; *Kent Herald*, 18 January and 8 February 1827; Waugh, *Smuggling in Kent and Sussex*, 81–4; *Maidstone Journal*, 3 December 1828 and 20 January 1829.

70. E. Cruickshanks and H. Erskine-Hill, 'The Waltham Black Act and Jacobitism', *Journal of British Studies*, 24, 3 (1985), 358–65.

71. Monod, 'Dangerous merchandise'; Platt, *Smuggling in the British Isles*, 126.

72. Daly, 'City of smugglers', 368; *Brighton Herald*, 30 October 1830.

73. C. Griffin, *The rural war: Captain Swing and the politics of protest* (Manchester, 2012), 87–90, 95–6.

74. Wells, 'Popular protest and social crime', 142–3; TNA, HO 52/10, fols 597–8.

75. On the partialities of judicial practice see: King, *Crime and law in England*, ch. 1.

76. D. Rollison, 'Property, ideology and popular culture in a Gloucestershire village 1660–1740', *P&P*, 93 (1981), 87.

77. J. Brewer, *The sinews of power: war, money, and the English state, 1688–1783* (London, 1989).

78. H. Dickinson, 'The Hexham militia riot of 1761', *Durham County Local History Bulletin*, 22 (1978), 2.

79. Randall, *Riotous assemblies*, 168.

80. Quoted in J. Caple, 'The militia riots of 1757', in A. Charlesworth (ed.), *An atlas of rural protest 1548–1900* (London, 1983), 126.

81. D. Neave, 'Anti-militia riots in Lincolnshire, 1757 and 1796', *Lincolnshire History and Archaeology* 11 (1976), 21–7; *London Chronicle*, 15 September 1757.

82. Caple, 'The militia riots'; G. Harris, *Life of Lord Chancellor Hardwicke; with selections from his correspondence, diaries, speeches and judgments*, Vol. 3 (London, 1847), 152; *Lloyd's Evening Post and British Chronicle*, 5 October 1757; *London Chronicle*, 18 October 1757.

83. *Kentish Post*, 21 and 28 July, 1 and 8 August 1759.
84. J. Western, *The English militia in the eighteenth century: the story of a political issue, 1660–1802* (London, 1965), 289.
85. T. Corfe, *Riot: the Hexham militia riot, 1761* (Hexham, 2004); Dickinson, 'The Hexham militia riot'.
86. *Sussex Weekly Advertiser*, 13 April, 1 and 8 June 1778.
87. Neave, 'Anti-militia riots'; Charlesworth, *Atlas of rural protest*, 127–9; Western, *The English militia*, 295–8.
88. J. Waylen, *A history military and municipal of the ancient borough of Devizes* (Longman, 1859), 493.

Chapter 3

1. For instance, see: R. Brown, *Church and state in modern Britain, 1700–1850* (London, 1991), 331.
2. D. Chambers and G. Mingay, *The agricultural revolution, 1750–1880* (London, 1965).
3. J. Bohstedt, *The politics of provisions: food riots, moral economy, and market transition in England, c. 1550–1850* (Farnham, 2010), ch. 4.
4. D. Hay and N. Rogers, *Eighteenth-century English society: shuttles and swords* (Oxford, 1997), 99; J.R. Wordie, 'The chronology of English enclosure, 1500–1914', *EcHR*, 36, 4 (1983), 483–505. For a useful survey of the temporality and spatiality of enclosure in Somerset see: M. Williams, 'The enclosure of waste land in Somerset, 1700–1900', *Transactions of the Institute of British Geographers*, 57 (1972), 101–05.
5. L. Shaw-Taylor, 'Parliamentary enclosure and the emergence of an English agricultural proletariat', *Journal of Economic History*, 61, 3 (2001), 659.
6. I. Whyte, '"Wild, barren and frightful": parliamentary enclosure in an upland county: Westmorland 1767–1890', *RH*, 14, 1 (2003), 21–38; G. Rogers, 'Custom and common right: waste land enclosure and social change in west Lancashire', *AgHR*, 41, 2 (1993), 137–54; H. French, 'Urban common rights, enclosure and the market: Clitheroe town moors, 1764–1802', *AgHR*, 51, 1 (2003), 67.
7. C. Griffin, 'More-than-human histories and the failure of grand state schemes: sylviculture in the New Forest, England', *Cultural Geographies*, 17, 4 (2010), 451–72; R. Anstis, *Warren James and the Dean Forest riots* (London, 1986); 41 Geo. III, c. 56, An Act for dividing, allotting, and inclosing, the Forest or Chase of Needwood, in the County of Stafford; C.S. Orwin and R.J. Sellick, *The reclamation of Exmoor* (Newton Abbot, 1970).
8. J. Chapman and S. Seeliger, *Enclosure, environment and landscape in southern England* (Stroud, 2001). For the initial assertion of the importance of enclosure by agreement and by unity of possession, see E. Gonner, *Common land and inclosure* (London, 1912).
9. J. Chapman and S. Seeliger, 'Formal agreements and the enclosure process: the evidence from Hampshire', *AgHR*, 43, 1 (1995), 35–46.

10. B. McDonagh, 'Women, enclosure and estate improvement in eighteenth-century Northamptonshire', *RH*, 20, 2 (2009), 143–62; J. Broad, *Transforming English society: the Verneys and the Claydons, 1600–1820* (Cambridge, 2004), 53–61.

11. *Portsmouth Gazette*, 28 September 1795; *Salisbury and Winchester Journal*, 28 September 1795. Titchfield was not subject to parliamentary enclosures until the 1860s: R. Kain, J. Chapman and R. Oliver, *The enclosure maps of England and Wales 1595–1918: a cartographic analysis and catalogue* (Cambridge, 2004), 394.

12. J.L. Hammond and B. Hammond, *The village labourer* (London, 1911/1978), 4th edn.

13. M. Turner, 'Economic protest in rural society: opposition to parliamentary enclosure in Buckinghamshire', *Southern History*, 10 (1988), 95; R. Wells, 'The moral economy of the English countryside', in A. Randall and A. Charlesworth (eds), *Moral economy and popular protest: crowds, conflict and authority* (London, 2000), 212–16.

14. A. Charlesworth (ed.), *An atlas of rural protest 1548–1900* (London, 1983), 39–62.

15. J. Pearson, 'Threshing out the common in community: the Great Tey riot of 1727', *RH*, 9, 1 (1998), 43–56; D. Hey, 'The north-west Midlands: Derbyshire, Staffordshire, Cheshire, and Shropshire', in J. Thirsk (ed.), *The agrarian history of England and Wales: 1640–1750: regional farming systems* (Cambridge, 1984), 148–9; A. Appleby, *Famine in Tudor and Stuart England* (Palo Alto, CA, 1978), ch. 11.

16. C. Searle, 'Custom, class conflict and agrarian capitalism: the Cumbrian customary economy in the eighteenth century', *P&P*, 110 (1986), 122.

17. J. Martin, 'The small landowner and parliamentary enclosure in Warwickshire', *EcHR*, 32 (1979), 328–43; J. Neeson, *Commoners: common right, enclosure and social change in England, 1700–1820* (Cambridge, 1993); M. Turner, 'Parliamentary enclosure and landownership change in Buckinghamshire', *EcHR*, 28 (1975), 565–81.

18. J. Humphries, 'Enclosures, common rights and women: the proletarianization of families in late eighteenth- and early nineteenth-century Britain', *Journal of Economic History*, 50, 1 (1990), 41–2; I. Pinchbeck, *Women Workers and the Industrial Revolution* (New York, 1969).

19. W. Tate, 'Opposition to parliamentary enclosure in eighteenth-century England', *Agricultural History*, 19, 3 (1945), 137.

20. Ibid., 142.

21. For instance, see J. Martin, 'Members of parliament and enclosure: a reconsideration', *AgHR*, 27, 2 (1979), 101–09.

22. Gonner, *Common land*; W.G. Hoskins, *The making of the English landscape* (Leicester, 1955); E.P. Thompson, *The making of the English working class* (London, 1980, first published 1963), 240–01.

23. J. Neeson, 'The opponents of enclosure in eighteenth-century Northamptonshire', *P&P*, 105 (1984), 114–39; Neeson, *Commoners*.

24. Whyte, 'Wild, barren and frightful', 37.
25. J. Stevenson, *Popular disturbances in England, 1700–1832* (London, 1992), 42.
26. Neeson, 'The opponents of enclosure', 118–20.
27. Ibid., 120.
28. *Reading Mercury*, 24 February 1800; *Morning Post and Gazetteer*, 15 May 1800; Neuman, *The Speenhamland county*, 36; P. Carter, 'Enclosure, waged labour and the formation of class consciousness: rural Middesex c.1700–1835', *Labour History Review*, 66, 3 (2001), 277–8.
29. N. Blomley, 'Making private property: enclosure, common right and the work of hedges', *RH*, 18, 1 (2007), 1–21.
30. *Kentish Gazette*, 17 January 1781.
31. *Hampshire Chronicle*, 26 March 1810.
32. *Salisbury and Winchester Journal*, 23 December 1816.
33. Dorset History Centre (herein DHC), NG/PR1/D1/1 Criminal process registers, 1782–1808 and 1809–1820, 106 and 41.
34. Neeson, 'The opponents of enclosure', 120.
35. Hamsphire County Record Office, 2M30/669, Petition entitled 'To the Right Honourable the Lords Spiritual and Temporal in Parliament Assembled' (no date, but 1792), and letter from Thomas Stone, Lyndhurst to George Rose, 22 October 1792.
36. DHC, NG/PR1/D1/2, Criminal process register, 1809–1820, p. 28; DHC, D/Pit/L35, various letters and notices in the case of the Pimperne enclosure, 1811; Neeson, *Commoners*, 265.
37. I. Whyte, *Transforming fell and valley: landscape and parliamentary enclosure in north-west England* (Lancaster, 2003), 57; M. Williams, *The Draining of the Somerset Levels* (Cambridge: Cambridge University Press, 1970), ch. 5.
38. L. Shaw-Taylor, 'Labourers, cows, common rights and parliamentary enclosure: the evidence of contemporary comment c.1760–1810', *P&P*, 171 (2001), 95–126.
39. Blomley, 'Making private property'; B. McDonagh, 'Subverting the ground: private property and public protest in the sixteenth-century Yorkshire Wolds, *AgHR*, 57, 2 (2009), 191–206.
40. A. Wood, *Riot, rebellion and popular politics in early modern England*, (Basingstoke, 2002), 94–5.
41. E.L. Jones, 'Eighteenth century changes in Hampshire chalkland farming', *AgHR*, 8, 1 (1960), 5–19; G. Bowie, 'Northern wolds and Wessex downlands: contrasts in sheep husbandry and farming practice, 1770–1850', *AgHR*, 38, 2 (1990), 117–26; M. Havinden, 'Lime as a means of agricultural improvement: the Devon example', in C. Chalkin and M. Havinden (eds), *Rural change and urban growth 1500–1800* (London, 1974), 104–34; J. Bettey, 'The development of water meadows on the Salisbury Avon, 1665–1690', *AgHR*, 51, 2 (2003), 163–72.
42. J. Chapman and S. Seeliger, *A guide to enclosure in Hampshire 1700–1900* (Winchester, 1997). Also see Chapman and Seeliger, *Enclosure, environment and landscape.*

43. B. McDonagh and S. Daniels, 'Enclosure stories: narratives from Northamptonshire', *Cultural Geographies*, 19, 1 (2012), 108. Also see: S. Hindle, 'Imagining insurrection in seventeenth-century England: representations of the Midland Rising of 1607', *History Workshop Journal*, 66, (2008), 21–61.

44. N. Whyte, 'Landscape, memory and custom: parish identities c.1550–1700', *SH*, 32, 2 (2007), 167–8. On taskscapes see: T. Ingold, *The perception of the environment: essays on livelihood, dwelling and skill* (Routledge, 2000).

45. C. Griffin, '"Cut down by some cowardly miscreants": plant-maiming, or the malicious cutting of flora, as an act of protest in eighteenth- and nineteenth-century rural England', *RH*, 19, 1 (2008), 38–40. For the creation of copses and plantations as cover for game birds see: E. Jones, 'The environmental effects of blood sports in lowland England since 1750', *RH*, 20, 1, (2009), 54–6.

46. M. Williams, 'The enclosure and reclamation of the Mendip Hills, 1770–1870', *AgHR*, 19, 1 (1974), 65–81.

47. Hindle, 'Power, poor relief, and social relations', 71. For the long battle over the enclosure of Holland Fen, see H.C. Darby, *The draining of the fens*, 2nd edn (Cambridge, 1956), 48–58; and K. Lindley, *Fenland riots and the English revolution* (London, 1982), 54–5, 60–02, 105–06, 111–12, 140, 161–4, 258.

48. D. Eastwood, 'Communities, protest and police in early nineteenth-century Oxfordshire: the enclosure of Otmoor reconsidered', *AgHR*, 44, 1 (1996), 35–46.

49. J. Virgoe, 'The Croston drainage scheme: co-operation and conflict in the development of the south-west Lancashire landscape', *Landscape History*, 32, 1 (2011), 59–77.

50. Griffin, *The rural war*, 73–4.

51. B. Duckham, 'The Fitzwilliams and the navigation of the Yorkshire Derwent', *Northern History*, 2 (1967), 45–61; E. Hadfield, 'The Thames navigation and the canals, 1770–1830', *EcHR*, 14, 2 (1944), 172–9; S. Oliver, 'Navigability and the improvement of the river Thames, 1605–1815', *Geographical Journal*, 176, 2 (2010), 164–77.

52. A. Charlesworth, R. Sheldon, A. Randall and D. Walsh, 'The Jack-a-Lent riots and opposition to turnpikes in the Bristol region in 1749', in A. Randall and A. Charlesworth (eds), *Markets, market culture and popular protest in eighteenth-century Britain and Ireland* (Liverpool, 1996), 46–68; P.D. Jones, 'The Bristol Bridge riot and its antecedents: eighteenth-century perceptions of the crowd', *Journal of British Studies*, 19 (1980), 77–8; Charlesworth, *Atlas of Rural Protest*, 119–20.

53. Duckham, 'The Fitzwilliams', 48; TNA, Assi 24/40, Western Circuit process book, 1734–44; *Hampshire Chronicle*, 9 June 1794.

54. Jones, 'Eighteenth-century changes', 7.

55. For instance, see J. Bohstedt, *Riots and community politics in England and Wales, 1790–1810* (Cambridge, MA, 1985), 27, 75; Wells, 'Popular protest and social crime'.

56. K. Navickas, 'Captain Swing in the north: the Carlisle riots of 1830', *History Workshop Journal*, 71 (2011), 11.
57. I. Waites, 'The common field landscape, cultural commemoration and the impact of enclosure', in M. Cragoe and P. Readman (eds), *The land question in Britain, 1750–1950* (Basingstoke, 2010), 24.

Chapter 4

1. In addition to the analysis in the Introduction, see the recent essays by Steve Poole, and Katrina Navickas's thoughtful reflections on this shift: S. Poole, 'Forty years of rural history from below: Captain Swing and the historians', *Southern History*, 32 (2010), 1–20; K. Navickas, 'What happened to class? New histories of labour and collective action in Britain', *SH*, 36, 2 (2011), 192–204.
2. E. Hobsbawm and G. Rudé, *Captain Swing* (London, 1969).
3. D. Hay, P. Linebaugh, J. Rule, E.P. Thompson and C. Winslow, *Albion's fatal tree: crime and society in eighteenth-century England* (London, 1975); E.P. Thompson, *Whigs and hunters: the origin of the Black Act* (London, 1975).
4. R. Wells, 'The development of the English rural proletariat and social protest, 1700–1850', *JPS*, 6, 2 (1979), 115–39; A. Charlesworth, 'The development of the English rural proletariat and social protest, 1700–1850: a comment', *JPS*, 8, 1 (1980), 101–11; M. Reed and R. Wells (eds), *Class, conflict and protest in the English countryside, 1700–1880* (London, 1990).
5. For a more detailed analysis see my Introduction, pp. 12–14.
6. Quoted in P. Jones, 'Swing, Speenhamland and rural social relations: the "moral economy" of the English crowd in the nineteenth century', *SH*, 32, 3 (2007), 281.
7. T. Shakesheff, 'Wood and crop theft in rural Herefordshire, 1800–60', *RH*, 13, 1 (2002), 1.
8. C. Griffin, 'Protest practice and (tree) cultures of conflict: understanding the spaces of "tree maiming" in eighteenth- and early nineteenth-century England', *Transactions of the Institute of British Geographers*, 40, 1 (2008), 91–108; C. Griffin, '"Cut down by some cowardly miscreants": plant-maiming, or the malicious cutting of flora, as an act of protest in eighteenth- and nineteenth-century rural England', *RH*, 19, 1 (2008), 29–54.
9. The Labourers' Friend Society, *A selection from the publication of The Labourers' Friend Society showing the utility and national advantage of allotting land for cottage husbandry* (London, 1835), 27.
10. 9 Geo. I c.22, i (1723), 'The Black Act'.
11. 6 Geo. 2d. c. 27. f.6 (1728), 'Attorneys and Solicitors Act': 'That if any person or persons shall unlawfully and maliciously cut any hop bines growing on poles in any plantation of hops, every person or persons so offending, being thereof lawfully convicted, shall be adjudged guilty of felony, without benefit of clergy.'

12. K.D.M. Snell, 'Deferential bitterness: the social outlook of the rural pro-letariat in eighteenth- and nineteenth-century England and Wales', in M. Bush (ed.), *Social orders and social classes in Europe since 1500: studies in stratification* (London, 1992), 164–5.
13. A. Wood, *Riot, rebellion and popular politics in early modern England* (Basingstoke, 2002), 101.
14. TNA, HO 64/1, fos 151–3.
15. E.P. Thompson, *Customs in common* (London, 1991), 49, 50, 51–2.
16. R. Lee, *Rural society and the Anglican clergy: encountering and managing the poor* (Woodbridge, 2006), ch. 5.
17. C. Griffin, *The rural war: Captain Swing and the politics of protest* (Manchester, 2012), 54, 74–5; R. Wells, 'Social protest, class, conflict and consciousness, in the English countryside, 1700–1880', in M. Reed and R. Wells (eds), *Class, conflict and protest in the English countryside, 1700–1880* (London, 1990), 158.
18. *Kentish Gazette*, 8 October 1830.
19. J. Obelkevich, *Religion in rural society: South Lindsey 1825–1875* (Oxford, 1976), 154–5; K.D.M. Snell and P. Ell, *Rival Jerusalems: the geography of Victorian religion* (Cambridge, 2000), *passim*.
20. Obelkevich, *Religion in rural society*, 148–9.
21. T. Hardy, *Under the Greenwood Tree* (London, 1872); *Hampshire Chronicle*, 13 December; *The Times*, 24 December 1830.
22. Obelkevich, *Religion in rural society, passim*; A. Urdank, *Religion and society in a Cotswold vale: Nailsworth, Gloucestershire 1780–1865* (Berkeley, CA, 1990); Snell and Ell, *Rival Jerusalems*.
23. C. Haydon, 'The Gordon Riots in the English provinces', *Historical Research*, 63 (1990), 354–9.
24. For a useful analysis of opposition to Catholic emancipation see: C. Tilly, *Contention and democracy in Europe, 1650–2000* (Cambridge, 2004), 149–56.
25. J. Oates, *York and the Jacobite rebellion of 1745*, Borthwick Paper no. 107 (York, 2005), 9–10.
26. G. Rudé, *Paris and London in the eighteenth century* (London, 1970), 289.
27. K. Navickas, *Loyalism and radicalism in Lancashire, 1798–1815* (Oxford, 2009), 97.
28. A. Gilbert, 'Methodism, dissent and political stability in early industrial England', *Journal of Religious History*, 10, 4 (1979), 381–99; J. Jaffe, 'The "chiliasm of despair" reconsidered: revivalism and working-class agitation in County Durham', *Journal of British Studies*, 28, 1 (1989), 28; Hobsbawm and Rudé, *Captain Swing*, 216.
29. E. Halevy, *A history of the English people in the nineteenth century, Vol. 3* (London, 1961); Halevy, *The birth of Methodism in England*, trans. Bernard Semmel (Chicago, 1971); E.P. Thompson, *The making of the English working class* (London, 1980/1963), 350–400; D. Hempton, *Methodism and politics in British society* (London, 1984), 74–6.
30. Gilbert, 'Methodism, dissent and political stability'.
31. N. Scotland, *Methodism and the revolt of the field* (Gloucester, 1981).

32. A. Gilbert, 'Religion and political stability in early industrial England', in P. O'Brien and R. Quinault (eds), *The industrial revolution and British society* (Cambridge, 1993), 93.

33. Thompson, *The making of the English working class*, 28; D. Hempton, *Religion and political culture in Britain and Ireland: from the Glorious Revolution to the decline of Empire* (Cambridge, 1995), 35.

34. Wood, *Riot, rebellion and popular politics*, 101–2.

35. A. Randall, *Riotous assemblies: popular protest in Hanoverian England* (Oxford, 2006), 77.

36. TNA, HO 42/61, fos 141–5.

37. TNA, HO 42/61, fos 5–6.

38. B. Reay, *The last rising of the agricultural labourers: rural life and protest in nineteenth-century England* (Oxford, 1990); Reay, 'The last rising of the agricultural labourers: the battle in Bossenden Wood, 1838', *History Workshop Journal*, 26, 1 (1988), 79–101.

39. C. Rose, *Property and persuasion: essays on the history, theory, and rhetoric of ownership* (Boulder, CO, 1994), 124.

40. Thompson, *Customs in common*, 97.

41. A. Randall, *Before the Luddites: custom, community and machinery in the English woollen industry, 1776–1809* (Cambridge, 1991), esp. ch. 6; L. Schwarz, 'Custom, wages and workload in England during industrialization', *P&P*, 197 (2007), 143–75. See also C. Fisher, *Custom, work and market capitalism: the Forest of Dean colliers, 1788–1888* (London, 1981).

42. P. Jones, 'Finding Captain Swing: protest, parish relations, and the state of the public mind in 1830', *IRSH*, 54, 3 (2009), 439–40.

43. J. Ruff, *Violence in early modern Europe, 1500–1800* (Cambridge, 2001), 160–82.

44. C. Griffin, 'The violent Captain Swing?', *P&P*, 209 (2010), 149–80; A. Charlesworth, R. Sheldon, A. Randall and D. Walsh, 'The Jack-a-Lent riots and opposition to turnpikes in the Bristol region in 1749', in A. Randall and A. Charlesworth (eds), *Markets, market culture and popular protest in eighteenth-century Britain and Ireland* (Liverpool, 1996), 46–68.

45. G. Seal, 'Tradition and agrarian protest in nineteenth-century England and Wales', *Folklore*, 99, 2 (1989), 146–69; D. Underdown, *Revel, riot, and rebellion: popular politics and culture in England 1603–1660* (Oxford, 1985).

46. A. Howkins and L. Merricks, 'Wee be black as hell': ritual, disguise and rebellion', *RH*, 4 (1993), 41–53.

47. *Lloyd's Evening Post and British Chronicle*, 25 July 1757.

48. Thompson, *Customs in common*, 261.

49. See especially, E.P. Thompson, 'The moral economy of the English crowd in the eighteenth-century', *P&P*, 50 (1971), 76–136; Thompson, 'Patrician society, plebeian culture', *Journal of Social History*, 7, 4 (1974), 382–405.

50. Ibid., 402.

51. Ibid., 397, 400.

52. See P. Langford, *Public life and the propertied Englishman, 1689–1798* (Oxford, 1991), 164. It is important to note, though, that as most turnpikes were

ancient thoroughfares, they had previously been maintained through parish-levied highway rates.

53. Charlesworth *et al.*, 'The Jack-A-Lent riots', 55; N. Rogers, *Mayhem: post-war crime and violence in Britain, 1748–53* (New Haven, CT, 2012), 117.

54. K. Binfield (ed.), *The writings of the Luddites* (Baltimore, MD, 2004) esp. 44–7; K. Navickas, 'The search for General Ludd: the mythology of Luddism', *SH*, 30, 3 (2005), 281–95.

55. T. Pettitt, '"Here comes I, Jack Straw": English folk drama and social revolt', *Folklore*, 95, 1 (1984), 11–12.

56. Rogers, *Mayhem*, 116; E. Muir, *Ritual in early modern Europe* (Cambridge, 1997), 4.

57. B. Bushaway, *By rite: custom, ceremony and community in England 1700–1880* (London, 1982), 191; P. Custer, 'Refiguring Jemima: gender, work and politics in Lancashire 1770–1820', *P&P*, 195 (2007), 131–2.

58. *Hampshire Advertiser*, 27 November 1830. For an excellent micro study of the rising at Owlesbury see: A. Howkins, 'The Owlesbury lads', *Southern History*, 32 (2010), 117–38.

59. J. Walter, *Crowds and popular politics in early modern England* (Manchester, 2006), 11.

60. Navickas, 'Moors, fields, and popular protest in south Lancashire and the West Riding of Yorkshire, 1800–1848', *Northern History*, 46, 1 (2009), 108–09.

61. B. Bushaway, 'From custom to crime: wood-gathering in eighteenth and early nineteenth-century England: a focus for conflict in Hampshire, Wiltshire and the South', in J. Rule (ed.), *Outside the law: studies in crime and order 1650–1850* (Exeter, 1982), 80–01.

62. C. Griffin, '"There was no law to punish that offence": re-assessing "Captain Swing": rural luddism and rebellion in East Kent, 1830–31', *Southern History*, 22 (2000), 153–4.

63. P. King, *Crime and law in England, 1750–1840: remaking justice from the margins* (Cambridge, 2006), 255–78; E. Griffin, 'Popular culture in industrializing England', *Historical Journal*, 45, 3 (2002), 619–35; Bushaway, *By rite*, ch. 7.

64. Hobsbawm and Rudé, *Captain Swing*, ch. 13; Griffin, *The rural war*, ch. 9.

65. R. Wells, *Wretched faces: famine in wartime England 1763–1803* (Gloucester, 1988), chs 15 and 16.

66. Wood, *Riot, rebellion and popular politics*, 109.

67. D. Eastwood, 'Communities, protest and police in early nineteenth-century Oxfordshire: the enclosure of Otmoor reconsidered', *AgHR*, 44, 1 (1995), 35.

68. As Karen Sayer notes, the conflation of the status of working women with that of their male relations might have cultural traction, but it also ignored the fact that the terms of women's protests were of their own making rather than set by men: 'Field-faring women: the resistance of women who worked in the fields of nineteenth-century England', *Women's History Review*, 2, 2 (1993), 185–98.

69. On the culture of migration see: K.D.M. Snell, 'Belonging and community: understandings of 'home' and 'friends' among the English poor, 1750–1850', *EcHR*, 65 (2012), 1–25. Also see: P. Hudson and S. King, 'Two textile

townships, *c.*1660–1820: a comparative demographic analysis', *EcHR*, 53 (2000), 706–41.

70. M. Reed, and R. Wells, 'An agenda for modern English rural history?', in Reed and Wells, *Class, conflict and protest*, 220–1.
71. These dynamics are brilliantly delineated in: K.D.M. Snell, *Parish and belonging: community, identity and welfare in England and Wales, 1700–1950* (Cambridge, 2006).
72. D. Underdown, 'The chalk and the cheese: contrasts among the English clubmen', *P&P*, 95 (1980), 25–48; J. Bohstedt, *Riots and community politics in England and Wales, 1790–1810* (Cambridge, MA, 1985).

Chapter 5

1. A. Charlesworth (ed.), *An atlas of rural protest, 1548–1900* (London, 1983).
2. D. Underdown, 'The chalk and the cheese: contrasts among the English clubmen', *P&P*, 85 (1979), 25–48; J. Bohstedt, *Riots and community politics in England and Wales, 1790–1810* (Cambridge, MA, 1985).
3. A. Randall, *Riotous assemblies: popular protest in Hanoverian England* (Oxford, 2006), 1–2.
4. J. Archer, *Social unrest and popular protest in England, 1780–1840* (Cambridge, 2001), 28.
5. Charlesworth, *An atlas of rural protest*, 83–111.
6. A. Charlesworth, 'From the moral economy of Devon to the political economy of Manchester, 1790–1812', *SH*, 18, 2 (1993), 210.
7. R.B. Rose, 'Eighteenth century price riots and public policy in England', *IRSH*, 6, 2 (1961), 288, 291. For an earlier acknowledgement of their importance see: M. Beloff, *Public order and popular disturbances, 1660–1714* (Oxford, 1938).
8. Charlesworth, 'From the moral economy of Devon', 210.
9. Archer, *Social unrest*, 39.
10. E.P. Thompson, *Customs in common* (London, 1991), 199.
11. Randall, *Riotous assemblies*, 76–7.
12. Ibid., 76; E.P. Thompson, 'Patrician society, plebeian culture', *Journal of Social History*, 7, 4 (1974), 382–405.
13. Forestalling was the purchasing of foodstuffs outside of the time of the market; regrating was the purchasing of foodstuffs at a lower price to create scarcity and then reselling at a higher price; while engrossing was the purchasing of all of a particular foodstuff in the market to create scarcity and thus push up prices.
14. For a useful summary of these ideas see: C. Schonhardt-Bailey, *From the corn laws to free trade: interests, ideas, and institutions in historical context* (Cambridge, MA, 2006), ch. 2.
15. R. Sheldon, 'Practical economics in eighteenth-century England: Charles Smith on the grain trade and the corn laws, 1756–72.', *Historical Research*, 81 (2008), 640.

16. See S. Brown, '"A Just and profitable commerce": moral economy and the middle classes in eighteenth-century London', *Journal of British Studies*, 32 (1993), 305–32.
17. *General Evening Post*, 23 and 28 May 1795; *Telegraph*, 16 July 1795.
18. *The Times*, 23 September 1800.
19. As early as the 1795 Shropshire Summer Assizes, Kenyon had pronounced that that the common law in relation to forestalling still held: D. Hay, 'The state and the market in 1800: Lord Kenyon and Mr Waddington', *P&P*, 162 (1999), 113–14.
20. Ibid., 102.
21. S. Poole, 'Scarcity and the civic tradition: market management in Bristol, 1753–1815', and W. Thwaites, 'Oxford food riots: a community and its markets', in A. Randall and A. Charlesworth (eds), *Markets, market culture and popular protest in eighteenth-century Britain and Ireland* (Liverpool, 1996), 91–114 and 137–62.
22. Archer, *Social unrest*, 39.
23. Bohstedt, *Riots and community politics*, 166, 169, 270.
24. Ibid., 168, 171–2.
25. For a neat summation of this revision see: Charlesworth, 'From the moral economy of Devon'. For Bohstedt's latest exposition see: *The politics of provisions: food riots, moral economy, and market transition in England, c. 1550–1850* (Farnham, 2010).
26. Randall, *Riotous assemblies*, 152.
27. R. Wells, *Wretched faces: famine in wartime England 1763–1803* (Gloucester, 1988), esp. 162–72.
28. A. Charlesworth and A. Randall, 'Morals, markets and the English crowd in 1766', *P&P*, 114 (1987), 202.
29. T. Richardson, 'The agricultural labourers' standard of living in Lincolnshire, 1790–1840: social protest and public order', *AgHR*, 41, 1 (1993), 6.
30. Wells, *Wretched faces*, 101–32, 162–80; Randall, *Riotous assemblies*, chs 4 and 5; Bohstedt, *Politics of provisions*, chs 4 and 5. On the Kingswood colliers see: R. Malcolmson, '"A set of ungovernable people": the Kingswood colliers in the eighteenth century', in J. Brewer and J. Styles (eds), *An ungovernable people: the English and their law in the seventeenth and eighteenth centuries* (London, 1980), 85–127.
31. TNA, HO 42/51 fos 455–7 and 42/52 fos 32–5.
32. *Sussex Weekly Advertiser*, 20 April; *Maidstone Journal*, 21 April 1795; TNA, WO 1/1092, fos 139–47.
33. Charlesworth, 'From the moral economy of Devon'; K. Navickas, *Loyalism and radicalism in Lancashire, 1798–1815* (Oxford, 2009), 169–71.
34. TNA, WO 1/1092 fos 139–47.
35. Navickas, *Loyalism and radicalism*, 32–4.
36. G. Rudé, *The crowd in the French revolution* (Oxford, 1959).
37. Charlesworth, *Atlas of rural protest*, 69; Boshtedt, *Riots and community politics*, ch. 2.

38. Wells, *Wretched faces*, 162.
39. The role of women in food riots remains a contentious area. See: J. Bohstedt, 'Gender, household and community politics: women in English riots, 1790–1810', *P&P*, 120 (1988), 88–122; Bohstedt, 'The myth of the feminine food riot: women as proto-citizens in English community politics, 1790–1810', in D. Levy and H. Applewhite (eds), *Women and politics in the age of democratic revolution* (Ann Arbor, MI, 1990), 21–60; and Thompson, *Customs in common*, ch.5.
40. *Reading Mercury*, 23 June 1800; *Sussex Weekly Advertiser*, 9 February 1801.
41. E. Fox Genovese, 'The many faces of the moral economy: a contribution to a debate', *P&P*, 58 (1973), 161–8.
42. L. Schwarz, 'Custom, wages and workload in England during industrialization', *P&P*, 197 (2007), 143–75.
43. For references see p. 136 (notes 62 and 63).
44. *Sussex Weekly Advertiser*, 9 March 1795.
45. Wells, *Wretched faces*, 426; TNA, Assi 94/1499, Indictment of William Brookes, labourer, Kent Summer Assizes 1800; TNA, HO 42/49 fos 359–60; Hampshire County Record Office (herein HCRO), Q9/1/481, Calendar for Hampshire Easter Quarter Sessions 1800; *Sussex Weekly Advertiser*, 21 April 1800; *Reading Mercury*, 16 and 23 June 1800.
46. HCRO, Q9/1/484, Calendar and indictments, Hampshire Epiphany Quarter Sessions 1801.
47. Wells, *Wretched faces*, 164.
48. Thompson, 'The moral economy', 128–31; C. Tilly, *Popular contention in Great Britain 1758–1834* (Cambridge, MA, 1995), see chs 1 and 2.
49. R. Wells, 'The development of the English rural proletariat and social protest, 1700–1850', in M. Reed and R. Wells (eds), *Class, conflict and protest in the English countryside, 1700–1880* (London, 1990), 45.
50. P. King, *Crime and law in England, 1750–1840: remaking justice from the margins* (Cambridge, 2006), 33, n.62; Randall, *Riotous assemblies*, ch. 6; R. Wells, 'The moral economy of the English countryside', in A. Randall and A. Charlesworth (eds), *Moral economy and popular protest: crowds, conflict and authority* (London, 2000), 209–72; P. Jones, 'Swing, Speenhamland and rural social relations: the 'moral economy' of the English crowd in the nineteenth century', *SH*, 32, 3 (2007), 271–90.
51. Boshtedt, *The politics of provisions*, 231–40.
52. *Sherborne and Yeovil Mercury*, 20 September 1756; *Salisbury Journal*, 31 January 1757.
53. *Sussex Weekly Advertiser*, 28 February 1757.
54. *Sussex Weekly Advertiser*, 7 February 1757.
55. TNA, HO 42/117, fos 448–9.
56. S. Poole, '"A lasting and salutary warning": incendiarism, rural order and England's last scene of crime execution', *RH*, 19, 2 (2008), 163.
57. E. Hobsbawm and G. Rudé, *Captain Swing* (London, 1969), 312, 98, 12. By contrast see: J.L. Hammond and B. Hammond, *The village labourer* (London, 1978, first published 1911), 179.

58. D. Jones, 'Thomas Campbell Foster and the rural labourer: incendiarism in East Anglia in the 1840s', *SH*, 1, 1 (1976), 5–37.

59. E.P. Thompson, *Whigs and hunters: the origin of the Black Act* (London, 1975), 83, 104, 143, 147, 165–6.

60. Jones, 'Thomas Campell Foster', 5.

61. Poole, 'A lasting and salutary warning', 163.

62. Wells, 'The development of the English rural proletariat', 45.

63. A. Charlesworth, 'The development of the English rural proletariat and social protest, 1700–1850: a comment', in Reed and Wells, *Class, conflict and protest*, 59–60.

64. R. Wells, 'Social conflict and protest in the English countryside in the early nineteenth century: a rejoinder', in Reed and Wells, *Class, conflict and protest*, 66–7.

65. Wells, *Wretched Faces*, 165; Wells, 'Social protest, class, conflict and consciousness, in the English countryside, 1700–1880', in Reed and Wells, *Class, conflict and protest*, 158.

66. Ibid., 158.

67. J. Archer, *By a flash and a scare: arson, animal maiming, and poaching in East Anglia 1815–1870* (Oxford, 1990), 177–97; Archer, 'A fiendish outrage?' A study of animal maiming in East Anglia: 1830–1870', *AgHR* 33, 2 (1985), 147–57; C. Griffin, '"Cut down by some cowardly miscreants": plant-maiming, or the malicious cutting of flora, as an act of protest in eighteenth- and nineteenth-century rural England', *RH*, 19: 1 (2008), esp. 42–5.

68. On the marginal position of lads see: P. King, 'The rise of juvenile delinquency in England 1780–1840: changing patterns of perception and prosecution', *P&P*, 160 (1998), 116–66. On the primary employment of married men see: S. Williams, 'Malthus, marriage and poor law allowances revisited: a Bedfordshire case study, 1770–1834', *AgHR*, 52, 1 (2004), 56–82.

69. Wells, 'Social protest', 137; C. Steedman, *Labours lost: domestic service and the making of modern England* (Cambridge, 2009), 181–98.

70. Archer, *By a flash and a scare*, 195, 293.

71. Ibid., 180–97, 160–01.

72. *Brighton Patriot*, 28 July 1835.

73. Poole, 'A lasting and salutary warning', 264.

74. *Morning Post*, 30 October 1822; *Salisbury and Winchester Journal*, 8 August 1825; *Kentish Gazette*, 31 August 1847.

75. TNA HO 42/149, fos 45–5.

76. TNA, HO 64/1, fos 310–13.

77. Archer, *By a flash and a scare, passim*.

78. K. Bawn, 'Social protest, popular disturbances and public order in Dorset, 1790–1838' (unpublished Ph.D. thesis, University of Reading, 1984), 103–4; Shakesheff, *Rural conflict, crime and protest*, 191–2; Archer, *By a flash and a scare*, 148.

79. C. Griffin, '"As lated tongues bespoke": popular protest in south-east England, 1790–1840' (unpublished Ph.D. thesis, University of Bristol, 2002), 296–8; R. Baxter, *The trial of the Rev. Robert Bingham* (Lewes, 1811).

80. P.G.M. Dickson, *The Sun Insurance office, 1710–1960* (Oxford, 1960), 141–2.
81. *Sussex Advertiser,* 25 August 1823; *The Times,* 6 September 1827; *Maidstone Journal,* 7 September 1842; *Rochester Gazette,* 4 January 1848; *Dover Telegraph,* 28 April 1849.
82. *Maidstone Journal,* 16 April 1850.
83. Jones, 'Thomas Campbell Foster', 13–14.
84. C. Griffin, *The rural war: Captain Swing and the politics of protest* (Manchester, 2012), 52–4.
85. A. Randall, *Before the Luddites: custom, community and machinery in the English woollen industry, 1776–1809* (Cambridge, 1991), 155–79; K. Navickas, 'Luddism, incendiarism, and the defence of rural "task–scapes" in 1812', *Northern History,* 48, 1 (2011), 64–70.
86. C. Griffin, 'More-than-human histories and the failure of grand state schemes: sylviculture in the New Forest, England', *Cultural Geographies,* 17, 4 (2010), 451–72.
87. J. Black, *The English press, 1621–1861* (Stroud, 2001), 8–9, 13; H.R. Fox Bourne, *English newspapers: chapters in the history of journalism* (London, 1887), 383.
88. Bawn, 'Social protest, popular disturbances and public order in Dorset', appendix 2.
89. T. Shakesheff, *Rural conflict, crime and protest: Herefordshire, 1800–1860* (Woodbridge, 2003), appendix 1; Griffin, *The rural war,* 50
90. Archer, *By a flash and a scare,* 166–7.
91. *Kentish Gazette,* 27 December 1831. On Dixon, see Griffin, *The rural war,* 305.
92. Bawn, 'Social protest, popular disturbances and public order in Dorset', 107.
93. Wells, 'Social protest', 158, 164, 170, 173.
94. See note 85; J. Archer, 'The Wells–Charlesworth debate: a personal comment on arson in Norfolk and Suffolk', in Reed and Wells, *Class, conflict and protest,* 86.
95. Hobsbawm and Rudé, *Captain Swing,* 200, 203.

Chapter 6

1. C. Tilly, *Social movements, 1768–2004* (Boulder, CO, 2004), 16–25.
2. W. Nicholls, 'Place, networks, space: theorising the geographies of social movements', *Transactions of the Institute of British Geographers,* 34, 1 (2009) 88.
3. S. Tarrow, *Power in movement: social movements and contentious politics* (Cambridge, 1998).
4. For a critique of Tilly's model see: K. Navickas, 'What happened to class?: New histories of labour and collective action in Britain', *SH,* 36, 2 (2011), 197.
5. For two fine surveys of theories of collective engagement see: R. Eyerman and A. Jamison, *Social movements: a cognitive approach* (Cambridge, 1991); S. Tarrow, 'Cycles of collective action', in M. Traugott (ed.), *Repertoires and cycles of contention* (Durham, NC, 1995), 89–116.
6. A. Wood, *The 1549 rebellions and the making of early modern England* (Cambridge, 2007).

7. P. Glennie and N. Thrift, *Shaping the day: a history of timekeeping in England and Wales, 1300–1800* (Oxford, 2009), 94.
8. H. Jennings, *Pandemonium: the coming of the machine as seen by contemporary observers, 1660–1885* (London, 1986).
9. A. Randall, *Before the Luddites: custom, community and machinery in the English woollen industry, 1776–1809* (Cambridge, 1991), 41–4.
10. J. Mokyr, *The lever of riches: technological creativity and economic progress* (Oxford, 1992).
11. A. Randall, *Riotous assemblies: popular protest in Hanoverian England* (Oxford, 2006), 246–8.
12. Ibid., 240–5.
13. A. Randall, 'The shearmen and the Wiltshire Outrages of 1802: trade unionism and industrial violence', *SH*, 7, 3 (1982), 283–304; Randall, *Riotous assembles*, 250–9.
14. J.L. Hammond and B. Hammond, *The skilled labourer 1760–1832* (London, 1919), 46–70; Randall, *Riotous assemblies*, 260–3.
15. K. Navickas, 'Luddism, incendiarism, and the defence of rural "task–scapes" in 1812', *Northern History*, 48, 1 (2011), 64–7.
16. Navickas, *Loyalism and radicalism in Lancashire, 1798–1815* (Oxford, 2009), 192.
17. Randall, *Riotous assemblies*, 263–70.
18. Ibid., 273.
19. See K. Binfield (ed.), *The writings of the Luddites* (Baltimore, MD, 2004), 168–9.
20. Information for these paragraphs is taken from: Randall, *Riotous assemblies*, 271–83.
21. Navickas, *Loyalism and radicalism*, 193.
22. Binfield, *Writings of the Luddites*, 169.
23. Randall, *Riotous assemblies*, 290.
24. Navickas, *Loyalism and radicalism*, 195–6.
25. Navickas, 'Luddism, incendiarism, and the defence of rural "task–scapes"', 65.
26. Navickas, 'The search for "General Ludd"', 284.
27. E.P. Thompson, *The making of the English working class* (London, 1980, first published 1963), 594. Also see: P. Linebaugh, *Ned Ludd & Queen Mab: machine-breaking, romanticism, and the several commons of 1811–12* (Oakland, CA, 2012), 13.
28. Binfield, *Writings of the Luddites*, 153–66; M. Thomis, *The Luddites: machine-breaking in Regency England* (Newton Abbot, 1970), 182.
29. N. Gash, 'After Waterloo: British society and the legacy of the Napoleonic wars', *Transactions of the Royal Historical Society* (fifth series), 28 (1978), 147. For a more detailed analysis of these dynamics see Chapter 1, especially pp. 30–4.
30. A. Peacock, *Bread or blood: a study of the agrarian riots in East Anglia in 1816* (London, 1965), 27–9.
31. See A. Charlesworth, *A comparative study of the spread of the agricultural disturbances of 1816, 1822 and 1830* (Liverpool, 1982).
32. Peacock, *Bread or blood*, 69–70; C. Griffin, *The rural war: Captain Swing and the politics of protest* (Manchester, 2012), 52.
33. Peacock, *Bread or blood*, 71–5.

34. TNA, HO 42/ 149, fos 1–2 and 13–15.
35. *Bury and Norwich Post*, 8 May 1816; TNA, HO 42, 150, fos 8–11.
36. Peacock, *Bread or blood*, 75–7. Stoke-by-Clare saw renewed machine-breaking on 22 May, while also in an isolated protest a demonstration occurred over food prices at nearby Haverhill on 15 May: *Morning Chronicle*, 25 May 1816; A. Charlesworth (ed.), *An atlas of rural protest, 1548–1900* (London, 1983), 146.
37. Peacock, *Bread or blood*, 77.
38. Charlesworth, *Atlas of rural protest*, 148.
39. *Bury and Norwich Post*, 27 May 1816.
40. *Bury and Norwich Post*, 27 May 1816; P. Warren (ed.) *Report of the trials for rioting at Ely and Littleport* (Wilburton, 1997), 1–42.
41. Ibid., 146; Peacock, *Bread or blood*, 116–19.
42. Charlesworth, *Atlas of rural protest*, 147.
43. For examples, see P. Muskett, 'The East Anglian agrarian riots of 1822', *AgHR*, 32, 1 (1984), 3.
44. For an exploration of these dynamics, see Chapter 1, pp. 30–4.
45. N. Fox, 'The spread of the threshing machine in central southern England', *AgHR*, 26, 1 (1978), 26–8.
46. *Ipswich Journal*, 2 February 1822; Muskett, 'East Anglian agrarian riots', 5.
47. Ibid., 5; *Bury and Norwich Post*, 20 February 1822.
48. *The Ipswich Journal*, 9 and 16 March; *Morning Chronicle*, 9 March; *Bury and Norwich Post*, 20 March 1822; P. Muskett, *Riotous assemblies: popular disturbances in East Anglia, 1740–1822* (Ely, 1984), 61–70.
49. TNA, HO 52/3, fos. 34–7 and 38–9.
50. Muskett, 'East Anglian agrarian riots', 6–7; Muskett, *Riotous assemblies*, 66–8.
51. Ibid., 68; Charlesworth, *Atlas of rural protest*, 148.
52. *Maidstone Gazette*, 9 April, 14 May and 4 June; *Hampshire Chronicle*, 22 April and 13 May; *Kentish Gazette*, 12 April and 5 July; *Times*, 28 June 1822; TNA, Assi 94/1849, indictment of John Wraith, Kent Summer Assizes 1822.
53. J. Archer, *By a flash and a scare: arson, animal maiming, and poaching in East Anglia, 1815–1870* (Oxford, 1990), 70, 85–6.
54. Quoted in Archer, *By a flash and a scare*, 88.
55. Griffin, *The rural war*, 67–8.
56. *Brighton Guardian*, 14 October 1829.
57. Archer, *By a flash and a scare*, 88; *Dorset County Chronicle*, 15 April 1830.
58. *Kent and Essex Mercury*, 13 and 27 January, 3, 17 and 24 February, 3, 10, 17 and 24 March 1829; J. Gyford, *Men of bad character: the Witham fires of the 1820s* (Chelmsford, 1991).
59. Archer, *By a flash and a scare*, 87–8.
60. *Devizies and Wiltshire Gazette*, 5 November 1829.
61. Griffin, *The rural war*, 87–90; E. Hobsbawm and G. Rudé, *Captain Swing* (London, 1969), 85; C. Griffin, 'Policy on the hoof': Sir Robert Peel, Sir Edward Knatchbull and the trial of the Elham machine breakers, 1830', *RH*, 15, 2 (2004), 131–5.
62. *Kentish Gazette*, 8 and 15 October; *Brighton Herald*, 16 October 1830.
63. Griffin, 'Policy on the hoof', 136–7.

64. Griffin, *The rural war*, 91, 92–3.
65. *Maidstone Journal*, 12 October 1830.
66. Centre for Kentish Studies, Q/SBw/124/7; TNA, HO 52/8, fos 365–6 and 361–2.
67. R. Wells, 'Mr. William Cobbett, Captain Swing and King William IV', *AgHR*, 45, 1 (1997), 35–6, 39; Griffin, *The rural war*, 95–7; East Sussex County Record Office, AMS 5995/3/10 and 13.
68. Griffin, *The rural war*, 97–103.
69. TNA, HO 52/8, fos 621–2; West Sussex County Record Office, QR/Q 51.
70. For the role of fires before the outbreak of collective actions see: C. Griffin, '"The mystery of the fires": "Captain Swing" as incendiarist', *Southern History*, 32 (2010), 31–4.
71. N. Gash, 'The rural unrest in England in 1830 with special reference to Berkshire' (unpublished B.Litt thesis, University of Oxford, 1934), 56–8; Hobsbawm and Rudé, *Captain Swing*, 134 and appendix 3.
72. Quantification based on Griffin, *The rural war*, appendix.
73. TNA, HO 52/7, fos 46–7; *Hampshire Advertiser*, 27 November 1830; TNA, HO 130/1 Calendar of the Winchester Special Commission, case numbers 98 and 154.
74. Hobsbawm and Rudé, *Captain Swing*, 122–3 and appendix 3.
75. I. Dyck, *William Cobbett and rural popular culture* (Cambridge, 1993), 171–7; D. Kent, *Popular radicalism and the Swing riots in central Hampshire*, Hampshire papers, no. 11 (Winchester, 1997), 3–9, 13–14; A. Somerville, *The whistler at the plough* (London, 1852), 262.
76. P. Jones, 'Finding Captain Swing: protest, parish relations, and the state of the public mind in 1830', *IRSH*, 54, 3 (2009), 443–54; Hobsbawm and Rudé, *Captain Swing*, 135–40.
77. A. Randall and E. Newman, 'Protest, proletarians and paternalists: social conflict in rural Wiltshire, 1830–1850', *RH*, 6, 2 (1995), 209–13.
78. Hobsbawm and Rudé, *Captain Swing*, 304–05.
79. R. Wells, 'Social protest, class, conflict and consciousness, in the English countryside, 1700–1880', in M. Reed and R. Wells (eds), *Class, conflict and protest in the English countryside, 1700–1880* (London, 1990), 165–6; C. Griffin, '"There was no law to punish that offence": re-assessing "Captain Swing": rural Luddism and rebellion in East Kent, 1830–31', *Southern History*, 22 (2000), esp. 139–40. Also see D. Kent and N. Townsend, *The convicts of the 'Eleanor': protest in rural England, new lives in Australia* (London, 2002), Ch. 5.
80. Griffin, *The rural war*, 104–05, 108–10 and 113–14.
81. Hobsbawm and Rudé, *Captain Swing*, 253–6.
82. *Dorset County Chronicle*, 2 and 9 December; *Sherborne Journal*, 2 December 1830; Bawn, 'Social protest, popular disturbances and public order in Dorset', ch.4; TNA, HO 52/7, fo. 321; *Dorset County Chronicle*, 2 and 9 December 1830; Hobsbawm and Rudé, *Captain Swing*, 129–30, 338–9, 344–5.
83. Ibid., 130–1; *Western Flying Post*, 6 December 1830; J. Maynard, 'The agricultural labourer in Worcestershire: responses to economic change and social dislocation 1790–1841' (unpublished Ph.D. thesis, Coventry

University, 2006), 184, 191–3, 198. On the relative paucity of protest but depth of paranoia in the West Midlands see: E. Richards, '"Captain Swing" in the West Midlands', *IRSH*, 19, 1 (1974), 86–99.

84. Hobsbawm and Rudé, *Captain Swing*, 128–9, 140, 141.
85. Ibid., 143–50; *The Standard*, 1 December 1830. Also see G. Chambers, *Buckinghamshire machine breakers: the story of the 1830 riots* (Lutterworth, 1991).
86. Archer, *By a flash and a scare*, 89–95; Hobsbawm and Rudé, *Captain Swing*, 152–62.
87. Ibid., 146–7.
88. T. Richardson, 'The agricultural labourers' standard of living in Lincolnshire, 1790–1840: social protest and public order', *AgHR*, 41, 1 (1993), 10–14; Hobsbawm and Rudé, *Captain Swing*, 135–6, appendix 1.
89. For a striking attempt to underpin the importance of diffusion to Swing through complex mathematical methods see: D. Myers and J. Przybysz, 'The diffusion of contentious gatherings in the Captain Swing uprising', *Southern History*, 32 (2010), 62–84.
90. Hobsbawm and Rudé, *Captain Swing*, appendix 3; Navickas, 'Captain Swing in the north: the Carlisle riots of 1830', *History Workshop Journal*, 71 (2011), 15, 17.
91. Jones, 'Finding Captain Swing', 457.
92. TNA, TS 11/1007, Prosecution brief prepared by the Treasury Solicitor against Richard Hodd and John Wickens for Riot, Lewes Winter Assizes 1830.
93. West Sussex County Record Office, QR/W/758 fos 280, 269, 270, 271 and 272.
94. TNA, HO 40/27/5 fos 440–01.
95. J. Burchard, *The allotment movement in England, 1793–1873* (Woodbridge, 2002), esp. 51–5.
96. Griffin, *The rural war*, 319.
97. Binfield, *Writings of the Luddites, passim*.
98. Griffin, *The rural war*, 218.
99. TNA, HO 52/10, fo. 373.
100. On this point see: S. Shave, 'The impact of Sturges Bourne's poor law reforms in rural England', *Historical Journal*, 56, 2 (2013), esp. 414–17.
101. *Brighton Gazette*, 11 November 1830 and 4 August 1831.
102. Hobsbawm and Rudé, *Captain Swing*, 281.
103. C. Griffin, 'Swing, Swing redivivus, or something after Swing? On the death throes of a protest movement, December 1830–December 1833', *IRSH*, 54, 3 (2009), 459–97; Wells, 'Resistance to the new poor law', *passim*; Archer, *By a flash and a scare*, 95–116; Neuman and Randall, 'Protest, proletarians and paternalists', 213–21.

Chapter 7

1. E.P. Thompson, *The making of the English working class* (London, 1980, first published 1963), 252, 201; J. Rule and R. Wells, *Crime, protest and popular politics in southern England, 1740–1850* (London, 1997), 2.

2. E.P. Thompson, 'Rural riots', *New Society*, 13 February 1969, 251–2; Thompson, *The making of the English working class*, 806; E. Hobsbawm and G. Rudé, *Captain Swing* (London, 1973), 2nd edn.

3. R. Wells, *Insurrection: the British experience 1795–1803* (Gloucester, 1983); Wells, *Wretched faces: famine in wartime England 1763–1803* (Gloucester, 1988); Wells, 'Social protest, class, conflict and consciousness, in the English countryside, 1700–1880' in M. Reed and R. Wells (eds), *Class, conflict and protest in the English countryside*, 1700–1880 (London, 1990), 121–98; I. Dyck, *William Cobbett and rural popular culture* (Cambridge, 1993); M. Chase, *The people's farm: English radical agrarianism, 1775–1840* (Oxford, 1988); K. Navickas, *Loyalism and radicalism in Lancashire, 1798–1815* (Oxford, 2009).

4. L. Colley, 'Eighteenth-century English radicalism before Wilkes', *Transactions of the Royal Historical Society*, 31 (1981), 1–19.

5. P. Monod, *Jacobitism and the English people, 1688–1788* (Cambridge, 1989), 170, 176; Thompson, *Whigs and hunters*, 164–5, 200.

6. J. Oates, 'Jacobitism and popular disturbances in Northern England, 1714–1719', *Northern History*, 41, 1 (2004), 127.

7. D. Szechi, *The Jacobites: Britain and Europe, 1688–1788* (Manchester, 1994), 24.

8. N. Rogers, *Mayhem: post-war crime and violence in Britain, 1748–53* (New Haven, CT, 2012), 111–4.

9. Monod, *Jacobitism*, 197; *Kentish Post*, 7 November 1757.

10. N. Rogers, *Crowds, culture, and politics in Georgian Britain* (Oxford, 1998), 57.

11. D. Wright, *Popular radicalism: the working class experience 1780–1880* (London, 1988), 31.

12. Rogers, *Crowds, culture, and politics*, esp. chs 1–3.

13. Navickas, *Loyalism and radicalism in Lancashire*, 131–75; K. Navickas, 'Moors, fields, and popular protest in south Lancashire and the West Riding of Yorkshire, 1800–1848', *Northern History*, 66, 1 (2009), 93–111.

14. R. Wells, *Insurrection*, 89, 241–6.

15. *Sussex Weekly Advertiser*, 20 April and 10 October 1795; Wells, *Insurrection*, 104–05.

16. F. O'Gorman, 'The Paine burnings of 1792–1793', *P&P*, 193 (2006), 111–55; Thompson, *Making of the English working class*, 430.

17. *Sussex Weekly Advertiser*, 31 December 1792; *Hampshire Chronicle*, 21 March 1793.

18. TNA, Assi 94/1387, indictment of John Thatcher, Kent Lent Assizes 1794.

19. G. Williams, *Artisans and sans-culottes: popular movements in France and Britain during the French Revolution* (London, 1968), 67.

20. *Hampshire Chronicle*, 10 March 1800; R. Wells, 'The development of the English rural proletariat and social protest, 1700–1850', in M. Reed and R. Wells (eds), *Class, conflict and protest in the English countryside, 1700–1880* (London, 1990), 45.

21. Navickas, *Loyalism and radicalism in Lancashire*, 169–70.

22. TNA, HO 42/35 fos 29–31.

23. TNA, HO 42/61, fos 141–5.

24. Navickas, *Loyalism and radicalism in Lancashire*, 209, 218; P. Spence, *The birth of romantic radicalism: war, popular politics, and English radical reformism, 1800–1815* (Aldershot, 1996), 81.

25. Navickas, *Loyalism and radicalism in Lancashire*, 222–3; Wright, *Popular radicalism*, 58–9.

26. Ibid., 66–7.

27. M. Chase, *The people's farm: English radical agrarianism, 1775–1840* (Oxford, 1988).

28. J. Belchem, *Popular radicalism in nineteenth-century Britain* (Basingstoke, 1996), 49; R. Poole, 'French revolution or Peasants' Revolt? Petitioners and rebels in England from the Blanketeers to the Chartists', *Labour History Review*, 47, 1 (2009), 6–26; Wright, *Popular radicalism*, 76.

29. Wells, 'Social protest', 183.

30. Ibid., 182.

31. *Hampshire Telegraph*, 10 March 1823.

32. For the outstanding study of Cobbett's rural radicalism see: Dyck, *William Cobbett, passim*.

33. See K. Beresford, '"Witnesses for the defence": the yeomen of old England and the Land Question, c.1815–1837', in M. Cragoe and P. Readman (eds), *The land question in Britain, 1750–1950* (Basingstoke, 2010), 37–51.

34. *Two-Penny Trash*, November 1830.

35. *Cobbett's Weekly Political Register*, 5 June 1830.

36. Quoted in Dyck, *William Cobbett*, 170–01.

37. Ibid., 171.

38. BPP. Commons, 'Report from His Majesty's Commissioners for inquiring into the administration and practical operation of the poor laws', (1834), vol. xxxiv, 475e, 478e and 503e.

39. R. Wells, 'Mr. William Cobbett, Captain Swing and King William IV', *AgHR*, 45, 1 (1997), 34–48; Dyck, *William Cobbett*, ch. 7.

40. For a detailed exposition of these arguments see: C. Griffin, *The rural war: Captain Swing and the politics of protest* (Manchester, 2012), chs 6 and 7.

41. *Sherborne Journal*, 13 January 1831.

42. J. Stevenson, *Popular disturbances in England, 1700–1832* (London, 1992) (2nd edn), 290–3.

43. See J. Caple, *The Bristol riots of 1831 and social reform in Britain* (Lewiston, NY, 1990).

44. Dorset History Centre (herein DHC), NG/PR1/D2/2: Prison Register, 1827–38, 113–18.

45. See: J. Wasserman and E. Jaggard, 'Electoral violence in mid-nineteenth-century England and Wales', *Historical Research*, 80 (2006), 124–55.

46. N. Lopatin, *Political unions, popular politics, and the Great Reform Act of 1832* (Basingstoke, 1999); *Kent Herald*, 19 April and 24 May 1832.

47. *Hampshire Telegraph*, 2 July 1832. *Cobbett's Weekly Political Register*, 30 June; *Brighton Gazette*, 26 July; *Sussex Advertiser*, 6 August 1832. According to Ian Dyck, Melbourne thought the Chopsticks' Festival to be 'a seditious affair', but as no report of the Festival was made no prosecution could be brought: *William Cobbett*, 198–9.

48. *Hampshire Advertiser*, 11 August 1832.

49. *Berrow's Worcester Journal*, 10 November 1831.

50. Dyck, *William Cobbett*, 198; *Poor Man's Guardian*, 1 December 1832.

51. Griffin, *The rural war*, 309–11; *Hampshire Advertiser*, 19 May 1832.

52. J. Parry, *The rise and fall of liberal government in Victorian Britain* (New Haven, CT, 1993), 99; Belchem, *Popular radicalism*, 72.

53. H. Fraser, *A history of British trade unionism, 1700–1998* (Basingstoke, 1999), 1; C.R. Dobson, *Masters and journeymen: a prehistory of industrial relations, 1717–1800* (London, 1980), 2, appendix.

54. Ibid., 21, 154–65.

55. R. Wells, 'Tolpuddle in the context of English agrarian labour history, 1780–1850', in J. Rule (ed.) *British trade unionism: the formative years* (London, 1988), 11; *Salisbury and Winchester Journal*, 3 May 1790.

56. Wells, 'Tolpuddle', 118.

57. *Kentish Gazette*, 19 October 1821.

58. TNA, HO 52/15, fo. 15; Wells, 'Tolpuddle', 121.

59. University of Southampton Special Collections, WP4/4/3/34.

60. Wright, *Popular radicalism*, 104; TNA HO 64/15, fo.106, cited in Wells, 'Tolpuddle', 122.

61. J. Marlow, *The Tolpuddle Martyrs* (London, 1971), 165–6.

62. DHC, D/FSI, Accession 99, 5, uncatalogued ('Rural disorders' file: Frampton, Moreton to the Earl of Ilchester, 25 November 1830).

63. *Southampton Herald*, 30 January 1826; *Dorset County Chronicle*, 28 February; *Morning Post*, 15 March 1833; Wells, 'Tolpuddle', 121; G. Loveless, *The victims of Whiggery* (1887, first published 1838), 5.

64. *Western Flying Post*, 20 and 27 January 1834.

65. Wells, 'Tolpuddle', 121–2.

66. DHC, D/FSI/Box 242, James Frampton, Moreton to the Earl of Ilchester, n.d. (but March 1834).

67. Quoted in Wells, 'Tolpuddle', 122; Marlow, *The Tolpuddle Martyrs*, 41–8.

68. Information from which this and the previous paragraph is drawn is from W. Citrine, *The book of the Martyrs of Tolpuddle, 1834–1934* (London, 1934), passim; Marlow, *The Tolpuddle Martyrs*, Chs 4–10, 13; Wells, 'Tolpuddle', 122–3; A. Norman, *The story of George Loveless and the Tolpuddle Martyrs* (Wellington, 2008).

69. Marlow, *Tolpuddle Martyrs*, 160–73 and ch. 15.

70. Loveless, *The victims of Whiggery*; Marlow, *Tolpuddle Martyrs*, 207.

71. Ibid., 205–13, 217–26. On Gipps see: Griffin, *The rural war*, 92, 119, n.34.

72. Wells, 'Tolpuddle', 123; *Hampshire Advertiser*, 8 November; *Brighton Herald*, 29 November and 6 December 1834.

73. C. Griffin, '"As lated tongues bespoke": popular protest in south-east England, 1790–1840' (unpublished Ph.D. thesis, University of Bristol, 2002), 225–30; J. Lowerson, 'The aftermath of Swing: anti-poor law movements and rural trades unions in the south-east of England', in. A. Charlesworth (ed.), *Rural social change and conflicts since 1550* (Hull, 1983); and Wells, 'Resistance to the New Poor Law', 101–05.

74. *Essex Standard*, 15 July 1835; Wells, 'Tolpuddle', 125.

75. *The People's Charter*, 2.

76. M. Chase, *Chartism: a new history* (Manchester, 2007), 1–19.

77. The outstanding recent study of Chartism is Malcolm Chase's *Chartism*. Other excellent recent studies are: C. Frank, *Master and servant law: Chartists, trade unions, radical lawyers and the magistracy in England, 1840–1865* (Farnham, 2010); Navickas, 'Moors, fields and popular protest'; Poole, 'French revolution or Peasant's Revolt?'; R. Swift, 'Policing Chartism, 1839–1848: the role of the Specials reconsidered', *English Historical Review*, 497 (2007), 669–99. For a slightly older but vital revisionist account of Chartism beyond its major centres see: R. Wells, 'Southern Chartism', *RH*, 2, 1 (1991), 37–59.

78. J. Martin, 'Oratory, itinerant lecturing and Victorian popular politics: a case study of James Acland (1799–1876)', *Historical Research*, 86 (2013), 31.

79. Chase, *Chartism*, 31, 35.

80. Ibid., 31–2. On the 'tradition' of meeting on the moors, see: Navickas, 'Moors, fields, and popular protest', 93–111.

81. Wells, 'Southern Chartism', 39–49; DHC, D/FRA/X32, Undersecretary Phillips, Home Office to James Frampton, 26 November 1838.

82. Chase, *Chartism*, 41.

83. A.F.J. Brown, *Chartism in Essex and Suffolk* (Chelmsford, 1982), 96–7.

84. On rich, associational, radical cultures see: C. Calhoun, *The question of class struggle: social foundations of popular radicalism during the industrial revolution* (Blackwell, 1982), chs 6 and 7; A. Randall and E. Newman, 'Protest, proletarians and paternalists: social conflict in rural Wiltshire, 1830–1850', *RH*, 6, 2 (1995), 220.

85. J. Rule, 'The Chartist mission to Cornwall', in Rule and Wells, *Crime, Protest and Popular Politics*, 67–80; Chase, *Chartism*, 65.

86. *Kent Herald*, 24 January 1839; Wells, 'Southern Chartism', 40.

87. *Sussex Agricultural Express*, 30 March, 1, 8 and 27 April 1839; Wells, 'Southern Chartism', 42–3.

88. Chase, *Chartism*, 65–6.

89. Ibid., 68–87, 95–110.

90. D. Jones, *The last rising: the Newport Chartist insurrection of 1839* (Cardiff, 1999), *passim*; Chase, *Chartism*, 127–9.

91. Ibid., 163.

92. At this time land reform ran deep through Chartist thought: M. Chase, 'Chartism and the land: "the mighty people's question"', in M. Cragoe and P. Readman (eds), *The land question in Britain, 1750–1950* (Basingstoke, 2010), 65–6.

93. Wells, 'Southern Chartism', 46–51; R. Hastings, *Chartism in the North Riding of Yorkshire and south Durham, 1838–48*, Borthwick Papers 105 (York, 2004), 26–8; Chase, *Chartism*, ch. 7. The 'Plug-Plot' riots remain little studied. For the landmark account see: F.C. Mather, 'The general strike of 1842: a study in leadership, organisation and the threat of revolution during the Plug Plot disturbances', in R. Quinault and J. Stevenson (eds), *Popular protest and public order: six studies in British History 1790–1920* (London, 1974), 115–35.

94. Wells, 'Southern Chartism', 52.

95. Brown, *Chartism in Essex and Suffolk*, 77.

96. Chase, *Chartism*, 259–61, 277, 291–2.

97. Quoted in Brown, *Chartism in Essex and Suffolk*, 80.

98. Chase, *Chartism*, 296–7, 300–03.

99. Chase, *Chartism*, 313.

100. Ibid., 315, 319–5.

101. M. Chase, 'Labour's candidates: Chartist challenges at the parliamentary polls, 1839–1860', *Labour History Review*, 74, 1 (2009), 78; Chase, *Chartism*, 326–40.

Conclusion

1. J. Bohstedt, *Riots and community politics in England and Wales, 1790–1810* (Cambridge, MA, 1985), ch. 2. For later riots see: A. Charlesworth (ed.), *An atlas of rural protest 1548–1900* (London, 1983), ch. 3, 11; *Salisbury and Winchester Journal*, 15 and 22 May 1826; *Bath Chronicle*, 11 and 25 May 1826. In his latest survey, Bohstedt underestimates the resort to food rioting in the immediate post-Napoleonic period: *The politics of provisions: food riots, moral economy, and market transition in England, c. 1550–1850* (Farnham, 2010), 246–50.

2. A. Randall, *Riotous assemblies: popular protest in Hanoverian England* (Oxford, 2006), 46.

3. G. Stedman-Jones, *Languages of class: studies in working class history, 1832–1982* (Cambridge, 1983), 33.

4. C. Griffin, 'Knowable geographies? The reporting of incendiarism in the eighteenth- and early nineteenth century English provincial press', *Journal of Historical Geography*, 32, 1 (2006), 38–56.

5. R. Wells, *Wretched faces: famine in wartime England, 1763–1803* (Gloucester, 1988), 162–70; S. Poole, '"A lasting and salutary warning": incendiarism, rural order and England's last scene of crime execution', *RH*, 19, 2 (2008), 163–77; D. Jones, 'Thomas Campbell Foster and the rural labourer: incendiarism in East Anglia in the 1840s', *SH*, 1, 1 (1976), 5–37; C. Griffin, '"The mystery of the fires": "Captain Swing" as incendiarist', *Southern History*, 32 (2010), 22–44.

6. E.P. Thompson, 'The moral economy of the English crowd in the eighteenth-century', *P&P*, 50 (1971), 76–136; A. Charlesworth, 'From the moral economy of Devon to the political economy of Manchester, 1790–1812', *SH*, 18, 2 (1993), 210.

7. R. Wells, 'The development of the English rural proletariat and social protest, 1700–1850', *JPS*, 6, 2 (1979), 115–39.

8. W. Rostow, *British economy of the nineteenth century* (Oxford, 1948), 124; Cobbett quoted in *Birmingham Journal*, 12 November 1836.

9. Thompson, 'The moral economy'.

10. J. Stevenson, *Popular disturbances in England 1700–1832* (London, 1992), 316.

11. For which see: P. Jones, 'Swing, Speenhamland and rural social relations: the "moral economy" of the English crowd in the nineteenth century', *SH*, 32, 3 (2007), 272–91; and C. Griffin, 'The violent Captain Swing?', *P&P*, 209 (2010), 149–80.

12. N. Verdon, *Rural women workers in nineteenth-century England: gender, work and wages* (Woodbridge, 2002), 198.

13. For a full account, see: C. Griffin, *The rural war: Captain Swing and the politics of protest* (Manchester, 2012), 182.

14. On these issues see the essays in M. Cragoe and P. Readman (eds), *The land question in Britain, 1750–1950* (Basingstoke, 2010).

15. See J. Burchardt, *Paradise lost? Rural idyll and social change 1800–2000* (London, 2002).

16. K.D.M. Snell, *Parish and belonging: community, identity and welfare in England and Wales, 1700–1950* (Cambridge, 2006).

Select Bibliography

J. Archer, 'The Wells–Charlesworth debate: a personal comment on arson in Norfolk and Suffolk', *JPS*, 9, 4 (1982), 277–84.

J. Archer, *By a flash and a scare: arson, animal maiming, and poaching in East Anglia, 1815–1870* (Oxford, 1990).

J. Archer, 'Poaching gangs and violence: the urban–rural divide in nineteenth-century Lancashire', *British Journal of Criminology*, 39, 1 (1999), 25–38.

J. Belchem, *Popular radicalism in nineteenth-century Britain* (Basingstoke, 1996).

M. Berg, *The age of manufactures, 1700–1820: industry, innovation and work* (Routledge, 1994).

K. Binfield (ed.), *The writings of the Luddites* (Baltimore, MD, 2004).

J. Bohstedt, *Riots and community politics in England and Wales, 1790–1810* (Cambridge, MA, 1985).

J. Bohstedt, 'Gender, household and community politics: women in English riots, 1790–1810', *P&P*, 120 (1988), 88–122.

J. Bohstedt, *The politics of provisions: food riots, moral economy, and market transition in England, c. 1550–1850* (Farnham, 2010).

J. Burchardt, *The allotment movement in England, 1793–1873* (Woodbridge, 2002).

J. Burnette, *Gender, work and wages in industrial revolution Britain* (Cambridge, 2008).

B. Bushaway, *By rite: custom, ceremony and community in England, 1700–1880* (London, 1982).

P. Carter, 'Enclosure, waged labour and the formation of class consciousness: rural Middlesex c.1700–1835', *Labour History Review*, 66, 3 (2001), 269–93.

J. Chapman and S. Seeliger, *Enclosure, environment and landscape in southern England* (Stroud, 2001).

A. Charlesworth, *Social protest in a rural society: the spatial diffusion of the Captain Swing disturbances of 1830–1831* (Norwich, 1979).

A. Charlesworth, 'The development of the English rural proletariat and social protest, 1700–1850: a comment', *JPS*, 8, 1 (1980), 101–11.

A. Charlesworth (ed.), *An atlas of rural protest, 1548–1900* (London, 1983).

A. Charlesworth, 'An agenda for historical studies of rural protest in Britain, 1750–1850', *RH*, 2, 2 (1991), 231–40.

A. Charlesworth, 'From the moral economy of Devon to the political economy of Manchester, 1790–1812', *SH*, 18, 2 (1993), 205–17.

A. Charlesworth, R. Sheldon, A. Randall and D. Walsh, 'The Jack-a-Lent riots and opposition to turnpikes in the Bristol region in 1749', in A. Randall and A. Charlesworth (eds), *Markets, market culture and popular protest in eighteenth-century Britain and Ireland* (Liverpool, 1996), 46–68.

M. Chase, *The people's farm: English radical agrarianism, 1775–1840* (Oxford, 1988).

M. Chase, *Chartism: a new history* (Manchester, 2007).

P. Custer, 'Refiguring Jemima: gender, work and politics in Lancashire 1770–1820', *P&P*, 195 (2007), 127–58.

G. Daly, 'Napoleon and the city of smugglers', *Historical Journal*, 50, 2 (2007), 333–52.

I. Dyck, *William Cobbett and rural popular culture* (Cambridge, 1993).

D. Eastwood, 'Communities, protest and police in early nineteenth-century Oxfordshire: the enclosure of Otmoor reconsidered', *AgHR*, 44, 1 (1996), 35–46.

M. Freeman, 'Plebs or predators? Deer-stealing in Whichwood Forest, Oxfordshire in the eighteenth and nineteenth centuries', *SH*, 21, 1 (1996), 1–21.

R. Ganev, *Songs of protest, songs of love: popular ballads in eighteenth-century Britain* (Manchester, 2009).

C. Griffin, '"Cut down by some cowardly miscreants": Plant-maiming, or the malicious cutting of flora, as an act of protest in eighteenth- and nineteenth-century rural England', *RH*, 19, 1 (2008), 29–54.

C. Griffin, '"The mystery of the fires": "Captain Swing" as incendiarist', *Southern History*, 32 (2010), 22–44.

C. Griffin, 'The violent Captain Swing?', *P&P*, 209 (2010), 149–80.

C. Griffin, 'Animal maiming, intimacy and the politics of shared life: the bestial and the beastly in eighteenth- and early nineteenth-century England', *Transactions of the Institute of British Geographers*, 37, 2 (2012), 301–16.

C. Griffin, *The rural war: Captain Swing and the politics of protest* (Manchester, 2012).

J.L. Hammond and B. Hammond, *The village labourer* (London, 1911/1978), 4th edn.

R. Hastings, *Chartism in the North Riding of Yorkshire and south Durham, 1838–48*, Borthwick Paper 105 (York, 2004).

D. Hay, 'War, dearth and theft in the eighteenth century: the record of the English courts', *P&P*, 95 (1982), 117–60.

D. Hay, 'The state and the market in 1800: Lord Kenyon and Mr Waddington', *P&P*, 162 (1999), 101–62.

D. Hay, P. Linebaugh, J. Rule, E.P. Thompson and C. Winslow, *Albion's fatal tree: crime and society in eighteenth-century England* (London, 1975; 2nd edn London, 2011).

C. Haydon, 'The Gordon Riots in the English provinces', *Historical Research*, 63 (1990), 354–9.

S. Hindle, 'Power, poor relief, and social relations in Holland Fen, c. 1600–1800', *Historical Journal*, 41, 1 (1998), 67–96.

E. Hobsbawm, *Labouring men: studies in the history of labour* (London, 1964).

E. Hobsbawm and G. Rudé, *Captain Swing* (London, 1969; 2nd edn 1973).

H. Hopkins, *The long affray: the poaching wars in Britain* (London, 1985).

A. Howkins and L. Merricks, '"Wee be black as hell": ritual, disguise and rebellion', *RH*, 4, 1 (1993), 41–53.

P. Hudson, *The genesis of industrial capital: a study of the West Riding wool textile industry, c.1750–1850* (Cambridge, 1986).

J. Humphries, 'Enclosures, common rights and women: the proletarianization of families in late eighteenth- and early nineteenth-century Britain', *Journal of Economic History*, 50, 1 (1990), 17–42.

D. Jones, 'Thomas Campbell Foster and the rural labourer: incendiarism in East Anglia in the 1840s', *SH*, 1, 1 (1976), 5–37.

P. Jones, 'Swing, Speenhamland and rural social relations: the "moral economy" of the English crowd in the nineteenth century', *SH*, 32, 3 (2007), 272–91.

P. Jones, 'Finding Captain Swing: protest, parish relations, and the state of the public mind in 1830', *IRSH*, 54, 3 (2009), 429–58.

D. Kent, *Popular radicalism and the Swing riots in central Hampshire*, Hampshire papers, no. 11 (Winchester, 1997).

D. Kent and N. Townsend, *The convicts of the 'Eleanor': protest in rural England, new lives in Australia* (London, 2002).

P. King, *Crime, justice and discretion in England, 1740–1820* (Oxford, 2000).

P. King, *Crime and law in England, 1750–1840: remaking justice from the margins* (Cambridge, 2006).

S. King, *Poverty and welfare in England, 1700–1850* (Manchester, 2000).

J. Knott, *Popular opposition to the 1834 poor law* (Croom Helm, 1986).

P. Linebaugh, *The London hanged: crime and civil society in the eighteenth century* (London, 1991/2003).

P. Linebaugh, *Ned Ludd and Queen Mab: machine-breaking, romanticism, and the several commons of 1811–12* (Oakland, CA, 2012).

N. Lopatin, *Political unions, popular politics, and the Great Reform Act of 1832* (Basingstoke, 1999).

B. McDonagh, 'Women, enclosure and estate improvement in eighteenth-century Northamptonshire', *RH*, 20, 2 (2009), 143–62.

B. McDonagh and S. Daniels, 'Enclosure stories: narratives from Northamptonshire', *Cultural Geographies*, 19, 1 (2012), 107–21.

R. Malcolmson, '"A set of ungovernable people": the Kingswood colliers in the eighteenth century', in J. Brewer and J. Styles (eds), *An ungovernable people: the English and their law in the seventeenth and eighteenth centuries* (London, 1980), 85–127.

J. Martin, 'Oratory, itinerant lecturing and Victorian popular politics: a case study of James Acland (1799–1876)', *Historical Research*, 86 (2013), 30–52.

P. Monod, *Jacobitism and the English people, 1688–1788* (Cambridge, 1989).

P. Monod, 'Dangerous merchandise: smuggling, Jacobitism, and commercial culture', *Journal of British Studies*, 30, 2 (1991), 150–82.

P. Muskett, 'The East Anglian agrarian riots of 1822', *AgHR*, 32, 1 (1984), 1–13.

K. Navickas, 'The search for General Ludd: the mythology of Luddism', *SH*, 30, 3 (2005), 281–95.

K. Navickas, *Loyalism and radicalism in Lancashire, 1798–1815* (Oxford, 2009).

K. Navickas, 'Moors, fields, and popular protest in south Lancashire and the West Riding of Yorkshire, 1800–1848', *Northern History*, 46, 1 (2009), 93–111.

K. Navickas, 'Luddism, incendiarism, and the defence of rural "task–scapes" in 1812', *Northern History*, 48, 1 (2011), 59–73.

K. Navickas, 'What happened to class?: New histories of labour and collective action in Britain', *SH*, 36, 2 (2011), 192–204.

J. Neeson, 'The opponents of enclosure in eighteenth-century Northamptonshire', *P&P*, 105 (1984), 114–39.

J. Neeson, *Commoners, common right, enclosure and social change in England, 1700–1820* (Cambridge, 1993).

J. Oates, 'Jacobitism and popular disturbances in Northern England, 1714–1719', *Northern History*, 41, 1 (2004), 111–28.

J. Oates, *York and the Jacobite rebellion of 1745*, Borthwick Paper no. 107 (York, 2005).

F. O'Gorman, 'The Paine burnings of 1792–1793', *P&P*, 193 (2006), 111–55.

A. Peacock, *Bread or blood: a study of the agrarian riots in East Anglia in 1816* (London, 1965).

J. Pearson, 'Threshing out the common in community: the Great Tey riot of 1727', *RH*, 9, 1 (1998), 43–56.

T. Pettitt, '"Here comes I, Jack Straw": English folk drama and social revolt', *Folklore*, 95, 1 (1984), 3–20.

R. Platt, *Smuggling in the British Isles: a history* (London, 2007).

R. Poole, 'The march to Peterloo: politics and festivity in late Georgian England', *P&P*, 192 (2006), 109–53.

R. Poole, 'French revolution or Peasants' Revolt? Petitioners and rebels in England from the Blanketeers to the Chartists', *Labour History Review*, 47, 1 (2009), 6–26.

S. Poole, '"A lasting and salutary warning": incendiarism, rural order and England's last scene of crime execution', *RH*, 19, 2 (2008), 163–77.

S. Poole, 'Forty years of rural history from below: Captain Swing and the historians', *Southern History*, 32 (2010), 1–20.

A. Randall, *Before the Luddites: custom, community and machinery in the English woollen industry, 1776–1809* (Cambridge, 1991).

A. Randall, *Riotous assemblies: popular protest in Hanoverian England* (Oxford, 2006).

A. Randall and A. Charlesworth (eds), *Markets, market culture and popular protest in eighteenth-century Britain and Ireland* (Liverpool, 1996).

A. Randall and A. Charlesworth (eds), *Moral economy and popular protest: crowds, conflict and authority* (London, 2000).

A. Randall and E. Newman, 'Protest, proletarians and paternalists: social conflict in rural Wiltshire, 1830–1850', *RH*, 6, 2 (1995), 205–27.

B. Reay, *The last rising of the agricultural labourers: rural life and protest in nineteenth-century England* (Oxford, 1990).

220   SELECT BIBLIOGRAPHY

B. Reay, *Microhistories: demography, society, and culture in rural England, 1800–1930* (Cambridge, 1996).

B. Reay, *Rural Englands: labouring lives in the nineteenth-century* (Basingstoke, 2004).

M. Reed, 'Social change and social conflict in nineteenth-century England: a comment', *JPS*, 12, 1 (1984), 109–23.

M. Reed, 'Gnawing it out': a new look at economic relations in nineteenth-century rural England', *RH*, 1, 1 (1990), 83–94.

M. Reed, 'Class and conflict in rural England: some reflections on a debate', in M. Reed and R. Wells (eds), *Class, conflict and protest in the English countryside, 1700–1880* (London, 1990), 1–28.

T. Richardson, 'The agricultural labourers' standard of living in Lincolnshire, 1790–1840: social protest and public order', *AgHR*, 41, 1 (1993), 1–19.

I. Robertson, 'The role of women in protests in the Scottish Highlands', *Journal of Historical Geography*, 23, 2 (1997), 187–200.

N. Rogers, *Crowds, culture, and politics in Georgian Britain* (Oxford, 1998).

N. Rogers, *Mayhem: post-war crime and violence in Britain, 1748–53* (New Haven, CT, 2012).

D. Rollison, 'Property, ideology and popular culture in a Gloucestershire village 1660–1740', *P&P*, 93 (1981), 70–97.

G. Rudé, *The crowd in history: a study of popular disturbances in France and England, 1730–1848* (London, 1964).

J. Rule, 'Social crime in the rural south in the eighteenth and nineteenth centuries', *Southern History*, 1 (1979), 135–53.

J. Rule, *The experience of labour in eighteenth-century industry* (London, 1981).

J. Rule and R. Wells, *Crime, protest and popular politics in southern England, 1740–1850* (London, 1997).

K. Sayer, 'Field-faring women: the resistance of women who worked in the fields of nineteenth-century England', *Women's History Review*, 2, 2 (1993), 185–98.

J. Scott, *Weapons of the weak: everyday forms of peasant resistance* (New Haven, CT, 1985).

J. Scott *Domination and the arts of resistance: hidden transcripts* (New Haven, CT, 1990).

G. Seal, 'Tradition and agrarian protest in nineteenth-century England and Wales', *Folklore*, 99, 2 (1989), 146–69.

C. Searle, 'Custom, class conflict and agrarian capitalism: the Cumbrian customary economy in the eighteenth century', *P&P*, 110 (1986), 106–33.

T. Shakesheff, *Rural conflict, crime and protest: Herefordshire, 1800–1860* (Woodbridge, 2003).

S. Shave, 'The impact of Sturges Bourne's poor law reforms in rural England', *Historical Journal*, 56, 2 (2013), 399–429.

L. Shaw-Taylor, 'Labourers, cows, common rights and parliamentary enclosure: The evidence of contemporary comment c.1760–1810', *P&P*, 171 (2001), 95–126.

L. Shaw-Taylor, 'Parliamentary enclosure and the emergence of an English agricultural proletariat', *Journal of Economic History*, 61, 3 (2001), 640–62.

B. Short, 'Environmental politics, custom and personal testimony: memory and life space on the late Victorian Ashdown Forest, Sussex', *Journal of Historical Geography*, 30, 3 (2004), 470–95.

K.D.M. Snell, 'Deferential bitterness: the social outlook of the rural proletariat in eighteenth- and nineteenth-century England and Wales', in M. Bush (ed.), *Social orders and social classes in Europe since 1500: studies in stratification* (London, 1992), 158–84.

K.D.M. Snell, 'The culture of local xenophobia', *SH*, 28,1 (2003), 1–30.

K.D.M. Snell, *Parish and belonging: community, identity and welfare in England and Wales, 1700–1950* (Cambridge, 2006).

K.D.M. Snell and P. Ell, *Rival Jerusalems: the geography of Victorian religion* (Cambridge, 2000).

R. Soderlund, 'Resistance from the margins: the Yorkshire worsted spinners, policing, and the transformation of work in the early industrial revolution', *IRSH*, 51 (2006), 217–42.

P. Spence, *The birth of romantic radicalism: war, popular politics, and English radical reformism, 1800–1815* (Aldershot, 1996).

G. Stedman-Jones, *Languages of class: studies in working class history, 1832–1982* (Cambridge, 1983).

D. Szechi, *The Jacobites: Britain and Europe, 1688–1788* (Manchester, 1994).

E.P. Thompson, *The making of the English working class* (London, 1980, first published 1963).

E.P. Thompson, 'The moral economy of the English crowd in the eighteenth-century', *P&P*, 50 (1971), 76–136.

E.P. Thompson, 'Patrician society, plebeian culture', *Journal of Social History*, 7, 4 (1974), 382–405.

E.P. Thompson, 'The crime of anonymity', in D. Hay, P. Linebaugh, J. Rule, E.P. Thompson and C. Winslow, *Albion's fatal tree: crime and society in eighteenth-century England* (London, 1975), 255–344.

E.P. Thompson, *Whigs and hunters: the origin of the Black Act* (London, 1975).

E.P. Thompson, 'Eighteenth-century English society: class struggle without class?', *SH*, 3, 2 (1978), 133–65.

E.P. Thompson, *Customs in common* (London, 1991).

C. Tilly, *Contention and democracy in Europe, 1650–2000* (Cambridge, 2004).

C. Tilly, *Social movements, 1768–2004* (Boulder, CO, 2004), 16–25.

N. Verdon, *Rural women workers in nineteenth-century England: gender, work and wages* (Woodbridge, 2002).

J. Walter, *Crowds and popular politics in early modern England* (Manchester, 2006).

R. Wells, 'The development of the English rural proletariat and social protest, 1700–1850', *JPS*, 6, 2 (1979), 115–39.

R. Wells, 'Social conflict and protest in the English countryside in the early nineteenth century: a rejoinder', *JPS*, 8, 4 (1981), 514–30.

R. Wells, *Insurrection: the British experience, 1795–1803* (Gloucester, 1983).

R. Wells, *Wretched faces: famine in wartime England, 1763–1803* (Gloucester, 1988).

R. Wells, 'Tolpuddle in the context of English agrarian labour history, 1780–1850', in J. Rule (ed.) *British trade unionism: the formative years* (London, 1988), 98–142.

R. Wells, 'Social protest, class, conflict and consciousness in the English countryside, 1700–1880', in M. Reed and R. Wells (eds), *Class, conflict and protest in the English countryside, 1700–1880* (London, 1990), 121–98.

R. Wells, 'Southern Chartism', *RH*, 2, 1 (1991), 37–59.

R. Wells, 'Mr. William Cobbett, Captain Swing and King William IV', *AgHR*, 45, 1 (1997), 34–48.

R. Wells, 'The moral economy of the English countryside', in A. Randall and A. Charlesworth (eds), *Moral economy and popular protest: crowds, conflict and authority* (London, 2000), 209–72.

R. Wells, 'Historical trajectories: English social welfare systems, rural riots, popular politics, agrarian trade unions, and allotment provision, 1793–1896', *Southern History*, 25 (2003), 85–245.

N. Whyte, 'Landscape, memory and custom: parish identities c.1550–1700', *SH*, 32, 2 (2007), 166–86.

S. Williams, 'Malthus, marriage and poor law allowances revisited: a Bedfordshire case study, 1770–1834', *AgHR*, 52, 1 (2004), 56–82.

S. Williams, *Poverty, gender and the life-cycle under the English poor law* (Woodbridge, 2011).

A. Wood, *The politics of social conflict: the Peak Country, 1520–1770* (Cambridge, 1999).

A. Wood, *Riot, rebellion and popular politics in early modern England* (Basingstoke, 2002).

D. Wright, Popular radicalism: the working class experience, 1780–1880 (London, 1988).

Index

226

Printed by Printforce, the Netherlands